LOGISTICS & RETAIL MANAGEMENT

Emerging issues and new challenges in the retail supply chain

3RD EDITION

EDITED BY
JOHN FERNIE & LEIGH SPARKS

The Chartered Institute of
Logistics and Transport (UK)

KoganPage

LONDON PHILADELPHIA NEW DELHI

First published in Great Britain and the United States in 1999 by Kogan Page Limited
Second edition published in 2004
Third edition published in 2009
Reprinted 2009, 2010

120 Pentonville Road	525 South 4th Street, #241	4737/23 Ansari Road
London N1 9JN	Philadelphia PA 19147	Daryaganj
United Kingdom	USA	New Delhi 110002
www.koganpage.com		India

© John Fernie, Leigh Sparks and individual contributors, 1999, 2004, 2009

ISBN 978 0 7494 5407 4

British Library Cataloguing-in-Publication Data

A CIP record for this book is available from the British Library.

Library of Congress Cataloging-in-Publication Data

Logistics and retail management : emerging issues and new challenges in the retail supply chain / John Fernie and Leigh Sparks.
    p. cm.
  Includes index.
  ISBN 978-0-7494-5407-4
  1. Business logistics. 2. Retail trade--Management. I. Fernie, John, 1948- II. Sparks, Leigh.
  HD38.5.L614 2009
  658.5--dc22
                           2008049601

Typeset by Saxon Graphics Ltd, Derby
Printed and bound in India by Replika Press Pvt Ltd

Contents

Contributors

Nobu Azuma is Associate Professor in Marketing and Distribution Studies at the School of Business, Aoyama Gakuin University in Tokyo. He is also engaged in a variety of research activities at the School of Management and Languages, Heriot-Watt University, Edinburgh, on a part-time basis. His current research interests cover fashion, culture, and consumption, industrial/commercial agglomeration, market orientation and supply chain management in the fashion industry. He emphasizes the importance of the 'soft variables' in management studies by employing an interdisciplinary research approach.

Johanna Bergvall-Forsberg is Lecturer in Supply Chain Management in the School of Materials at the University of Manchester. Since 2003 she has been involved in research investigating strategic agile merchandizing as a route to competitiveness for the European textile sector. She has published in internationally rated journals and has also authored a number of sector policy reports for the European Social Fund sponsored Textiles Advanced Skills (TASk) Equal project. She is a member of the Institute of Operations Management and has been invited to teach at the College of International Education, Zhongyuan University of Technology, China.

Martin Christopher is Professor of Marketing and Logistics at Cranfield School of Management. He has published widely and his recent books include *Logistics and Supply Chain Management* and *Marketing Logistics*. Martin Christopher was the founding co-editor of the *International Journal of Logistics Management*. He is a regular contributor to conferences and workshops around the world. At Cranfield, he chairs the Centre for Logistics and Supply Chain Management, the largest activity of its type in Europe. In addition to leading a number of ongoing research projects in logistics and supply chain management, he is active as an adviser to many organizations. Martin Christopher is an Emeritus Fellow of the Chartered Institute of Logistics and Transport on whose Council he sits. He is also a Fellow and Foundation Professor of the Chartered Institute of Purchasing and Supply and a Fellow of the Chartered Institute of Marketing. In 1988 he was awarded the Sir Robert Lawrence Gold Medal for his contribution to logistics education, in 1997 he was given the US Council of Logistics Management's Foundation Award and in 2005 he received the Distinguished Service Award from the US Council of Supply Chain Management Professionals (This is North America's highest accolade for work in the area of supply chain management and was the first time it has been given to anyone outside North America.) In 2007 he was appointed a Foundation Professor of the UK Chartered Institute of Purchasing and Supply.

Dr Julia Edwards is a Research Associate at the Logistics Research Centre in the School of Management and Languages at Heriot-Watt University, Edinburgh. She joined Heriot-Watt in 2006, as part of the multi-university 'Green Logistics' project. Prior to that, she was a Senior Lecturer of Environmental Management at the University of Wales, Newport. Dr Edwards has been researching and teaching in the areas of transport and environmental issues for the last 15 years. Currently, her research interests include carbon auditing of supply chains, e-commerce and the environment, and consumer travel and shopping behaviour.

John Fernie is Professor of Retail Marketing at Heriot-Watt University, Edinburgh. He has written and contributed to numerous textbooks and papers on retail management, especially in the field of retail logistics and the internationalization of retail formats. He is editor of the *International Journal of Retail & Distribution Management*, published by Emerald, and received the prestigious award of Editor of the Year in 1997 in addition to Leading Editor awards in 1994, 1998 and 2000. He is on the editorial boards of the *Journal of Product and Brand Management*, and the *International Journal of Logistics Management*, both published by Emerald. He is a Fellow of the Institute of Logistics and Transport and an active member of the Chartered Institute of Marketing in the United Kingdom. He has also held office in the American Collegiate Retail Association. In 2001 he became a member of the Logistics Directors Forum, a group of leading professionals in supply chain management and logistics in the United Kingdom.

David B Grant is Professor in Logistics and Deputy Academic Director at the University of Hull Logistics Institute and an Adjunct Faculty member at Mannheim Business School in Germany. Prior to joining Hull, he was Senior Lecturer and Deputy Director of the Logistics Research Centre at Heriot-Watt University in Edinburgh. David's doctoral thesis investigated customer service, satisfaction and service quality in UK food processing logistics and received the James Cooper Memorial Cup PhD Award from the Chartered Institute of Logistics and Transport (UK) in 2003. David has published over 70 papers in various refereed journals, books and conference proceedings and is on the editorial board of the *International Journal of Physical Distribution & Logistics Management*, *International Journal of Business Science and Applied Management* and *Supply Chain Forum: An International Journal*. David is a member of the US Council of Supply Chain Management Professionals, the UK Logistics Research Network, and the NOFOMA Nordic logistics research group.

Tomakazu Higashi is Associate Professor of Marketing at the University of Marketing and Distribution Sciences (UMDS), Kobe, Japan. Prior to joining UMDS, he completed Master's and Doctoral Courses at the Graduate School of Commerce, Keio University, Tokyo. He specializes in general marketing studies. His ongoing research projects tackle the issues of strategic marketing and relationship marketing. He places a particular focus on the salience of entrepreneurship and 'intrepreneurship' in directing a firm's customer orientation strategies.

The late **Robert Lowson** was the Professor of Operations and Supply Chain Management and Director of the Strategic Operations Management Centre (SOMC) at the Norwich Business School. Professor Lowson received his PhD from Cardiff Business School, for work examining the flexibility and responsiveness of retailers and manufacturers in the Fast Moving Consumer Goods (FMCG) sector. His research interests encompassed the supply chain and operations strategies; supply chain management; supply pipeline linkages between retailers and their suppliers; the use of agility for responsiveness and flexibility (Quick Response) in the modern commercial organization; the role and agility of the Small and Medium-sized Enterprise (SME) in modern economies; and complex adaptive systems, non-linear dynamics, organizational ecology and their implications for organizational theory.

Alan McKinnon is Professor and Director of the Logistics Research Centre in the School of Management and Languages at Heriot-Watt University, Edinburgh. Alan has been researching and teaching in the field of logistics for 30 years and has published widely on the subject. He has been an adviser to several UK government departments and consultant to numerous public and private sector organizations on a variety of logistics and transport issues. In 2000–2001 he was chairman of the UK government's Retail Logistics Task Force. He has recently been advising government committees, trade associations and companies on the 'decarbonization' of logistics operations and is involved in a large multi-university research project on 'green logistics'. Alan is a fellow of the Chartered Institute of Logistics and Transport, founder member of its Logistics Research Network and recipient of it highest distinction, the Sir Robert Lawrence Award.

Dr Helen Peck is Senior Lecturer in Commercial and Supply Chain Risk at Cranfield University. She joined Cranfield in 1983 from a major UK retail bank, working initially with the School's Library and Information Services and Management Development Unit, before taking up a research post within the Marketing and Logistics Group, where she completed her PhD. Helen has led Cranfield University's ground-breaking government-funded research programme into all aspects of supply chain related risk and resilience since its inception. She teaches corporate and supply chain risk on graduate programmes and short courses at Cranfield University and guest lectures at other leading univer-sities in the United Kingdom and Europe. Her research-based teaching brings together themes of risk, resilience and complex systems theory with practical management disciplines such as supply chain management and business continuity. Her work contributes directly to the devel-opment of UK national emergency planning policy as well as management practice. Helen's research and consultancy interests span mainstream commercial, defence and other public service contexts. She is a regular speaker at academic, business and defence conferences around the world. Her published work includes papers and journal articles, joint editor- and authorship of several books, with contributions to many others. She is also an award-winning writer of management case studies.

Dr David Smith was Head of Primary Distribution at Tesco. After working in other sectors of high street retail distribution he joined Tesco in 1984 in the distribution division and worked in the fast moving food consumer and temperature controlled distribution networks in both secondary and primary distribution. In 1993 he completed an MBA at Stirling University with a dissertation on 'Integrated supply chain management: the case of fresh produce in Tesco'. Since 1998 he has been an independent consultant in retail supply chain logistics. In 1998 he was seconded to the Department of the Environment, Transport and the Regions best-practice programme on freight distribution and logistics, and worked with several cross-industry working groups for road, rail and packaging. A Fellow of the Institute of Logistics and Transport, he has written articles, given lectures on logistics and co-authored *Packaging Logistics and Fresh Food Retailing: managing change in the supply chain.* He completed his PhD at the University of Stirling in 2006 with the thesis: 'The role of retailers as channel captains in retail supply chain change: the example of Tesco'.

Leigh Sparks is Professor of Retail Studies at the Institute for Retail Studies, University of Stirling, Scotland. Leigh has been previously the Head of the Department of Marketing, the Director of the Institute for Retail Studies and the Dean of the Faculty of Management (1995–2000). In 1989 Leigh was awarded a Winston Churchill Travelling Fellowship for a study of customer service in retailing in the United States and Canada, and has been a Visiting Professor at Florida State University and the University of Tennessee at Knoxville. He is co-editor of *The International Review of Retail, Distribution and Consumer Research,* the leading academic journal on retailing in Europe. Leigh is also on the editorial boards of the *Journal of Marketing Management* and the *Journal of Marketing Channels.* He is a member of the Chartered Institute of Logistics and Transport and Chair of the Academy of Marketing Research Committee. Leigh's research concentrates on structural and spatial change in retailing, including logistics and supply chain issues. This research has been disseminated widely through a number of books, many reports and over 100 academic and professional articles.

Neil Towers is Senior Lecturer in Supply Chain Management at Heriot-Watt University, Edinburgh. His research, teaching and scholarly activity have been developed in the area of fashion retail marketing, supply chain management and operations management with extensive international, industrial and commercial supply chain management experience. His research investigates the relationship between retail marketing and production planning controls within the context of textile supply chain management, with particular reference to small and medium-sized manufacturing enterprises. He publishes widely in internationally rated journals and is on the editorial board of *the Journal for Business Advancement.* He has authored a number of sector policy reports that have included the lead chapter in the European Social Fund sponsored Textiles Advanced Skills (TASk) Equal project report and the Global Excellence for Textiles Businesses Project. He has regularly been invited to teach at the University of Lille and ESSCA in France and the Asia Pacific International Institute at Zhongyuan University of Technology, China. He is a Fellow of the Institute of Operations Management, including Chair of the Qualifications and Awards Committee, Deputy Senior Examiner at the Chartered Institute of Marketing and a Fellow of the Chartered Management Institute.

Preface

As educators involved in the teaching of logistics and the supply chain, particularly in the context of retailing, it is increasingly hard to get over to students how much things have changed in the retail supply chain, but also how many challenges remain. Many approaches and results are taken for granted and it is assumed that supply chains have always been at the forefront of retail innovation and have always delivered the goods. Nothing of course could be further from the truth. For a long time, the supply of products into retail outlets was controlled by manufacturers and was very much a hit or miss affair. Consumers had to put up with the product they found (or did not find) on the shelves and retailers and manufacturers operated in something of an efficiency vacuum. This situation has now been transformed. Retailers have recognized the need to have more involvement in supply chains and noted that benefits can be achieved in both service levels and cost reduction. Massive efforts have been made to reorganize and reprioritize activities in moving products from production to consumption. Notwithstanding the major strides made, some challenges remain, and new issues have emerged.

In 1990 John Fernie edited *Retail Distribution Management* for Kogan Page. This volume, one of the first to look explicitly at distribution (as it then was) in retailing, combined retail academic and practitioner studies and viewpoints to provide a glimpse into what was a fast-changing situation. This groundbreaking volume pointed to a revolution in logistical support to retail stores over the 1980s in the United Kingdom. Through academic work and practical case examples the volume showed how retailers were gaining control of supply chains and reorganizing their own operations, and those of manufacturers, suppliers and distribution specialists, to transform the flow of goods and information in supply chains. In the process, new forms of working, using new technologies, were improving the quality of products moving through the system, both in physical terms and in terms of time appropriateness. Through the building of relationships with supply partners, efficiency and effectiveness were introduced into previously inefficient and ineffective supply systems. From a concentration on functional silos in physical distribution and materials management, the logistics concept and a focus on end-to-end supply chains were developed.

By 1998, John Fernie and Leigh Sparks were in a position to put together a second edited volume, again combining academic and practitioner viewpoints on changes in the retail supply chain. This volume showed that the 1990s had experienced further change, mainly focused on incremental improvements and relationship change, though in some circumstances major one-off efficiency gains were still possible. Through the adoption of further technological developments and the integration of the entire retail supply chain, costs were squeezed out of the system, yet at the same time service improvements were still possible.

The 1998 edited volume, by now entitled *Logistics and Retail Management*, was a considerable success. It became recommended reading in both academic and practitioner situations. It was no surprise therefore that the publishers, on seeing it go out of print, requested a revised second edition. Between 1998 and 2002 there was another transformation in many retail supply chains. Allied to changes in the retail sector itself, with global developments of supply and concentration, the supply of products took on new dimensions. This is not to say that the subject matter of retail logistics was totally changed. Many of the issues remained the same, but the way these were tackled, and the dimensions of the issues, altered. The second edition thus had only one chapter identical to the first edition. Some were lightly changed, as the issues remain broadly the same, but many were brand new and developed especially for the second edition.

The second edition was finally published in 2004 and has been even more successful than its predecessors. It has been reprinted a number of times as well as translated into a number of different languages. Modern production and supply methods have allowed it to have a considerable shelf-life, but from 2005 onwards, the publishers began to lobby for a third revised edition. In finally succumbing to this idea, we have again been confronted with a dilemma: how much of the previous edition should survive?

In our afterword to the second edition we identified a number of challenges to retailers and their supply chains. These revolved around issues of availability, retailer control of channels, time in replenishment, technology (and in particular RFID) and e-tailing. It is notable that we focused on the latter two elements. RFID at the time of the second edition was a 'hot topic' (and indeed remains so), though the debates between the 'zealots' and the 'Luddites' remained inconclusive. We took a moderate path suggesting data were a bigger issue than recognized and that a focus on 'obvious issues and bottlenecks in the supply chain' would provide more benefits than a blanket imposition of RFID as the panacea in the supply chain. As will be seen in this current volume these debates and issues remain live and recent RFID efforts have indeed been focused on real issues (not least availability).

Secondly, we focused on e-tailing and the various models that were being developed. Internet-based retailing is now a reality and e-tailing is a channel for consumers and retailers. It continues to evolve, though. In our afterword we commented, 'The sharing of the same inventory between store and online shopper could ultimately lead to poor customer service levels for both sets of shoppers. Thus there may come a time in the near future when investment in "stand-alone" picking centres will be necessary in specific geographic markets.' Time has, we feel, begun to prove us correct here, with varied practices now being introduced as circumstances change. No doubt retailers are keeping this under close review.

In 2004 we also concluded that retail logistics would continue to be exciting and interesting, and identified the challenges in the following way:

> Existing supply chains will be affected by changes in retailers, consumers and the environment, and technologies will be applied to meet specific operational issues. Some companies may transform their supply systems through the relationships they build with key suppliers, logistics services providers and even other retailers. New ways of meeting changing consumer demands will be the focus of much effort, though the cost bases remain uncertain. Retailers will be concerned to ensure they obtain the right balance between lean and agile approaches to their supply systems in order to meet the challenges of spatial reach and rapid reaction. Whatever the broad outcomes, leading retailers will be those with quality management able to apply change in supply, to drive effectiveness and efficiency within an appropriately balanced concern for people, processes and technology. (p 236)

In putting together this third edition we have tried to remain faithful to the ethos set down by John in 1990 and to meet the challenges and approaches identified in our previous edition and noted above. This has involved the removal of some material from the second edition and its replacement by some different chapters and topics. A couple of chapters remain totally untouched with a couple more having 'cosmetic' updating. Others have been substantially rewritten to take into account changing circumstances. The aim has been to maintain relevance and reflect the changing dimensions of retail supply chains and logistics. Most of the substantive changes have occurred towards the end of the volume, with new chapters on availability and on environmental issues combined with strongly revised chapters on e-tailing and RFID.

There are four main sections to the book. First, three chapters provide a context for the more detailed sectoral considerations that follow. The second and third parts each contain three chapters, on non-food and food logistics, respectively. For a long time, food retail logistics was seen to be at the forefront of techniques and results, as exemplified by Tesco in the United Kingdom. In the late 1990s however, fashion retailers such as Zara have shown how supply chain reorganization in non-food sectors can produce dramatic results and competitive advantage. Finally, there are three chapters covering particular aspects of technology adoption and implementation in the supply chain and environmental concerns. If one thing has been learnt since Drucker's 1962 claim about distribution being the last cost frontier, it is that logistics is as much about information use as it is about product movement. It is also clear that the environmental impact of supply chains cannot be ignored given the broad issues of climate change and current issues of energy costs and availability. In some cases environmental concerns and best supply chain practice also provide commercial benefits for businesses, but in others real questions have to be asked about the sustainability of practices.

The opening chapter of the book (Retail logistics: changes and challenges) has been written by us. The aim of this chapter is to provide a context for the remainder of the volume. It begins by pointing to the way in which many people tend to forget that supplying products and services is not necessarily a straightforward task. Rather, it is the managed integration of a range of tasks, both within and increasingly beyond the boundaries of the company. The traditional functional silos of warehousing and transport have been removed by the need to integrate the logistics tasks and to develop a stronger sense of supply chain management. Through a close examination of the needs in different situations and the development of techniques such as Quick Response and Efficient Consumer Response, leading to ideas of lean and agile supply systems, so effectiveness and efficiency have been attained in very different circumstances. This is not to say that challenges do not exist but rather to point to the great strides forward that have been taken. Retailers that have not critically examined their supply systems are now realizing that they need to catch up. To meet national and potentially global competitors, many retailers are re-examining their supply chains. Often the steps they are taking are not new, but rather have become the standards required of major retailers. Other retailers are recognizing that they also need to look at every aspect of their supply systems. This is certainly the case when retailers get involved in e-commerce, where challenges to efficiency are fundamental, and throughout supply systems when waste and environmental impact reductions are potential hazards for all retailers.

One of the biggest areas of change for retailers has been the development of pan-company relationships. It has been remarked that retailers now compete not on the basis of their activities alone, but on the basis of the effectiveness and efficiency of their whole supply chain. If problems are present in production and primary distribution then these will inevitably have an effect on the price, quality and availability of the products on the shelves for consumers. Relationships in the supply chain are therefore now fundamental. Analysis of these changing relationships forms the basis of the second chapter, prepared by John Fernie. In this chapter key themes in relationships, such as power and dependence, trust and commitment, and cooperation and co-opetition, are examined initially. Much of the emphasis on relationships in supply chains, as noted in the introductory chapter, has focused on the concepts of Quick Response (QR) and Efficient Consumer Response (ECR). These are analysed in detail in this chapter, along with ideas of Collaborative Planning, Forecasting and Replenishment (CPFR). Finally, the role of third-party logistics providers in helping retailers meet their strategic objectives is considered. As the retail logistics environment changes, so logistics service providers can capitalize on a range of opportunities.

One of these logistics environment changes occurs in the spatial component of supply. 'Globalization' is an overused term, but there can be no doubt that there has been a greater internationalization in retail supply, both in terms of the internationalization of the major retailers themselves and also in the sources of product supply. Chapter 3, by John, focuses therefore on the internationalization of the retail supply chain. In this chapter he points initially to the major changes that have occurred in the sourcing of products in recent decades. In both food and non-food there has been an increasing internationalization of product supply, developed both through the potential of low cost supply, but also simply because of the increasing international operations generally by major retailers. 'Internationalization' is probably a better term than 'globalization' in this area (as in some others) as it is clear that the distribution and supply practices ('culture') and infrastructure in different countries and parts of the world are substantially different. There is no global logistics approach that can be identified, though it is becoming increasingly clear that the growing internationalization of retailing is leading to the internationalization of logistics practices, both within retailers and through their supply partners. Perhaps the closest to a global approach can be found in some of the logistics services providers.

These first three chapters provide a context for the detailed studies that follow. Together they suggest that retail supply has been transformed in recent decades, not without problems in some cases. Chief amongst the issues being confronted by many retailers are the relationships throughout the supply chain and the increasing breadth in spatial terms of the sources of supply. The next six chapters provide illustrations of these issues in the non-food and food sectors.

Chapter 4 by Nobukaza Azuma, John Fernie and Toshikazu Higashi is on market orientation and supply chain management in the fashion industry. The fashion industry has recently been changed by enhancements in time-based competition and, to a considerable extent, such techniques and time compression are becoming the de facto standard in the sector. The chapter therefore considers the market orientation of firms in the sector, with a particular focus on the supply chain and the possibilities of organizational learning. An integrated approach to market orientation and supply chain management has potential to provide competitive advantage, but in the fashion industry such potential is mitigated by the short-term nature of fashion and by the ability of retailers to learn from the past and from competitors.

This broad examination of the fashion industry is complemented by a more detailed consideration of fashion logistics and QR by Martin Christopher, Bob Lowson and Helen Peck. This chapter integrates three of the issues that have thus far formed the core of the book: issues of time, internationalization and quick response systems. Through a detailed examination of the fashion sector, they show how an agile or quick response supply chain is essential to compete effectively.

In Chapter 6, Neil Towers and Johanna Bergvall-Forsberg consider these issues further. They point to the requirements of the European textile fashion industry and the ways in which these are met by combinations of lean and agile solutions. They focus on market mediation strategies that allow companies to continuously adjust the delivery process in response to actual customer demand, but recognize that practical implementation is hard to achieve. They illustrate the issues through a case study of 11 European small and medium-sized manufacturing enterprises in the textile fashion industry.

The case of Tesco has received considerable academic and practitioner attention over the last decades. Initially this was probably due to the very public transformation of the business that was being attempted. More recently this attention has been due to the success of this transformation and the growing realization that Tesco has been a pioneer in the supply chain and has developed a world-class logistics approach. To some extent this success was due to the particular circumstances in the United Kingdom, which allowed a conforming and standard retail offer to be serviced by a straightforward and regular supply system. Such circumstances no longer apply, as the market in the United Kingdom has been altered and Tesco itself has become a much more international retailer (and product sourcing has also become more international). Chapter 7 provides therefore a review of Tesco's supply chain management. David Smith and Leigh Sparks, who have been involved in studying Tesco's logistics for a number of years, have written the chapter. Particular emphasis is placed on the need to change logistics and supply to reflect the changing nature of the retail operations. With the store component transformation of the business well known, the chapter considers the less well known developments for logistics and supply. One component of this is the way in which Tesco has been influenced by dimensions of lean supply in its thinking. This is most seen in their food business and in new start-ups such as Fresh and Easy in the United States. At the same time the global nature of Tesco and its movement into non-food has complicated its supply and logistics operations.

Whilst there are particular aspects of fashion logistics that require special consideration and handling, such issues are probably as pointed in the food sector. Chapter 8 for example, also by David Smith and Leigh Sparks, is concerned with temperature controlled supply chains (TCSCs). These chains are essential to the safe supply of food to consumers, not least because breakdowns in such systems can cause serious health hazards in the general population. At a time when food scares have become more common, retailers have therefore had to pay special attention to channels that need specially controlled handling systems. Smith and Sparks review the importance of TCSCs before outlining the issues that are confronting retailers in meeting legal and other standards and then examining the future concerns that are likely to arise.

One of the key topics identified by retailers, and in our second edition as a major challenge, is that of availability. If products are not available for sale then retailers struggle and consumers will be attracted to competitors that have availability and choice. Chapter 9, by John Fernie and David B Grant uses a case study of on-shelf availability in UK grocery retailing. Despite the belief that the United Kingdom had a good retail supply chain, concern was raised from 2003 onwards that availability was variable and provided an opportunity for retailers and manufacturers. Through a case study with a major UK grocery retailer, the authors show how on-shelf availability has been improved. In particular they argue that simple techniques focusing on human resources can overcome many on-shelf availability problems.

The final three chapters in the book take a somewhat different approach, by looking at aspects of technology use and environmental concerns in logistics. Whilst technology is implicit in many of the chapters that have gone before, here the focus is more explicit. Similarly, many of the practices identified in the early chapters can be seen as having environmental or 'green' aspects, though the direction of impact varies considerably. Here again, the focus is made explicit.

The first of these chapters is by John Fernie and Alan McKinnon, who consider the development of e-tail logistics. Non-store shopping is of course not new. Systems to deliver products to homes have been around for a long time. The late 1990s, however, saw massive hype around the development of e-commerce and predictions that over time (though this varied enormously) a significant proportion of retail sales would migrate to the internet. The collapse of the dot com boom has brought such claims into stark reality. Nonetheless, successful internet shopping does occur using a variety of models, and many retailers have essentially become multi-channel (albeit skewed) businesses. The future rate of growth will partly depend on the quality and efficiency of the supporting system of order fulfilment. Many e-tailers have developed effective logistical systems and built up consumer confidence in the supply and delivery operations. Challenges remain however, particularly in the grocery sector, where options for picking and the 'last mile' delivery remain to be resolved. The retailers themselves drive some of these choices, whereas other options may be constrained by consumer acceptance and desires from local government to manage the environmental issues of home delivery from multiple sources. This chapter reviews the development of e-tail logistics and considers the decisions that remain to be worked through.

Chapter 11, by Leigh Sparks, considers Radio Frequency Identification Devices (RFID). Since supply chains became the focus of attention some decades ago, many wild claims for various technologies have been made. Technology implementation has held out promise of supply chain transformation. These promises have not often materialized. Today, RFID is seen as another technology that will transform the retail supply chain. But, despite its overt promise, RFID may have many implementation problems to overcome. The chapter asks whether one issue in technology introduction is the problem of matching people, processes and technology at a time when the technology is both simultaneously unready and being hyped, and the ramifications of extensive implementation inside an organization are under-analysed. By focusing too much on technology and emphasizing the all-encompassing transformative properties, businesses may be missing opportunities for more specific benefits. In terms of RFID it would seem that the initial transformative promise has given way to a more measured consideration of where and how the technology is useful and precisely what benefits it can bring to retailers and their supply partners. RFID has not lived up to its hype, but neither is it a 'busted flush'.

The final chapter in this volume is by Alan McKinnon and Julia Edwards and is entitled 'The greening of retail logistics'. Whilst environmental concerns were around at the time of the second edition of this book, there can be little doubt that the intervening five or so years have seen a tremendous upsurge in concern both generally and specifically by retailers. Logistical activities are responsible for much of the environmental cost associated with modern retailing and it is thus not surprising that logistics is a key component of environmental strategy developed by retailers. This chapter examines the adverse effects of retail logistics on the environment and reviews a series of measures that companies can take to minimize them. The authors conclude that large retailers have been a fertile source of logistical innovation and have pioneered many practices and technologies. However, many of the environmental costs of retail distribution currently are borne by the community at large and not by the retailer's balance sheet. If this changes, as seems likely, then those retailers already trying to minimize their logistical environmental footprint will have a significant financial advantage and will also probably be viewed more positively by consumers.

In any book on a topic as wide as retail logistics it is inevitable that some issues will be missed. We hope that those that we have included are of interest and demonstrate the complexity and challenge of modern retail logistics. As before, we have resisted the temptation to have a chapter focusing on future issues. Rather, we provide a brief afterword to highlight some of the issues we believe are important in our examination of changes and challenges in retail logistics. Product supply has been transformed in recent years. The only thing we can be reasonably sure of is that changes will continue to be made as retailers continue to search for the most appropriate systems and practices to meet the changing consumer and operational demands. As before, the future remains challenging and exciting.

John Fernie and Leigh Sparks
Scotland, August 2008

Part 1

Concepts in retail logistics and supply chain management

1

Retail logistics: changes and challenges

John Fernie and Leigh Sparks

It is often taken for granted that appropriate products will be available to buy in the shops. The cornucopia of goods that are available in a hypermarket or a department store sometimes means that we forget how the products were supplied or what demands are being met. We expect our lettuces to be fresh, the new Wii Fit to be available on launch day and our clothes to be in good condition and ready to wear. With the introduction of e-commerce we have come to demand complete availability and home delivery at times of our choosing.

Consumer beliefs and needs have altered. How consumers behave and what we demand have changed. Our willingness to wait to be satisfied or served has reduced and we expect instant product availability and gratification. It should be obvious from this that the supply or logistics system that gets products from production through retailing to consumption has also had to be transformed. Physical distribution and materials management have been replaced by logistics management and a subsequent concern for the whole supply chain (Figure 1.1). This consideration for the supply chain as a whole has involved the development of integrated supply chain management. More recently there has been a concern to ensure that channels of distribution and supply chains are both anticipatory (if appropriate) and reacting to consumer demand, at general and detailed segment levels. There has also been a stronger realization of the

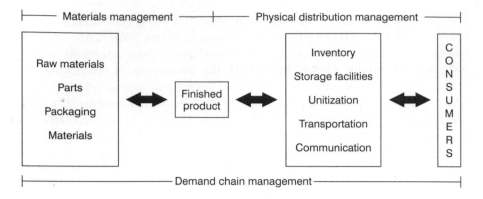

Figure 1.1 From physical distribution management to demand chain management

need for reverse flows of data and product in supply chains, both to inform demand-driven supply and to ensure appropriate recycling, reuse and other handling and sustainable systems.

This transformation in conceptualization and approach derives from cost and service requirements as well as consumer and retailer change (see Fernie, 1990; Fernie and Sparks, 1998, 2004). Elements of logistics are remarkably expensive, if not controlled effectively. Holding stock or inventory in warehouses just in case it is needed is a highly costly activity. The stock itself contains value and might not sell or could become obsolete. Warehouses and distribution centres generally are expensive to build, operate and maintain. Vehicles to transport goods between warehouses and shops are not cheap, both in terms of capital and, increasingly, running costs. Building and managing data networks and data warehouses remain pricey, despite the huge cost reductions for equipment in recent years. There is thus a cost imperative to making sure that logistics is carried out effectively and efficiently, through the most appropriate allocation of resources along the supply chain.

At the same time, there can be service benefits. By appropriate integration of demand and supply, mainly through the widespread use of information technology and systems, retailers can provide a better service to consumers by, for example, having fresher, higher quality produce arriving to meet consumer demand for such products. With the appropriate logistics, products should be of a better presentational quality, could possibly be cheaper, have a longer shelf-life and there should be far fewer instances of stock-outs. Reaction time to 'spurts' in demand can be radically improved through the use of information transmission and dissemination technologies. If operating properly, a good logistics system can therefore both reduce costs and improve service, providing a competitive advantage for the retailer.

Increasingly, there is also an environmental or 'green' dimension to logistics and supply chains. This occurs in many situations and has become increasingly important. This importance is both externally and, to a degree, internally driven. Externally, the awareness of environmental and sustainability issues has increased exponentially and retailers have had to respond to these pressures, both voluntarily and under legal requirement. Internally, retailers have become more aware that the benefits of having a system that is efficient and effective in meeting consumer demands can generate environmental benefits. Being environmentally sensible can also sometimes improve efficiency and effectiveness. This is clearly not always the case, but doing logistics 'properly' can bring benefits for all (eg reduced packaging). This is predicated on being fully aware of the impacts of decisions in logistics and on correctly mapping the processes and activities from both a supply and a demand point of view.

As might be anticipated, as the practical interest and involvement in retail supply chains have risen, so too academic consideration has expanded. Previous editions of this volume have garnered considerable interest. Since the last edition was published in 2004, three books explicitly on the retail supply chain have been produced (Ayers and Odegaard, 2008; Hugos and Thomas, 2006; Kotzab and Bjerre, 2005). Our revised edition continues to develop the subject. This chapter sets the scene for the changes and challenges confronting retailers and their supply chains.

THE LOGISTICS TASK

Retailing and logistics are concerned with product availability. Many have described this as 'getting the right products to the right place at the right time'. Unfortunately that description does not do justice to the amount of effort that has to go into a logistics supply system and the multitude of ways that supply systems can go wrong. The very simplicity of the statement suggests logistics is an easy process. As Box 1.1 shows, problems and mistakes can be all too apparent. The real management 'trick' is in making product availability look easy, day in and day out, whilst understanding consumer demand and reacting to its sometimes volatile dimensions.

For example, if the temperature rises and the sun comes out in an untypical Scottish summer, then demand for ice cream, soft drinks and even salad items rises dramatically. How does a retailer make sure they remain in stock and satisfy this perhaps transient demand? Or how about Valentine's Day, when demand for certain products in the days before increases exponentially? If a retailer stocks Valentine's cards and demand

Box 1.1 Mothercare

Carelessness at Mothercare leaves cupboard bare

Sales at Mothercare have dived by 6 per cent in the last three weeks after its move to a new hi-tech distribution centre caused problems.

The childrenswear retailer admitted yesterday that staff shortcomings meant its heralded autumn/winter clothing range had languished at the new Northamptonshire warehouse, causing huge stock shortages in its stores.

Chief Executive Chris Martin, who was recruited to turn around the chain, admitted the setback was 'exceptionally frustrating' given that like-for-like sales until this period had been up about 10 per cent, and that the new range had been well received.

It was doubly frustrating, he said, as management of the Daventry warehouse is subcontracted to a third party, Tibbett & Britten. 'Some of their staff just weren't doing their job', said a source.

Tibbett has responded by placing a senior director at the building to sort out the problems and establish a proper flow of stock to the stores. Asked if he was considering legal action, Mr Martin said: 'This is a five-year relationship. We are working it through together.'

He added that a fifth less stock than usual had been in the shops but stressed that it was 'now coming through'. In a trading statement Mr Martin revealed that sales rose by 9.6 per cent for the 26 weeks to September 28 with like-for-like sales up by 7.6 per cent. Brokers at Charterhouse Securities cut their recommendation from hold to sell after the news. But Seymour Pierce retail analyst Richard Ratner said: 'If they sort the warehouse problems out in the next few weeks I won't be unduly concerned, particularly as the 2.1 percentage point improvement in margin was better than expected.' Mothercare will forge ahead with the roll-out of its larger Mothercare World format after Christmas.

Helen Slingsby
Guardian, *Tuesday 9 October 9 2001*

---

does not materialize, then the retailer has stock that will not sell. There is little demand for Valentine's cards on 15 February. Whilst overstocks in this case will not perish, the cost of their storage and handling for the intervening year can be considerable.

The examples above demonstrate that retailers must be concerned with the flows of product and information both within the business and in the wider supply chain. In order to make products available retailers have to manage their logistics in terms of product movement and demand management. They need to know what is selling in the stores and both anticipate and react quickly to changes in this demand. At the same time they need to be able to move less demand-volatile products in an efficient and cost-effective manner.

The logistics management task is therefore initially concerned with managing the components of the 'logistics mix'. We can identify five components:

1. *Storage facilities:* these might be warehouses or distribution centres or simply the stock rooms of retail stores. Retailers manage these facilities to enable them to keep stock in anticipation of or to react to demand for products.
2. *Inventory:* all retailers hold stock to some extent. The question for retailers is the amount of stock or inventory (finished products and/or component parts) that has to be held for each product and the location of this stock to meet demand changes.
3. *Transportation:* most products have to be transported in some way at some stage of their journey from production to consumption. Retailers therefore have to manage a transport operation that might involve different forms of transport, different sizes of containers and vehicles and the scheduling and availability of drivers and vehicles.
4. *Unitization and packaging:* consumers generally buy products in small quantities. They sometimes make purchase decisions based on product presentation and packaging. Retailers are concerned to develop products that are easy to handle in logistics terms, do not cost too much to package or handle, yet retain their selling ability on the shelves.
5. *Communication:* to get products to where retailers need them, it is necessary to have information, not only about demand and supply, but also about volumes, stock, prices and movements. Retailers have thus become increasingly concerned with being able to capture data at appropriate points in the system and to use that information to have a more efficient and effective logistics operation.

It should be clear that all of these elements are interlinked. In the past they were often managed as functional areas or 'silos' and whilst potentially optimal within each function, the business as a whole was sub-optimal in logistics terms. More recently the management approach has been to integrate these logistics tasks and reduce the functional barriers. So, if a retailer gets good sales data from the checkout system, this can be used in scheduling transport and deciding levels and locations of stock holding. If the level of inventory can be reduced, then perhaps fewer warehouses are needed. If communication and transport can be effectively linked, then a retailer can move from keeping stock in a warehouse to running a distribution centre that sorts products for immediate store delivery, ie approaching a 'stockless' system. If standardized decisions about handling systems are made then the physical handling system can be built around the facilitating movement and aiding reusability. Internal integration has therefore been a major concern.

It should also be clear, however, that retailers are but one part of the supply system. Retailers are involved in the selling of goods and services to the consumer. For this they draw upon manufacturers to provide the necessary products. They may outsource certain functions, eg transport, warehousing to specialist logistics services providers. Retailers therefore have a direct interest in the logistics systems of their suppliers and other intermediaries. If a retailer is effective, but its suppliers are not, then errors and delays in supply from the manufacturer or logistics services provider will impact the retailer and the retailer's consumers, either in terms of higher prices or stock-outs (no products available on the store shelves). This was the essence of the problem in the Mothercare example in Box 1.1. If a retailer can integrate effectively its logistics system with that of its suppliers, then such problems may be minimized. Much more importantly, the entire supply chain can then be optimized and managed as a single entity. This brings potential advantages of costs reduction and service enhancement, not only for the retailer but also for the supplier. It should also mean that products reach the stores more rapidly, thus better meeting sometimes-transient customer demand. In some instances it may mean the production of products in merchandizable-ready units, which flow through the distribution systems from production to the shop floor without the need for assembly or disassembly. Such developments clearly require supply chain cooperation and coordination (Gustafsson et al, 2006).

We may be describing highly complex and advanced operations here. Retail suppliers have been increasingly spread across the world. A retailer may have thousands of stores in a number of countries, with tens of thousands of individual product lines. It may make millions of individual sales per day. Utilising data to ensure effective operation amongst retailers, manufacturers, suppliers, logistics services providers, head office, shops and distribution centres is not straightforward. There is thus always a tension between overall complexity and the desire for the simplest possible process.

Managing the logistics mix in an integrated retail supply chain while aiming to balance cost and service requirements are the essential elements of logistics management (Figure 1.2). As retailers have begun to embrace

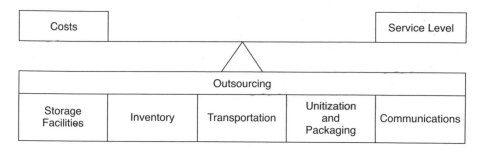

Figure 1.2 The management task in logistics

this logistics approach and examine their wider supply chains, many have realized that to carry out logistics properly, there has to be a transformation of approach and operations (Sparks, 1998).

It is also important to be aware of the dangers of an internally focused supply chain or set of logistics operations. The 'tipping point' in Figure 1.2 is between cost and service and it is always important to ensure that the appropriate balance is achieved. If the system is too cost-focused then it may not meet the consumer demands, with potentially dire business consequences (eg Walters and Rainbird, 2004). Being aware of consumer demands and requirements is vital. Conversely, too much focus on consumer demands and the provision of too high service levels will cause cost problems for retailers. If the system is too responsive at any price, then again the operation is likely to be unsustainable. The transformation in retail supply chains is thus about appropriate balances and activities and the right approach to supply and demand.

RETAIL LOGISTICS AND
SUPPLY CHAIN TRANSFORMATION

Retailers were once effectively the passive recipients of products, allocated to stores by manufacturers in anticipation of demand. Today, retailers are the active designers and controllers of product supply in reaction to known customer demand. They control, organize and manage the supply chain from production to consumption. This is the essence of the retail logistics and supply chain transformation that has taken place.

Times have changed and retail logistics has changed also. Retailers are the channel captains and set the pace in logistics. Having extended their channel control and focused on efficiency and effectiveness, retailers are now attempting to engender a more cooperative and collaborative stance in many aspects of logistics. They are recognizing that there are still gains to be made on standards and efficiency, but that these are probably only obtained as channel gains (ie in association with manufacturers and logistics services providers) rather than at the single firm level.

McKinnon (1996) reviewed and summarized the key components required for this retail logistics transformation. He identified six closely related and mutually reinforcing trends:

1. Increased control over secondary distribution: retailers have increased their control over secondary distribution (ie warehouse to shop) by channelling an increasing proportion of their supplies through distribution centres (DCs). In some sectors such as food this process is now virtually complete. British retailers exert much tighter control over the supply chain than their counterparts in many other countries. Their logistical operations are heavily dependent on information technology (IT), particularly the large integrated stock replenishment systems that control the movement and storage of an enormous number of separate products.
2. Restructured logistical systems: retailers have reduced inventory and generally improved efficiency through, for example, the development of 'composite distribution' (the distribution of mixed temperature items through the same distribution centre and on the same vehicle) and centralization in specialist warehouses of slower-moving stock. In the case of mixed retail businesses the establishment of 'common stock rooms' (where stock is shared across a number of stores, with demand deciding to which store stock is allocated) is developed.
3. Adoption of Quick Response (QR): the aim has been to cut inventory levels and improve the speed of product flow. This has involved reducing order lead time and moving to a more frequent delivery of smaller consignments both internally (between DC and shop) and externally (between supplier and DC). This has greatly increased both the rate of stock-turn and the amount of product being 'cross-docked', rather than stored at DCs. QR (Lowson et al, 1999) was made possible by the development of EDI (Electronic Data Interchange) and EPOS (Electronic Point of Sale), the latter driving the Sales Based Ordering (SBO) systems that most of the larger retailers have installed. In other words, as an item is sold and scanned in a shop, this information is used to inform replenishment and reordering systems and thus react quickly to demand. Sharing such data with key suppliers further integrates production with the supply function. Major British retailers have been faster to adopt these technologies than their counterparts in other European countries, though the technologies still have to diffuse to many small retail businesses.

4. Rationalization of primary distribution (ie factory to warehouse): partly as a result of QR pressures and partly as a result of intensifying competition, retailers have extended their control upstream of the DC (ie from the DC to the manufacturer). In an effort to improve the utilization of their logistical assets, many have integrated their secondary and primary distribution operations and run them as a single 'network system'. This reduces waste and improves efficiency.

5. Increased return flow of packaged material and handling equipment for recycling/reuse: retailers have become much more heavily involved in this 'reverse logistics' operation. This trend has been reinforced by the introduction of the EU packaging directive. Although the UK currently lags behind other European countries, particularly Germany, in this field, there remain opportunities to develop new forms of reusable container and new reverse logistics systems to manage their circulation.

6. Introduction of Supply Chain Management (SCM) and Efficient Consumer Response (ECR): having improved the efficiency of their own logistics operations, many retailers have begun to collaborate closely with suppliers to maximize the efficiency of the retail supply chain as a whole. SCM (and within this, ECR) provide a management framework within which retailers and suppliers can more effectively coordinate their activities. The underpinning technologies for SCM and ECR have been well established in the UK, so conditions have been ripe for such developments.

It is clear that many of these trends identified by McKinnon have been the focus for retailers in the intervening decade or so. Issues such as primary distribution and factory gate pricing, consolidation centres and stockless depots and Collaborative Planning Forecasting and Replenishment (CPFR) have occupied much attention. The overall focus in retail logistics has been altered from an emphasis on the functional aspects of moving products to an integrative approach that attempts to develop end-to-end supply chains. This outcome is normally referred to as 'supply chain management'.

SUPPLY CHAIN MANAGEMENT

The roots of supply chain management are often attributed to Peter Drucker and his seminal 1962 article on 'the economy's dark continent'. At this time he was discussing distribution as one of the key areas of business where major efficiency gains could be achieved and costs saved. Then, and through the next two decades, the supply chain was still viewed as a series of disparate functions. Once the functions began to be integrated and considered as a supply chain rather than separately, several key themes emerged:

- a shift from a push to a pull, ie a demand-driven supply chain;
- customers gaining more power in the marketing channel;
- an enhanced role of information systems to gain better control of the supply chain;
- the elimination of unnecessary inventory in the supply chain;
- a focus upon core capabilities and increased outsourcing of non-core activities to specialists.

To achieve maximum effectiveness of supply chains, it became clear that integration, ie the linking together of previously separated activities within a single system, was required. Companies have had therefore to review their internal organization to eliminate duplication and ensure that total costs can be reduced, rather than allow separate functions to control their costs in a sub-optimal manner. Similarly, supply chain integration can be achieved by establishing ongoing relationships with trading partners throughout the supply chain.

In industrial markets supply chain integration focused upon the changes promulgated by the processes involved in improving efficiencies in manufacturing. Total quality management, business process re-engineering and continuous improvement brought Japanese business thinking to western manufacturing operations. The implementation of these practices was popularized by Womack *et al's* (1990) book *The Machine that Changed the World,* which focused on supply systems and buyer–seller relationships in car manufacturing. In a retail context it is claimed that food retailers such as Tesco have increasingly embraced such lean principles for parts of their business (eg Jones, 2002). The update by Womack and Jones (2005) of the state of 'lean solutions' puts retailing (or at least some retailers) at the heart of the changes under way.

During the 1990s this focus on so-called 'lean production' was challenged in the United States and the United Kingdom, because of an over-reliance on efficiency measures ('lean') rather than innovative ('agile') responses. Agility as a concept was developed in the United States in response to the Japanese success in lean production. Agility plays to US strengths of entrepreneurship and information systems technology. An agile supply chain (Figure 1.3) is highly responsive to market demand. Harrison *et al* (2002) argue that the improvements in the use of information technology to capture 'real time' data means less reliance on forecasts and creates a virtual supply chain between trading partners. By sharing information, process integration takes place between partners who focus upon their core competencies. The final link in the agile supply chain is the network where a

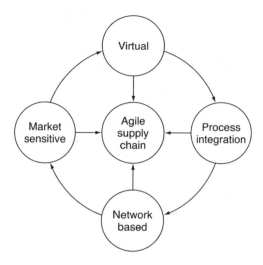

Figure 1.3 The agile supply chain
Source: Harrison and van Hoek, 2002, p 174

confederation of partners structures, coordinates and manages relation-ships to meet customer needs (Aldridge and Harrison, 2000).

Both approaches of course have their proponents. There is, however, no reason why supply systems may not be a combination of both lean and agile approaches, with each used when most appropriate (the so-called 'leagile' approach: Mason-Jones *et al*, 2000; Naylor *et al*, 1999; Towill and Christopher, 2002). Table 1.1 provides a summary comparison of lean, agile and leagile supply chains (Agarwal *et al*, 2006). It can be seen that they have value in particular circumstances.

It can be suggested that the key concepts within supply chain management include the value chain, resource-based theory of the firm, transaction cost economics and network theory. The thrust of all these concepts is the obtaining of competitive advantage through managing the supply chain (ie within and beyond the single firm) more effectively. They all explore possible benefits of a pan-firm orientation. Figure 1.4 illustrates a supply chain model showing how value may be added to the product through manufacturing, branding, packaging, display at the store and so on. At the same time, at each stage cost is added in terms of production costs, branding costs and overall logistics costs. The aim for retailers (and their supply partners) is to manage this chain to create value for the customer at an acceptable cost. The managing of this so called 'pipeline' has been a key challenge for logistics professionals, especially with the realization that the reduction of time not only reduced costs, but also gave competitive advantage.

Table 1.1 Comparison of lean, agile and leagile supply chains

Distinguishing attributes	Lean supply chain	Agile supply chain	Leagile supply chain
Market demand	Predictable	Volatile	Volatile and unpredictable
Product variety	Low	High	Medium
Product lifecycle	Long	Short	Short
Customer drives	Cost	Lead time and availability	Service level
Profit margin	Low	High	Moderate
Dominant costs	Physical costs	Marketability costs	Both
Stock-out penalties	Long-term contractual	Immediate and volatile	No place for stock-out
Purchasing policy	Buy goods	Assign capacity	Vendor managed inventory
Information enrichment	Highly desirable	Obligatory	Essential
Forecast mechanism	Algorithmic	Consultative	Both/either
Typical products	Commodities	Fashion goods	Product as per customer demand
Lead-time compression	Essential	Essential	Desirable
Muda elimination	Essential	Desirable	Arbitrary
Rapid reconfiguration	Desirable	Essential	Essential
Robustness	Arbitrary	Essential	Desirable
Quality	Market qualifier	Market qualifier	Market qualifier
Cost	Market winner	Market qualifier	Market winner
Lead time	Market qualifier	Market qualifier	Market qualifier
Service level	Market qualifier	Market winner	Market winner

Source: Agarwal et al, 2006, p 212

According to Christopher and Peck (2003) there are three dimensions to time-based competition that must be managed effectively if an organization is going to be responsive to market changes. These are:

1. time to market: the speed at bringing a business opportunity to market;
2. time to serve: the speed at meeting a customer's order;
3. time to react: the speed at adjusting output to volatile responses in demand.

Christopher and Peck (2003) use these principles to develop strategies for strategic lead-time management. By understanding the lead times of the integrated web of suppliers necessary to manufacture a product, they argue

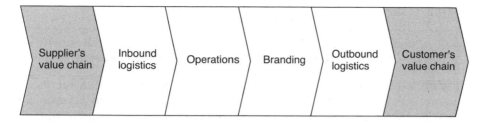

Figure 1.4 The extended value chain

that a 'pipeline map' can be drawn to represent each stage in the supply chain process from raw materials to customer. In these maps it is useful to differentiate between 'horizontal' and 'vertical' time. Horizontal time is time spent on processes such as manufacture, assembly, in-transit or order processing; vertical time is the time when nothing is happening, no value is added but only cost and products/materials are standing as inventory.

It was in fashion markets that the notion of 'time-based competition' had most significance, in view of the short time window for changing styles. In addition, the prominent trend in the last 20 years has been to source products globally, often in low-cost Pacific Rim nations, which lengthened the physical supply chain pipeline. These factors combined to illustrate the trade-offs that have to be made in supply chain management and suggested an imperative to develop closer working relationships with supply chain partners. Box 1.2 details these processes through the example of Zara.

Another catalyst for many of the initiatives in lead-time reduction came from work undertaken by Kurt Salmon Associates (KSA) in the United States in the mid-1980s. KSA was commissioned by US garment suppliers to investigate how they could compete with Far East suppliers. The results were revealing in that the United States-based supply chains were long (one and a quarter years from loom to store), badly coordinated and inefficient (Christopher and Peck, 1998). The concept of Quick Response was therefore initiated to reduce lead times and improve coordination across the apparel supply chain. In Europe, quick response principles have been applied across the clothing retail sector. Supply base rationalization has been a feature of the last decade as companies have dramatically reduced the number of suppliers and have worked much more closely with the remaining suppliers to ensure more responsiveness to the marketplace.

Complex webs of relationships have been formed in many supply chains. This has led Christopher and Peck (2003) to claim that as an outcome of supply chain management there is a strong case for arguing that individual companies no longer compete with other stand-alone companies, but rather that supply chain now competes against supply chain.

Box 1.2 Zara

Zara – time-based competition in a fashion market

Zara is one of Spain's most successful and dynamic apparel companies, producing fashionable clothing to appeal to an international target market of 18–35-year-olds. Zara's rapid growth and ongoing success in such a fiercely competitive environment is based on the dual objectives of working without stocks and responding quickly to market needs. It does this as well as, or even more effectively than, its internationally acclaimed rivals such as Benetton or Gap. Zara has developed one of the most effective quick response systems in its industry.

The process of supplying goods to the stores begins with cross-functional teams working within Zara's Design Department at the company headquarters in La Coruña. The designs reflect the latest in international fashion trends, with inspiration gleaned through visits to fashion shows, competitors' stores, university campuses, pubs, cafes and clubs plus any other venues or events deemed to be relevant to the lifestyles of the target customers. The team's understanding of directional fashion trends is further guided by regular inflows of EPOS data and other information from all of the company's stores and sites around the world.

If a proposed design is accepted, commercial specialists proceed to negotiate with suppliers, agree purchase prices, analyse costs and margins and fix a standard cross-currency price position for the garments. The size of the production run and launch dates are also determined at this point. A global sourcing policy, organized thorough the company's buying offices in the UK, China and the Netherlands, and using a broad supplier base, provides the widest possible selection of fashion fabrics, while reducing the risk of dependence on any source or supplier. Approximately 40 per cent of garments – those with the broadest and least transient appeal – are imported as finished goods from low-cost manufacturing centres in the Far East. The rest are produced by quick response in Spain, using Zara's own highly automated factories and a network of smaller contractors.

Only those operations that enhance cost efficiency through economies of scale are conducted in-house (such as dyeing, cutting, labelling and packaging). All other manufacturing activities, including the labour-intensive finishing stages, are completed by networks of more than 300 small exclusive subcontractors, each specializing in one particular part of the production process or garment type. The system is flexible enough to cope with sudden changes in demand, though production is always kept at a level slightly below expected sales, to keep stock moving. Zara has opted for under-supply, viewing it as a lesser evil than holding slow-moving or obsolete stock.

Finished goods are labelled, price-tagged and packed at the company's distribution centre in La Coruña. From there they travel by third-party contractors by road and/or air to their penultimate destinations. The shops receive deliveries of new stock on a twice-weekly basis, according to shop-by-shop stock allocations calculated by the Design Department. The whole production cycle takes only two weeks. In an industry where lead times of many months are still the norm, Zara has reduced its lead time to a level unmatched by any of its European or North American competitors.

The hub of the operation is the manufacturing and logistics centre near La Coruña. About 10,000 new items per year are turned out. New products are tested in particular stores before production runs are finalized, reducing failure rates to around 1 per cent, compared to the typical industry average of 10 per cent. The design, production and market cycle has been reduced to 22–30 days, in an industry where nine months has been the traditional lead time; see Figure 1.5.

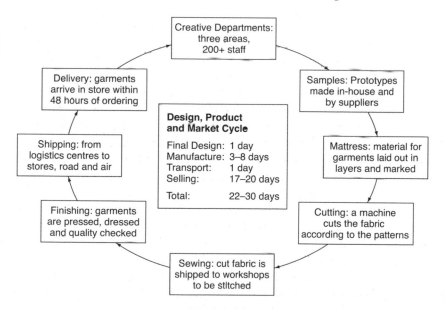

Figure 1.5 Zara: time-based competition in a fashion market

Significant investment in information technology drives the supply chain. The five-storey, 500,000 sq m logistics centre contains over 200 kilometres of moving rails, and automated routing systems deliver electronically tagged garments to the appropriate loading bays for dispersal via third-party subcontracted distributors. Products are ready for dispatch eight hours after arrival. It is claimed distribution is 98.9 per cent accurate, with shrinkage levels less than 0.5 per cent.

Zara's pre-season inventory level (the production committed before the season begins) is 15–20 per cent compared to 40–60 per cent norms in the industry, with its in-season commitment, allowed by the fast response, flexible production process in the 40–50 per cent region. This approach allows a closer alignment of production to sales forecasts, reducing the need to clear unwanted stock. Store sales are recorded daily on hand-held computers and store orders are made at predetermined times. This discipline allied to predetermined dispatch times at the logistics centre provides control and reduces costs.

Sources: Burt et al, *2006; Christopher, 1998, pp 155–7; Retail Week, 21 November 2003, pp 16–17*

In many supply chains, tiers of suppliers have been created to manufacture specific component parts. Other supplier associations have been formed to coordinate supply chain activities. In these businesses the trend has often been to buy rather than make and to outsource non-core activities. Benetton, which has been hailed as the archetypal example of a network organization, is however bucking this trend by increasing vertical integration and ownership of assets in the supply chain (Camuffo *et al*, 2001). While it is retaining its network structure, it is refining the network from product design through to distribution to its stores. While Benetton previously customized around 20 per cent of its ranges to satisfy national markets, it has reduced this to around 5 to 10 per cent in order to communicate one image of Benetton in global markets. The streamlining of its brands and in-store testing have allowed it to respond more quickly to changing market trends.

Benetton is renowned for its relationship with small and medium-sized enterprises (SMEs) in north-east Italy. These SMEs supplied the labour-intensive phases of production (tailoring, finishing and ironing) while the company kept 'in-house' the capital-intensive parts of the operation (weaving, cutting and dyeing). In the last decade it has established a high-tech production pole at Castrette, near its headquarters, to cope with increased volumes. The Castrette model has been recreated in foreign production poles in Spain, Portugal, Tunisia, Hungary, Croatia, South Korea, Egypt and India, with an SME network that focuses on specific products and skills in the area. Control also has been increased both upstream and downstream of production. The company now controls 85 per cent of its textile and thread suppliers to ensure speedy quality control and reduce lead times to workshops.

Walters and Rainbird (2004) conclude that if companies focus too much on the cost implications of supply chain management, they over-emphasize cost efficiency at the expense of meeting consumer demands (ie the service dimensions). As supply chains have become complex webs and networks with tiers of suppliers to be managed, the business answer to this complexity is to focus on cost efficiency. Walters and Rainbird (2004) argue that firms will be better placed if they combine their supply chain capabilities with demand chain effectiveness. They suggest that demand chains, which focus on demand, customers and markets and current and potential products and services, are vital for businesses, including retailers. As Table 1.2 suggests, there are differences between supply and demand chain processes and approaches. Others might argue that effective and efficient supply chains by definition include demand chain considerations. Walters (2006a, 2006b) presses the demand chain argument, and Canever *et al* (2008) provide an example of the approach. All recognize the links between supply and demand chain concepts. Here we intend supply chain management to

Table 1.2 Supply and demand chain comparison

Supply chain	Demand chain
Efficiency focus; cost per item	Effectiveness focus; customer-focused, product–market fit
Processes are focused on execution	Processes are focused more on planning and delivering value
Cost is the key driver	Cash flow and profitability are the key drivers
Short-term oriented, within the immediate and controllable future	Long-term orientated, within the next planning cycles
Typically the domain of tactical manufacturing and logistics personnel	Typically the domain of marketing, sales and strategic operations managers
Focuses on immediate resource and capacity constraints	Focuses on long-term capabilities, not short-term constraints
Historical focus on operations planning and controls	Historical focus on demand management and supply chain alignment

Source: Langabeer and Rose, 2001, in Walters, 2006b

mean incorporating a demand orientation and balance, and to include appropriate lean and agile principles, as shown below in the UK retail grocery chain.

THE GROCERY RETAIL SUPPLY CHAIN IN THE UNITED KINGDOM

The food retail supply chain is vital (Bourkakis and Weightman, 2004). The development of supply chain management and the consequent implementation of relationship initiatives have been identified as the fourth and final stage of the evolution of grocery logistics in the United Kingdom (Fernie et al, 2000). This relationship stage relates to a more collaborative approach to supply chain management after decades of confrontation. The United Kingdom is often mooted to have the most efficient grocery supply chain in the world and this is a key contributor to the profit margins of its grocery retailers.

This logistical transformation of UK retailing has occurred in a short period of time (Sparks, 1998). In the first stage of evolution (pre-1980) the dominant method of distribution to stores was by manufacturers that stored products at their factories or field warehouses for multiple drops to numerous small shops. As the retail multiple gained in prominence (especially after the abolition of resale price maintenance in 1964), retailers invested in regional distribution centres to consolidate deliveries from suppliers for onward delivery to stores. This was the first step-change in the supply of FMCGs in that buying and distribution became a headquarter function in retailing and the logistical infrastructure created a market for third-party logistics service providers.

To all intents and purposes, this marked the removal of suppliers from controlling the supply chain. This period of centralization throughout the 1980s enabled retailers to reduce lead times, minimize inventory and give greater product availability to customers in their stores. The 1990s witnessed a consolidation of this process. In many cases inventory had only been moved from store to RDC. By implementing JIT principles, retailers began to focus on their primary distribution networks (from supplier to RDC), demanding more frequent deliveries of smaller quantities. Clearly this created a problem for many suppliers in that they could not deliver full vehicle loads of product. To ensure that vehicle utilization could be maximized, consolidation centres have been created upstream of the RDC and retailers have established supplier collection programmes to pick up products from suppliers' factories on return trips from stores.

In the early years of this century, retail networks continue to be upgraded as ECR initiatives are enacted and grocery retailers accommodate the increase in non-food products through their distribution centres. Furthermore, the greater sharing of information, especially through internet exchanges, has fostered collaborative planning, forecasting and replenishment (CPFR) initiatives to reduce supply chain response times.

It should be stressed that UK grocery retail logistics is relatively unique. Retailers not only control the supply chain but also have taken over marketing responsibilities that were once the sole domain of the manufacturer, eg product development, branding, advertising and distribution. The high level of retail brand penetration has enabled them to build up store loyalty and diversify into other businesses such as banking. Control of channels is a way of life for such companies.

In other countries a more fragmented store offering is apparent and different store choice attributes are evident. For example, price and promotions are key drivers of consumer choice in the United States, Germany and France when compared with the United Kingdom. This means the consumer buys in bulk and the retailer 'forward buys' promotional stock that needs to be housed in distribution centres. Of course, in these markets land and property costs are relatively low compared with the United Kingdom, so that the savings in buying costs can outweigh the additional logistics costs. When Safeway in the United Kingdom adopted a high/low promotional strategy to compete with Asda (Wal-Mart), this led to significant disruption and changes in the operation of its RDC network.

It is also true that not all British grocery retailers have had a smooth ride when it comes to their supply systems. There is little doubt that Tesco has led the way (Smith, 2006; Smith and Sparks, 2004) and that their success has put pressure on their competitors. This pressure has been felt in directly competitive ways and also in terms of perceptions of supply chains. As Tesco continued its journey in terms of supply chains, others struggled to catch up. Asda endured a transformative period as Wal-Mart systems were introduced. Morrisons had to spend a lot of time and effort on getting the merger with Safeway managed successfully, including in supply and logistics terms. Perhaps most dramatically, Sainsbury decided to go for an advanced technical and technological reorganization of its supply chain. Box 1.3 provides some of the details of the issues it faced and the ultimately disastrous consequences that ensued, and that then had to be recovered from. Perhaps what Box 1.3 shows most strongly is that supply chains and logistics systems have to evolve constantly to meet the changing supply and demand situations and that supply chains have to consider the demand requirements of consumers. Being satisfied with the current situation is not an option.

Box 1.3 Sainsbury

Sainsbury: Supply chain transformation goes wrong

In 2000 a study of Sainsbury's supply chain revealed starkly what had become obvious – the company was operating outdated systems and facilities in its supply chain and these were adding to its costs and substantially under-performing its rivals. As a consequence the new CEO opted for an 'all-or-nothing' supply chain re-engineering strategy involving network renewal, systems and technology, and pressures and partnerships. This would involve:

- replacing the current depots with automated fulfilment factories (FF) and a primary consolidation centre (PCC);
- an integrated management of transportation from the factory gate to the store back door;
- replacing of core supply chain systems that were old and inflexible;
- ensuring clear performance measurement by reorganizing the supply chain structure and processes.

The new system would be paperless, stockless, accurate, simple and automated where appropriate. Martin White, the Director of Supply Chain stated the task in 2003:

> The core strategy is a fundamental transformation for our supply chain, it is fundamental change for our business and it is fundamental transformation for what people are doing across Europe. We are really moving forward to do something very simple; all the supply chain has to do is provide excellent service at an unbeatable cost and deliver it through having highly motivated great colleagues, particularly at a time when the tough environment is making it difficult to get people to come and work for you.
>
>   One of the core elements of the strategy was to get rid of most of the physical networks, and start again and build sheds that were fit for purpose. We needed to change all the systems; our functionality was way behind the times, and we were not giving colleagues the right tools for the job. We needed to lift their heads and let them see a new and more modern way of doing it, to change fundamentally the way we operate. It is a huge task. No one in Europe is doing anything of this size or this complexity and most importantly at this pace.

> It is end-to-end. It is substantial. It is a radical new programme. We are implementing differently to the way anyone else has tried to go about it. Clearly, it is critical.

Despite the fundamental and critical nature of the re-engineering process, the reality on implementation was not pretty. The business simply could not get the right products to the stores in sufficient volume and on time. Empty shelves in its stores were testimony to how great a failure the new system was. Poor stock availability is unacceptable. Marketing becomes impotent when the products involved are buried away in some depot instead of being at the end of the supply chain. Some Sainsbury outlets struggled to even provide an acceptable percentage of staple products. Dissatisfied customers understandably went elsewhere.

By October 2004, the problems had become acute. Sainsbury had not made up ground on its rivals generally. Another new CEO (Justin King) had been brought in. From the summer of 2004, customers had been unable to find many products on the shelves of its stores. King stated bluntly, 'Sainsbury blew millions on IT systems and automated depots that were too complex and couldn't deliver the goods to the shop.' Product availability in 2004 was worse than before the change process started. Additionally, exceptional costs of £550 million were incurred, including writing off £140 million of useless IT assets and £120 million of automated equipment for depots. There is an irony in the dissonance between the aim of 'excellent service at an unbeatable cost' and its associated cost-reduction supply chain claims, and the reality of poor availability and huge financial write-downs, let alone the damage to brand reputation.

Lawrence Christensen (the ex-Supply Chain Director of Safeway) was brought in and mandated to sort out the problems. He opted to go back to basics and revert to manual processes for stock-level management. After problem identification, he began to sort out the automated warehouses, draw up an action plan to get the best out of what already existed, and improve communication between the distribution facilities and Witron and Siemens, the companies behind the automation equipment. Furthermore, about 3,000 new employees were hired to manually sort products where needed. At their lowest point, Hams Hall, Waltham Point and Rye Park were turning away 50 per cent of supplier deliveries. In October 2004, the fulfilment factories were each operating at a capacity of only 800,000 cases a week being picked and delivered (around 30 per cent of capacity) and systems were breaking down regularly.

The Annual Report for 2006 noted the steps to put things right:

> We've made big changes in the supply chain, reorganising processes to ensure we get the right products to the right stores at the right time. Getting the supply chain right has required decisive action. We transferred our operation at Charlton to a third-party operator, closed our depots at Northfleet and Rotherham and reorganised our Basingstoke and St Albans depots into multi-purpose facilities, providing chilled, ambient and fresh products to stores. We have used our Buntingford facility to provide additional capacity at Christmas for the past two years, but will now keep it open to help us keep pace with sales growth. We worked successfully to win support for our actions from colleagues and unions.
>
> Our Waltham Point and Hams Hall depots are now processing an average of two million cases a week, significantly up on 2004/05.
>
> In January 2006 Roger Burnley joined us as Supply Chain Director and Lawrence Christensen moved into a part-time consulting role. Roger will now concentrate on consolidating the numerous changes already made. Replenishment orders are being delivered faster and in a store-friendly way, with products already sorted according to the aisles in which they are found in store, and we're working with suppliers to help us improve availability even further and reduce costs.

The 2008 Annual Report commented on the success of this 'back to basics' programme:

> Within the distribution network there has been significant improvement to depot productivity and store deliveries. These have been driven by new processes, network re-organisation, a new transport management system and the introduction of new facilities such as a new 530,000 sq ft depot at Northampton, built under carbon-negative conditions, which opened in November 2007. In April 2008 we announced the appointment of Roger Burnley, previously supply chain director, into the new role of retail and logistics director on our operating board. This reflected in part that the task had changed from fixing the basics to ongoing operational improvements by consolidating the responsibility for both store and depot operations. A 355,000 sq ft ambient facility was acquired in Staffordshire in March 2008 and a 550,000 sq ft centre in north Yorkshire, to be operated by logistics specialist Wincanton, will be used to consolidate the convenience store supply chain operation currently based in two centres at Maltby and Skelton. These will close later this year. The new depot will also provide relief for the supermarket estate this Christmas and when fully operational will employ around 500 colleagues. At Waltham Point,

some of the automated equipment has been removed and similar refurbishment is planned at Hams Hall later this year.

What is noticeable from this saga is the sheer effort involved in unravelling a very complicated initial re-engineering. Once the problem had been recognized, basic business solutions were imposed to get back on track. After this it was realized that substantial investment and system alteration still remained. The recent changes have begun to produce a modern supply chain for the business. But Sainsbury can not neglect to adapt further in the future if it wants to avoid a similar story of decline and then chaos.

Sources: BBC, 2004; Sainsbury Annual Reports (various); White, 2003; Zentes et al, 2007

SUPPLY CHAIN CHALLENGES

In 2005, Auton produced a paper for the CILT on the challenges confronting retail logistics. In a survey of various stakeholders, he asked, 'What are the three most important issues in retail logistics?' There were 23 answers but the clear top three were:

1. Increasing on-shelf availability and replenishment.
2. RFID.
3. Factory gate pricing.

On-shelf availability was revealed in particular by in-store internet picking, which showed that there were extensive voids in availability. These had previously been hidden by consumers' product substitutions and store-switching to shopping elsewhere. Lack of availability was focused on promotions and produce.

RFID was an emerging issue at the time and remains so. Dictat by retailers has not helped introduction, but the experimentation occurring suggests that RFID has something to offer, despite the costs. But what precisely are the benefits and issues?

Factory gate pricing had become an issue as its prevalence had increased. It had meant that manufacturers focused on the product and retailers on transport. It seemed valuable where volume and distribution could be driven up, to the benefit of the retailer.

After these top three, another common group of five topics emerged covering multiple channels (multi-channel retailing and returns), planning skills, global stretch of sourcing and selling, returns management and postponement and localization. With the exception of skills (which to an extent are a consequence of the others) these topics all show the concern with increasing complexity in retail logistics. At a time when there is a need for as much simplicity and transparency as possible, so the retail logistics world is getting more complex and possibly opaque. These issues also suggest how data collection and transmission across supply chains can help partners work closely together for overall benefit.

However, Auton's paper is operationally focused. More generally we might argue that there are some overriding challenges for retailers, and here we focus on technology/channels (e-commerce) and sustainability.

E-commerce

Whilst members of the supply chain have sought ways to foster collaboration, the rise of e-commerce has posed a set of challenges for retailers (Burt and Sparks, 2003). The rise and subsequent fall of many dot com companies in 1998–2002 led to a high degree of speculation as to the reconfiguration of the business to consumer (B2C) channel. Ultimately, e-fulfilment, especially the 'last mile' problem of delivering goods to the final customer, holds the key to success in this channel. The business to business (B2B) channel, however, has more to offer members of the supply chain because of the number and complexity of transactions and the greater adoption of internet technology by businesses compared with consumers. There have been numerous B2B exchange marketplaces created since the late 1990s with most of these exchanges being created in highly concentrated global markets sectors with a 'streamlined' number of buyers and sellers, for example in the automobile, chemical and steel industries. The more proactive retailers developed B2B internet exchanges as an extension of the EDI platforms created a decade earlier. This has enabled companies such as Tesco, Sainsbury and Wal-Mart to establish their own private exchanges with suppliers to share data on sales, product forecasting, promotion tracking and production planning. There are major benefits to be derived from replacing EDI efforts into a smaller number of B2B platforms. For example it is easier to standardize processes for communication, reduce development costs and give members access to a larger customer base. Internal and external systems have thus been developed.

In 2000, several retailer-based internet trading exchanges were created promising a revolution in product procurement. The two major exchanges, Global Net Exchange (GNX) and World Wide Retail Exchange

(WWRE), made some progress. They have now merged to become Agentrics (www.agentrics.com). Although the Global Commerce Initiative established draft standards for global internet trading, many issues needed to be resolved to ensure the seamless flow of data across the supply chain. The complexity of dealing with thousands of SKUs has meant that retailers have had to be selective in the projects that can be routed through their private exchanges compared with these global exchanges.

In the business to consumer (B2C) channel, the rise and fall of internet retailers around 2000–2002 brought a touch of realism to the evolving market potential of online shopping. In Europe, grocery retailers are powerful 'bricks and mortar' companies and the approach to internet retailing has been reactive rather than proactive. Most internet operations have been small and few pure players have entered the market to challenge the conventional supermarket chains. Tesco is one of the few success stories in e-grocery, having adopted what was initially an unconventional model (see Box 1.4).

Why have 'pure players' failed in this channel? Laseter *et al* (2000) identify four key challenges:

1. limited online potential;
2. high cost of delivery;
3. selection–variety trade-offs;
4. existing entrenched competition.

Ring and Tigert (2001) came to similar conclusions when comparing the internet offering with the conventional 'bricks and mortar' experience. They looked at what consumers would trade away from a store in terms of the place, product, service and value for money by shopping online. They also detailed the 'killer costs' of the 'pure play' internet grocers, notably the picking and delivery costs. The gist of the argument presented by these critics is that the standard pure-play internet model is flawed.

The two main fulfilment models are illustrated in Figures 1.6 and 1.7. The store based model makes use of existing distribution assets as products pass through regional distribution centres (RDCs) to stores where orders are assembled for delivery to online customers (Figure 1.6). The advantages of the store model are the low initial investment required and the speed of rolling out the service to a wide geographical market. Customers also receive the same products online as are available in stores. The problem here, however, is that out-of-stocks and substitutions of products are more prevalent as online shoppers compete with in-store counterparts for products. This exposed the availability issue noted earlier.

Box 1.4   Tesco.com

Tesco.com: delivering home shopping

Tesco.com has become the world's largest internet grocery system in a very short time. Unlike many of its competitors, it has opted for an in-store picking and home delivery operation, rather than starting with a dedicated distribution centre system. This choice came about for three reasons:

1. Warehouse-based picking and delivery were not believed to be economic due to low penetration levels and drive times for vehicles being high.
2. Customers confirmed that they did not want a reduced offer online as this destroyed the point of shopping at Tesco.
3. Outside London, the penetration rates possible did not make a warehouse a valid option, even if other costs (eg picking) were solved.

Since introduction there has been a very rapid roll-out to effectively cover the UK through the network of stores. Each store involved has dedicated local delivery vehicles. The system in operation has thrown up a few surprises:

- Fresh food has been a big seller online, whereas people had initially expected big, bulky replenishment items to be the most popular.
- People plan their online order better than their in-store trip (aided by the Clubcard and internet item recall availability), so a higher proportion of spend is made with Tesco.
- The non-food item offer can be more extensive online than in-store so sales in this area can be expanded.
- Knowledge is gained from the online shopping process of what items customers wanted to buy, but were not actually in stock. This helps enhance the supply system.

Source: adapted from Jones, 2001

The dedicated order picking model (Figure 1.7) utilizes e-fulfilment centres to pick and deliver orders to customers. The advantage of this system is that it is dedicated purely to e-commerce customers so out-of-stocks should be low and delivery frequencies should be higher. These picking centres, however, have less of a product range and they need to be

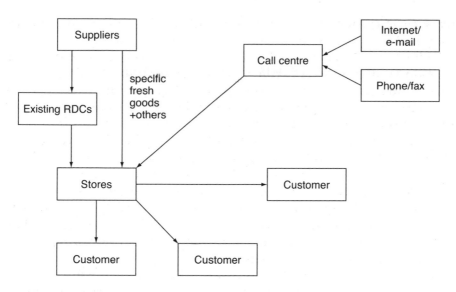

Figure 1.6　Logistics model for store based picking of e-commerce orders
Source: Foresight Retail Logistics Task Force, 2000, p 14

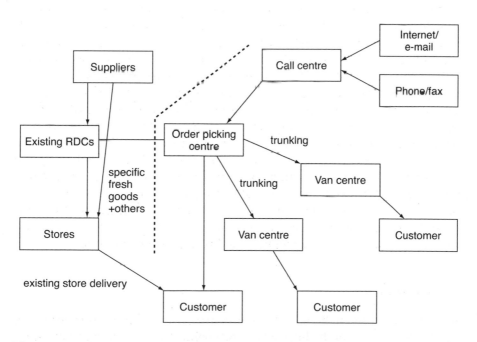

Figure 1.7　Logistics model for the e-fulfilment centre route
Source: Foresight Retail Logistics Task Force, 2000, p 15

working at capacity to justify investment costs. In non-food there are some highly successful operators of this model (eg asos.com).

Ultimately the picking centre model will possibly be the long-term solution to online grocery fulfilment. The problem is that the economics of order fulfilment and delivery are so poor in the short run that companies have abandoned this approach or gone bankrupt (Webvan). In the United Kingdom in the early 2000s, Asda closed two picking centres in London and Sainsbury developed a hybrid model. So why has the so-called least efficient fulfilment model proved successful? The answer is simple. You need to create market demand before you invest in costly infrastructure. It is interesting that recently Tesco moved to a dedicated picking operation in a part of London where volume and order density was high. With the success of other food and non-food operations, internet retailing clearly has now made its mark, but its exact logistics formula has to be monitored and adapted to demand.

E-commerce is here to stay and B2B and B2C channels will increase in importance once established standards for data transfer across the supply chain are realized. Already, the information revolution has been the catalyst for improving supply chain efficiency and for fostering stronger relationships between supply chain partners. Private internet exchanges developed by leading retailers, such as Wal-Mart with its Retail Link network, have enabled them to respond quickly to consumer choice at store level. Indeed, much of the focus of this chapter has centred on how competitive advantage can be achieved through companies cooperating and thus responding flexibly and quickly to market needs, hence the acronyms of JIT for lean supply chains and QR and ECR for agile supply chains.

Regardless of sector or industry, supply chain integration can only be achieved through greater collaboration and coordination of functions across supply chains. This means partnerships, alliances and networks that are created within and between organizations. Traditional functions can no longer be viewed in isolation or 'silos' independent from the workings of other parts of their own and other businesses. Cross-functional teamwork and inter-organizational cooperation will therefore hold the key to future developments in supply chain management. RFID for example does not fully realize its potential unless the data are shared and used to solve problems and create visibility across the channel.

Sustainability

In terms of future challenges it is necessary to mention another aspect of supply chains. One of the implicit reasons behind aspects of data communication in supply chains and the use of these data in such systems as outlined above is to reduce the demands for unnecessary product packaging and movement. It has long been recognized that cost performance and service can both be enhanced by appropriate movement of data and product. In essence this is a resource reduction strategy. More overtly, there has been growing concern with the environmental impact of logistics and companies have become increasingly concerned to ensure that their activities are appropriate. Through better use of data to understand activities, aspects of supply can be minimized. In addition, supply chains can be enhanced to ensure that resources are reused or recycled in the system and that reverse channels of logistics can reclaim valuable resources from packaging and product. Much more needs be done in this regard, but this issue will be one of the major challenges for the future.

It could be argued, for example, that many of the logistics efficiencies described above have been generated by operating systems that are insufficiently environmentally aware. Logistics can have a major adverse impact upon the environment. Whilst improvements in vehicle design, engine efficiency, reusable handling systems and building standards have reduced the impacts, the distances products now have to travel have accentuated the problems. Environmental issues are thus a major issue of future concern. They are also an issue that has become more important due to macro changes in the environment and perceptions and views over impact. The rise of awareness of climate change, environmental impact and sustainability has been dramatic. Retailers and their supply chain partners have no choice but to respond as customers expect appropriate responses and the impacts of logistics are so visible. Retail logistics is thus set to be transformed as the full issues in this area become clear and understood.

It has to be recognized, however, that terminology in this area has been the subject of some confusion. A reasonable starting point is:

> Reverse logistics is a process whereby companies can become more environmentally efficient through the recycling, reuse and reducing the amount of materials used. Viewed narrowly, it can be thought of as the reverse distribution of materials among channel members. A more holistic view of reverse logistics includes the reduction of materials in the forward system in such a way that fewer materials flow back, reuse of materials is possible, and recycling is facilitated. (Carter and Ellram, 1998, p 82)

In a retail context it is relatively straightforward to think of elements that fit these definitions. Many retailers operate a recycling policy for consumers to use and for aspects of their stores' waste. In some countries there may be legal or fiscal encouragement. Some recycling may be internalized in the company. Other material is sold on for external recycling purposes. The balance amongst these will swing towards resource reduction.

In the grocery industry, the use of plastic trays and boxes to carry and distribute fresh product has become standard (Gustafsson *et al*, 2006).

Many DCs contain specialist centres for cleaning and reusing such equipment. This is an example of a reverse logistics system in that a channel has had to be created to move containers back down the chain. In reality, the vehicles delivering to store often back-haul containers to distribution centres or to manufacturers. However, much more will have to be done to ensure that all activities are necessary and efficient from the outset.

CONCLUSIONS

This consideration of the changes and challenges in retail logistics allows us to summarize the key issues in retail logistics and supply chains. There are a number of changes in modern retail supply chains that are direct responses to the changing demands of consumers.

Pace

If nothing else, the modern consumer is more demanding and less patient than before. As a consequence, retailers, particularly in fashion goods, cannot afford to take a long time to develop, manufacture and then deliver the product. Speed or pace is vital. The concept of 'fast fashion', as developed by Zara and Hennes & Mauritz amongst others, shortens the product lifecycle in clothing from months and years to weeks and months. Development and manufacture time is slashed and demand response time is also shortened dramatically. The pace of the supply chain has also increased. This is not to say that speed in supply chains is the key priority: supply chains need to be fast on occasions but, more importantly, they have to accurately and reliably deliver the right products at the right time.

Span

Retailers are also now far more global in their outlook. As a consequence, they have to manage supply chains that span the globe. They are searching for low-cost production, but link this to an ability to distribute the product effectively from far-spread points of production to multiple locations for purchase and then consumption. There is little point in moving production points to faraway but low-cost sites if the cost and time of distribution and supply outweigh these production benefits. Retailers now talk about global supply rather than global production and are increasingly aware of the need to manage this business globally.

Availability

To meet the needs of ever more demanding consumers, retailers are increasingly more concerned about availability of products in store. Whereas increasing pace in supply chains and broadening spans of production would seem to be contradictory pressures on availability, both in fact can assist in enhancing broad supply chain availability. In part, this arises from the need to control supply chains more directly. But general availability is not what consumers require; consumers need specific on-shelf availability in front of them as they shop. Much attention has therefore been paid by retailers to ensure that the products are moved onto shelves more efficiently, rather than 'resting' in stock rooms. Any development that speeds up and simplifies this process (the so-called last 50 metres) is thus of importance. Concepts such as shelf-ready merchandise, retail-ready packaging or one-touch systems have found ready markets. Products have to be designed not only with their customer profile in mind, but with their supply and handling requirements iden-tified as well. Badly designed products and packaging from a supply chain viewpoint add cost and time to handling and reduce availability.

Information

Perhaps the critical element in retail supply chain change has been the ability to collect, disseminate and use data throughout the supply chain and the supply chain partners. Data collection on product levels and movements has allowed visibility in the supply chain (both vertically and horizontally) and has enabled stronger control of logistics and supply chain operations. By focusing on data and information, supply chain managers can increase the pace and accuracy of supply chains, allow a broader scope or span and focus on ensuring availability improvements. Data have become the lifeblood of retail supply chains. There can be difficulties in managing data on occasions and there is potential data overload if appropriate systems are not put in place. Similarly, technology systems introduction does not always go smoothly and can be highly disruptive to existing business practices. Nevertheless, the ability to collect, store and use greater amounts of data at more detailed levels and to transform these data into management infor-mation has undoubtedly enhanced retail supply systems, reducing stock levels and aiding appropriate and rapid response to consumer demand.

These changes to retail supply chains raise a number of implications for the management of retail supply chains. To a considerable extent they have had a transformative effect on how retailers (and their supply chain partners) view the management of retail supply chains. Here, we identify three implications of these changes.

1. Supply chains compete

In the traditional model of retailing, it was often believed that competition was amongst retailers alone, that is, at the horizontal level only. It is now increasingly realized that retailers are at the fulcrum of supply chains, between production and consumption. As such, the retail store is the recipient of both changing demand and supply. To the consumer, if a product is not on the shelf, then it is the retailer's fault, irrespective of where the true problem lies. As such, retailers compete not only horizontally amongst themselves, but vertically as well in terms of the efficiency and effectiveness of their supply systems. For a retailer, the implication of this is that it needs to extend its reach into the supply chain so as to make it as efficient and effective as possible.

2. Relationships matter

Given this need to extend reach into the supply chains, retailers are confronted with a major problem. The pace and scope of modern supply chains mean that, in most cases, it is not possible for retailers to actively undertake all the supply chain tasks themselves. Rather than vertical integration, vertical coordination may be the aim, but based perhaps on the integration of aspects of information systems. By properly managing supply chains, effectiveness and efficiency may be enhanced. However, this management task can be very large. To combat this, retailers have utilized logistics services providers (LSPs) to carry out many logistics activities, including a considerable degree of supply-chain management activities such as coordination, management and control. Additionally, in recognition of the pressures to make supply chains effective and efficient, there has been a tendency to simplify their structures. Thus, the number of direct partners and activities in many cases has been reduced considerably, such that the coordination activities are between a more limited number of supply chain partners, with a consequence potential for the deepening of relationships and activities.

3. Information, not product movement

The management task in supply chains has been aided by these processes of simplification and coordination. It has also been assisted by the considerable developments in data capture, storage and dissemination. Supply chains have become increasingly data-rich with these data often shared amongst the components of the supply chain partners. Data visibility means that to a large extent data movement has replaced product movement in supply chains. As supply chains have become coordinated and focused on getting closer to 'just in time' rather than operating as 'just in case', so the need for accurate management information increases. There remains much to be done in this regard, but the ability of retailers to 'see' the products at various stages in the supply chain has assisted their drives towards the development of effective and efficient supply chains. It does not matter if the supply chain orientation is towards 'lean' or 'agile' approaches, as all retailers and suppliers should be interested in having supply chains that simplify base flows and can respond rapidly to changing consumer demands when necessary.

References

Agarwal, A, Shankar, R and Tiwari, M (2006) Modelling the metrics of lean, agile and leagile supply chain: an ANP-based approach, *European Journal of Operational Research,* **173,** pp 211–25

Aldridge, D and Harrison, A (2000) Implementing Agile Methods in Retail Supply Chains: a scenario for the future, *International Journal of Agile Manufacturing,* **3,** (2), pp 37–44

Auton, B (2005) What's driving European logistics? Presentation available at http://www.ciltuk.org.uk/download/Emerging_Technologies_in_Retail_Logistics.pdf

Ayers, J B and Odegaard, M A (2008) *Retail Supply Chain Management,* Auerbach, Boca Raton

BBC (2004) Can Sainsbury's rise to the challenge? 19 October, downloaded from http://news.bbc.co.uk/go/pr/fr/-/1/hi/business/3756674.stm on 1 August 2008

Bourlakis, M A and Weightman, P W H (eds) (2004) *Food Supply Chain Management,* Blackwell, Oxford

Burt, S L and Sparks, L (2003) E-commerce and the retail process: a review, *Journal of Retailing and Consumer Services,* **10,** pp 275–86

Burt, S L, Dawson, J A and Larke, R (2006) Inditex-Zara: re-writing the rules in apparel retailing, in (eds) J A Dawson, R Larke and M Mukoyama, *Strategic Issues in International Retailing,* Routledge, London

Camuffo, A, Romano, P and Vinelli, A (2001), Back to the future: Benetton transforms its global network, *MIT Sloan Management Review,* Fall, pp 46–52

Canever, M D, Van Trijp, H C M and Beers, G (2008) The emergent demand chain management: key features and illustration from the beef business, *Supply Chain Management,* **13,** (2), pp 104–15

Carter, C R and Ellram, L M (1998) Reverse logistics : a review of the literature and framework for future investigation, *Journal of Business Logistics,* **19,** (1), pp 85–102

Christopher, M (1998) *Logistics and Supply Chain Management,* 2nd edn, FT/Prentice Hall, London

Christopher, M and Peck, H (1998) Fashion logistics, in (eds) J Fernie and L Sparks, *Logistics and Retail Management*, Kogan Page, London

Christopher, M and Peck, H (2003) *Marketing Logistics*, 2nd edn Butterworth-Heinemann, Oxford

Drucker, P (1962) The economy's dark continent, *Fortune*, April, pp 265–70

Fernie, J (1990) *Retail Distribution Management*, Kogan Page, London

Fernie, J and Sparks, L (1998), *Logistics and Retail Management*, Kogan Page, London

Fernie, J and Sparks, L (2004) *Logistics and Retail Management*, 2nd edn, Kogan Page, London

Fernie, J, Pfab, F and Marchant, C (2000) Retail grocery logistics in the UK, *International Journal of Logistics Management*, **11**, (2), pp 83–90

Foresight Retail Logistics Task Force (2000) @ Your Service: future models of retail logistics, DTI, London

Gustafsson, K, Jönson, G, Smith, D and Sparks, L (2006) *Retailing Logistics and Fresh Food Packaging*, Kogan Page, London

Harrison, A and van Hoek, R (2002) Logistics Management and Strategy. FT Prentice Hall, Harlow

Hugos, M and Thomas, C (2006) *Supply Chain Management in the Retail Industry*, Wiley, New York

Jones, D T (2001) Tesco.com: delivering home shopping, *ECR Journal*, **1**, (1), pp 37–43

Jones, D T (2002) Rethinking the grocery supply chain, in (eds) J-W Grievink, L Josten and C Valk, *State of the Art in Food*, Elsevier, Rotterdam (available from www.leanuk.org/articles.htm, downloaded 30 October 2003)

Kotzab, H and Bjerre, M (eds) (2005) *Retailing in a SCM Perspective*, Copenhagen Business School Press, Copenhagen

Langabeer, J and Rose, J (2002) *Creating Demand Driven Supply Chains*, Chandos, Oxford

Laseter, T, Houston, P, Ching, A, Byrne, S, Turner, M and Devendran, A (2000) The last mile to nowhere, *Strategy & Business*, (20), September

Lowson, B, King, R and Hunter, A, (1999) *Quick Response: Managing the supply chain to meet consumer demand*, Chichester, Wiley

Mason-Jones R, Naylor, B and Towill, D R (2000) Lean, agile or leagile? Matching your supply chain to the marketplace, *International Journal of Production Research*, **38**, (17), pp 4061–70

McKinnon, A C (1996) The development of retail logistics in the UK: A position paper, Technology Foresight: Retail and Distribution Panel, Edinburgh, Heriot-Watt University

Naylor, J B, Naim, M M and Berry, D (1999) Leagility: integrating the lean and agile manufacturing paradigm in the total supply chain, *International Journal of Production Economics*, **62**, pp 107–18

Retail Week (2003) At the heart of a retail giant, 21 November, pp 16–18

Ring, L J and Tigert, D J (2001) Viewpoint: the decline and fall of internet grocery retailers, *International Journal of Retail & Distribution Management,* **29,** (6), pp 266–73

Smith, D L G (2006) The role of retailers as channel captains in retail supply chain change: the example of Tesco, unpublished PhD thesis, University of Stirling

Smith, D L G and Sparks, L (2004) Logistics in Tesco: past, present and future, in (eds) J Fernie and L Sparks, *Logistics and Retail Management,* 2nd edn, Kogan Page, London

Sparks, L (1998) The retail logistics transformation, in (eds) J Fernie and L Sparks, *Logistics and Retail Management,* Kogan Page, London

Towill, D and Christopher, M (2002) The supply chain strategy conundrum: to be lean or agile or to be lean and agile?, *International Journal of Logistics,* **5,** (3), pp 299–309

Walters, D (2006a) Effectiveness and efficiency: the role of demand chain management, *International Journal of Logistics Management,* **17,** pp 75–94

Walters, D (2006b) Demand chain effectiveness – supply chain efficiencies, *Journal of Enterprise Information,* **19,** pp 246–51

Walters, D and Rainbird, M (2004) The demand chain as an integral component of the value chain, *Journal of Consumer Marketing,* **21,** pp 465–75

White, M (2003) Sainsbury's supply chain leading transformation, presentation and transcript, 3 October, downloaded from http://www.j-sainsbury.co.uk/files/presentations/pres100303/slides_mw.pdf on 1 August 2008

Womack, J P and Jones, D T (2005) *Lean Solutions,* Simon and Schuster, London

Womack, J P, Jones, D and Roos, D (1990) *The Machine that Changed the World: The story of lean production,* Harper-Collins, New York

Zentes, J, Marschett, D and Schramm-Klein, H (2007) *Strategic Retail Management, Sainsbury's,* Gabler, Weisbaden, pp 286–95

2

Relationships in the supply chain

John Fernie

INTRODUCTION

Relationship marketing (RM), Customer Relationship Marketing (CRM), e-CRM for online businesses and Collaborative Planning, Forecasting and Replenishment (CPFR) are only some of the acronyms to appear in the academic literature in the last 10 to 15 years. This represents a major paradigm shift in marketing and logistics away from a traditional transactional view of exchange between buyers and sellers to a more proactive, collaborative relationship approach. The purpose of this chapter is to discuss the conceptual framework of supply chain relationships and their applications to retailing through quick response and efficient consumer response initiatives. Finally, the role of logistical service providers in supply chain relationships will be reviewed.

CHANGING BUYER–SELLER RELATIONSHIPS

The origins of the relationship approach to understanding buyer–seller interaction at different parts of the supply chain go back several decades when the conventional marketing mix paradigm began to be challenged. The growth of the service sector, the move from mass marketing to micro marketing to mass customization, with the associated database infrastructure, allowed companies to target customers more effectively. Whilst consumer marketing embraced a relationship approach to improve customer retention, these trends were particularly prominent in industrial markets where the Industrial Marketing and Purchasing Group (IMP) initiated much of the business-to-business research in this area.

In parallel with these developments was a growing literature in logistics and supply chain management embodying similar paradigms and constructs. The fourth P of the marketing mix, Place, was traditionally centred on the wholesale and retail trade and how suppliers would channel their products to market. By the 1980s two key factors would begin to elevate logistics to greater prominence in the literature – the rise in power of the multiple retailers thereby changing power relationships and the need to eliminate inventory and non-value-added activities in getting products to market. Thus, to compete with Japanese manufacturing, European and US companies embraced just in time (JIT) techniques, reduced their supply base and worked more closely with the remaining suppliers. Throughout the 1990s debates emerged on the lean compared with the agile supply chain, the latter more relevant to the fast moving consumer goods (FMCG) market.

Interestingly, with a few exceptions such as Martin Christopher, the academic literature on relationships tends to be published in discrete camps as evidenced by readers on marketing (Hart, 2003) and logistics (Waters, 2007), which exhibit similar constructs when discussing relationships but very rarely cross-reference between 'marketing' and 'supply chain' literatures. Nevertheless, key themes are common – power and dependence, trust and commitment, cooperation and co-opetition, which will be discussed in turn.

Power and dependence

'Power in the supply chain can be defined operationally as the ability of one entity in the chain to control the decision of another entity' (Dapiran and Hogarth-Scott, 2003, p 259). It is generally agreed that the power base has shifted over time from supplier to retailer. When French and Raven (1959) produced their seminal work, the suppliers controlled the supply chain. The five power bases which they identified – reward power, coercive power, referent power, legitimate power and expert power – would lead to dependency of the retailer on the supplier, especially with regard to expert power in that the supplier had the marketing/logistics expertise in the channel. Clearly this has changed in the intervening years in that retailers can delist (coercive), reward, joint promote (referent) and dictate terms (legitimate) to suppliers because of their dominant market position (expert power).

The nature of such relationships between manufacturers and retailers was discussed by Kumar (1996) in a study of 400 relationships. He categorized them into different levels of dependence (Figure 2.1). The 'win-win' quadrant is the top right category where there is a high level of interdependence between parties. The 'hostage' and 'drunk with power' categories could lead to a breakdown in the relationship.

Trust and commitment

According to Kumar (1996) trust is the antithesis of power and it is trust that leads to cooperation. However, trust can easily be heralded as 'the glue that holds a relationship' (O'Malley, 2003, p 130) but it is difficult to measure because this involves social networks that are inherently fluid in a retail buying context. At an organizational level trust, and therefore commitment, can be related to the relationship lifecycle. Many UK private label suppliers have grown with the retailers they supplied, especially in the area of chilled fresh food where the category was developed by the retailer in partnership with these companies. This does not guarantee stability as evidenced by Marks & Spencer's breakdown in relationship with some UK clothing suppliers when it decided to source products offshore and thereby sever links that had been fostered for generations. Much of the discussion on the nature of competition in the UK grocery sector has focused on the possible abuse of power by retailers and their suppliers and the need for a strict code

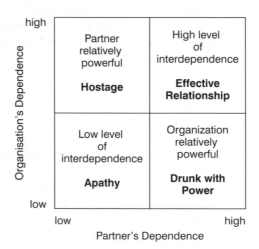

Figure 2.1 Effects of interdependence
Source: Kumar, 1996

of practice. The Competition Commission reporting in 2008 created a Groceries Supply Code of Practice (GSCOP) for retailers with over £1 million turnover to monitor their dealings with suppliers through a compliance officer and an ombudsman to arbitrate in disputes.

Cooperation and co-opetition

Much of the literature from ECR conferences and trade bodies implies greater collaboration between supply chain partners. This is discussed in more depth in the next section. In the academic literature, most attention has been focused on collaborative advantage rather than competitive advantage (Christopher and Peck, 2003) and co-opetition (Brandenburger and Naleboff, 1996) rather than competition. The thrust of this argument is that in sectors such as the FMCG industry where demand is stable, it is more appropriate for companies to 'grow the cake' in specific categories by boosting demand and compete on conventional marketing criteria. Similarly, companies have reviewed their logistics operations and are now willing to collaborate with competitors on 'invisible' shared resources but not on promotion or 'visible' marketing efforts. This mirrors the well-established approach by Japanese manufacturing companies, which cooperate on R&D but compete on the branded consumer goods in the marketplace.

The creation of value-added partnerships within industrial sectors is based on the tenets of resource-based theory, transaction cost analysis and network theory. In essence, the key decisions that have to be taken by companies within the supply chain relate to their core competencies, the allocation of resources and the network of organizations with which they interact. The best example of such a division of labour is in the clothing 'fast fashion' sector, which is discussed in much length elsewhere in the book. Benetton is the classic example of the network organization with its international poles throughout the world. Here Benetton keeps the capital-intensive parts of the operation 'in-house', contracting out to SMEs the labour-intensive phase of production (tailoring, knitting and ironing). Likewise, Zara has developed its production pole at La Coruña with its integrated network of SMEs in Galicia and northern Portugal.

In other parts of the retail sector, the rosy picture of collaboration and cooperation is less evident from published empirical research. An earlier edition of this volume cited work by Hogarth-Scott and Parkinson (1993) and Ogbonna and Wilkinson (1996) in the food sector of a more adversarial approach than the 'partnership' dialogue promulgated at the time. In the basic clothing sector similar trends were evident (Fernie, 1998) and the downward pressure in prices with the intense competition in the UK clothing market has done little to redress the emphasis on tough price negotiations. Indeed, Philip Green's takeovers of BHS and Arcadia have been marked by his public pronouncements on the renegotiating of supplier contracts.

The Competition Commission and Office of Fair Trading (OFT) reports from 2000 through to 2008 investigating the nature of competition in the UK supermarket sector were generally supportive of the status quo except for assessing the need for greater local competition and the need for a code of practice (discussed earlier) to eliminate the worst excesses of retailer power on suppliers. Also, anecdotal evidence would appear to suggest that prices were being driven down to unacceptable levels plus other 'contributions' for slotting allowances and other discounts for volume purchases. In their study of buyer–seller relationships in the UK and Australian markets, Dapiran and Hogarth-Scott (2003) challenge many of the conventional views on cooperation, trust and power. They claim that much of the literature argues that power is a negative construct and is invariably viewed as a distinctive independent construct divorced from the construct of cooperation. From their research, they would maintain that cooperation occurs as a result of compliant behaviour brought about by the application of power.

Using the results from their survey, Dapiran and Hogarth-Scott (2003) discuss dependence and power in relation to retail concentration and supplier dependency. Therefore, where retail concentration is high and there is low retailer dependence on the supplier, retailers will be more likely to use coercive power. Where concentration levels are high but dependence on suppliers is also high retailers are more likely to use expert power, probably through the use of category management. The use of such expert power leads to cooperative behaviour which in turn leads to greater trust within the relationship. This model is illustrated in Figure 2.2, which shows that the use of coercive/reward power can lead to capitulation in the relationship even if trust is broken within the context of category management and the referent/expert power in the right-hand quadrant disintegrates into coercive power.

Hingley's (2005) work on the fresh food supply chain in the United Kingdom concurs with the views of Dapiran and Hogarth-Scott (2003) in that 'the notion devised in mainstream RM (relationship marketing) literature that power is a negative and divisive influence that precludes relationshipping, is clearly flawed' (p 562). His research shows that there is an imbalance in power in such relationships but this does not exclude successful partnerships taking place. In all relationships friction and attempts to gain the upper hand will exist and will change over time.

Research by Fearne (2005) and his colleagues at Kent Business School offers further evidence that relationships are complex in the fresh food supply chain. Their research was carried out in the wake of the initial implementation of the Code of Practice referred to earlier and sought to

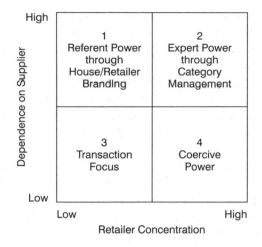

Figure 2.2   Power strategies of retailers
Source: Dapiran and Hogarth-Scott, 2003

measure fairness in exchange relationships. Their findings show considerable variation in behaviours across the sector from supermarket chains with EDLP (everyday lowprice) strategies to those embracing niche, regional strategies. Notably, the EDLP company exposed the myth that low price equates with squeezing suppliers' margins. Category leadership was another feature of successful relationships in fresh food supply chains. In their sample, a company developed relationships with a category champion which held responsibility for sourcing and distributing in the meat and dairy sectors. By coordinating the supply base to the retailer, greater efficiency in logistics operations can be achieved. This approach of using an intermediary is a feature of the fresh food supply chain.

QUICK RESPONSE

The term Quick Response (QR) was coined in the US in 1985 (Fernie, 1994; Hines, 2001) when Kurt Salmon Associates (KSA) recognized deficiencies in the fashion supply chain. According to KSA, only 11 weeks out of the 66-week lead time in the pipeline are spent on the actual processes (value-adding time / horizontal time), and the rest (non-value-adding time / vertical time) are wasted in the form of WIP and finished inventories at various stages of the complex system (Christopher, 1997,1998; Christopher and Peck, 1998; KSA, 1997). The resultant losses arising from this was estimated at US$25 billion, due to stocking too large an inventory of unwanted items and too small of the fast movers.

In response to this situation, the US textiles, apparel and retail industries formed VICS (Voluntary Interindustry Commerce Standards Association) in 1986 as their joint effort to streamline the supply chain and make a significant contribution in getting the in-vogue style at the right time in the right place (Fernie, 1994, 1998) with increased variety (Giunipero *et al*, 2001; Lowson, 1998; Lowson *et al*, 1999) and inexpensive prices. This is done by applying an industry standard in information technologies (eg bar code, EDI, shipping container marking, roll ID, etc) and contractual procedures (Giunipero *et al*, 2001; Ko *et al*, 2000; Lowson *et al*, 1999) among the supply chain members. Not only is QR an IT-driven systematic approach (Forza and Vinelli, 1996, 1997, 2000; Hunter, 1990; Riddle *et al*, 1999) to achieve supply chain efficiency from raw materials to retail stores, but it is also a partnership in which each member of the supply chain shares the risks and the benefits of the partnership on an equal basis to realize the philosophy of 'the whole is stronger than the parts'.

QR, in principle, requires the traditional buyer–supplier relationship, which is too often motivated by opportunism, to transform into a more collaborative partnership. In this QR partnership, the objectives of the vendor are to develop the customer's business. The benefit to the vendor is the likelihood that it will be treated as a preferred supplier. At the same time, the costs of serving that customer should be lower as a result of a greater sharing of information, integrated logistics systems and so on (Christopher, 1997; Christopher and Juttner, 2000). Thus, partnership among the supply chain members is a prerequisite of QR programmes.

QR's ultimate goal, nonetheless, is to give customers the savings that are gained through the initiative (Giunipero *et al*, 2001). The last, and perhaps one of the most important tenets of the original proposition of the QR concept is that QR is a survival strategy of the domestic manufacturing sector in the advanced economies against competition from low-cost imports (Finnie, 1992; METI, 2002; MITI, 1993, 1995, 1999). In the case of the United States, the QR initiative was expected to make a considerable contribution to the 'Pride with the USA' campaign, which promoted the excellence of US-made products to US consumers, who had already been familiar with inexpensive imported casual clothing.

With the basic fashion category, relatively steady demand is a feature of the market, therefore the United States-born QR concept places much focus on the relationship between retailers and the apparel manufacturers. The eventual benefits on both parties are detailed in Table 2.1. Giunipero *et al* (2001) summarize the hierarchical process of QR adaptation as an integral part of QR as business process re-engineering (BPR) (Table 2.2). This model, most appropriate for the apparel–retail linkage in basic clothing, has become a role model for QR programmes in other advanced economies. Quick response implementation, however, has been patchy as evidenced from studies undertaken in the last decade. Birtwistle *et al* (2003) in a study of quick response implementation in UK clothing retailing noted the slow progress made towards external integration of the textile supply chain with most gains being made in stages 1 and 2 of the QR development model (Table 2.2). Even in the United States, the financial benefits of QR implementation are inconclusive. Brown and Buttross (2008) measured the financial performance of companies that had adopted QR compared to those that had not. They found that adopters did not achieve significantly better results on profitability, cost efficiency or inventory levels than non-adopters and cited increased transport costs, carrying of more lines and corporate culture issues pertaining to collaboration as possible reasons for this outcome.

Having established many of the QR goals, VICS has implemented a CPFR (Collaborative Planning, Forecasting, and Replenishment) programme, to synchronize market fluctuations and the supply chain in a more real-time fashion. Through establishing firm contracts among supply chain members and allowing them to share key information, CPFR makes the forecasting, production and replenishment cycle ever closer to the actual demands in the marketplace (VICS, 1998). While the US practices have played a leading role in the QR and SCM initiatives in the apparel industry, much of the success is in the basic fashion segment, where the manufacturing phase is normally the first to be transferred offshore. In this sense, the philosophy of QR as the survival strategy of fashion manufacturing in the industrial economies has not been realized.

QR in Japan

While the US apparel industry competes largely on a cost basis in the basic fashion segment, Japanese firms have forged their success on bridge fashion with flexible specialization (Piore and Sable, 1984) in a subcontracting network of process specialists in the industrial districts (Sanchi)

Table 2.1 Retailers' and suppliers' QR benefits

Retailers' QR benefits	Suppliers' QR benefits
Reduced costs	Reduced costs
Reduced inventories	Predictable production cycles
Faster merchandise flow	Frequency of orders
Customer satisfaction	Closer ties to retailers
Increased sales	Ability to monitor sales
Competitive advantage	Competitive advantage

Source: Quick Response Services, 1995

Table 2.2 Technological and organizational QR development stages

STAGE 1	**(Introduction of basic QR technologies)** SKU Level Scanning JAN (Standard) Bar code Use of EDI Use of Standard EDI
STAGE 2	**(Internal process re-engineering via technological and organizational improvement)** Electronic Communication for Replenishment Use of Cross-docking Small Amounts of Inventory in the System Small Lot Size Order Processing ARP (Automatic Replenishment Program) JIT (Just-in-time) Delivery SCM (Shipping Container Marking) ASN (Advanced Shipping Notice)
STAGE 3	**Realization of a collaborative supply chain and Win-Win relationship)** Real-time Sales Data Sharing Stock-out Data Sharing QR Team Meets with Partnerships MRP (Material Resource Planning)

Source: Giunipero et al, 2001; KSA, 1997

led by the 'apparel firms' with design and marketing expertise. The US fashion industry essentially produces for the international market that is mostly controlled by the largest retailers, which are the real promoters and the first to profit from QR (Scarso, 1997; Taplin and Ordovensky, 1995). Thus, the Japanese fashion industry shows clear contrasts to its US and most of the European counterparts, where large retailers control the supply chain (Azuma, 2001).

Harsh competition from offshore and stagnant domestic consumption in the past decade has come to highlight the costly structure and the lack of partnership in the Japanese fashion supply chain (MITI, 1993, 1999; METI, 2002). This led to the formation of QRPA (Quick Response Promotion Association; now FISPA – Fashion Industry SCM Promotion Association) in 1994, as a joint endeavour of the Japanese TAR (Textiles, Apparel and Retailing) industries to regain competitiveness of the overall domestic industry in order to effectively and efficiently serve ever-changing customers' needs.

Since the introduction of the first QR initiative in the Japanese fashion industry, a series of programmes have been implemented in an orderly manner; from the Retail–Textiles, Textiles–Apparel, to Apparel–Sewing interfaces (Figure 2.3). FBA (Fashion Business Architecture) is an application of CPFR to the interface of the Japanese department stores and apparel firms. With an increasing adaptation of the industry standard platforms, such as EDI (JAIC: Japan Apparel Industry Council format), JAN (Japan article number) code, and ASN (Advanced Shipping Notice), department stores and apparel firms have achieved some of the expected QR benefits by eliminating the labour-intensive and costly processes of ticketing and inspections in a smooth flow of information. Elsewhere in the supply chain, however, there are fewer QR initiatives, apart from some positive results at a T–A collaboration programme in men's heavy garments manufacturing, and a fibre sourcing network at the highly concentrated sector upstream of the supply chain.

Thus, QR initiatives have not necessarily worked out throughout all of the domestic apparel manufacturing sector. Unless the ongoing partnership programme in the mid-stream of the supply chain is accomplished, the Japanese QR in the longrun is likely to be limited to retailing and apparel firms, providing that offshore sourcing locations are becoming less important. Nevertheless, Apparel–Sewing (A–S) Net, one of the current initiatives linking the apparel firms with their sewing subcontractors, is designed to be applied for sourcing in China.

EFFICIENT CONSUMER RESPONSE

Efficient Consumer Response (ECR) emerged in the United States partly through the joint initiatives between Wal-Mart and Proctor and Gamble and the increased competition in the traditional grocery industry in the

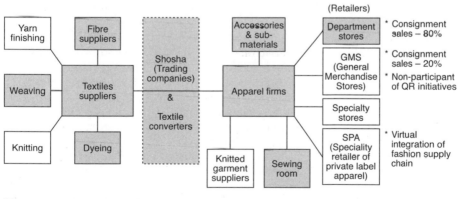

HIGHLIGHTED: (Partial) participation in the industry-wide QR initiatives

Figure 2.3 The structure of the Japanese fashion industry

early 1990s due to recession and competition from new retail formats. Once again, KSA was commissioned to analyse the supply chain of a US industrial sector. Similar trends were evident to its earlier work in the apparel sector: excessive inventories, long uncoordinated supply chains and estimated potential savings of $30 billion, 10.8 per cent of sales turnover (see Table 2.3).

ECR programmes commenced in Europe in 1993, a European Executive Board was created in 1994 and a series of projects and pilot studies were commissioned. For example, the Coopers & Lybrand survey of the grocery value chain estimated potential savings of 5.7 per cent of sales turnover (Coopers & Lybrand, 1996). Since then ECR has been adopted by around 50 countries in all of the continents of the world. The European ECR initiative defines ECR as a 'global movement in the grocery industry focusing on the total supply chain – suppliers, manufacturers, wholesalers and retailers, working closer together to fulfil the changing demands of the grocery consumer better, faster and at least cost' (Fiddis, 1997, p 40).

Despite the apparent emphasis on the consumer, much of the early studies focused mainly on the supply side of ECR. Initially reports sought efficiencies in replenishment and the standardization of material handling

Table 2.3 Comparison of scope and savings from supply chain studies

Supply chain study	Scope of study	Estimated savings
Kurt Salmon Associates (1993)	US dry grocery sector	1. 10.8% of sales turnover (2.3% financial, 8.5% cost) 2. Total supply chain $30 billion, warehouse supplier dry sector $10 billion 3. Supply chain cut by 41% from 104 days to 61 days
Coca-Cola Supply Chain Collaboration (1994)	1. 127 European companies 2. Focused on cost reduction from end of manufacturers' line 3. Small proportion of category management	1. 2.3 – 3.4 percentage points of sales turnover (60% to retailers, 40% to manufacturer)
ECR Europe (1996 ongoing)	1. 15 value chain analysis studies (10 European manufacturers, 5 retailers) 2. 15 product categories 3. 7 distribution channels	1. 5.7 percentage points of sales turnover (4.8% operating costs, 0.9% inventory cost) 2. Total supply chain saving of $21 billion 3. UK savings £2 billion

Source: Fiddis, 1997

equipment to eliminate unnecessary handling through the supply chain. The Coopers & Lybrand report in 1996 and subsequent re-prioritizing towards demand management, especially category management (see McGrath, 1997), has led to a more holistic view of the total supply chain being taken. Indeed, the greater cost savings attributed to the Coopers study compared with that of Coca-Cola can be attributed to a more narrow perspective of the value chain in the Coca-Cola survey (Table 2.3).

The main focus areas addressed under ECR are category management, product replenishment and enabling technologies. As can be seen from Figure 2.4, these are broken down into 14 further areas where improvements can be made to enhance efficiency. After the exceptional success of ECR Europe's annual conferences in the late 1990s / early 2000s, a series of initiatives were promulgated which encouraged much greater international collaboration. ECR movements began to share best practice principles, most notably the bringing together of the different versions of the US, Europe, Latin America and Asia scorecards to form a global scorecard. The scorecard was used to assess the performance of trading relationships. These relationships were measured under four categories – demand management, supply management, enablers and integrators

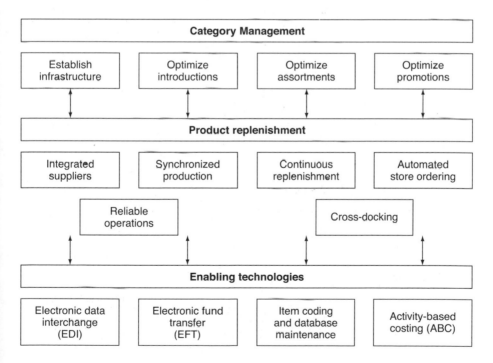

Figure 2.4 ECR improvement concepts
Source: Coopers & Lybrand, 1996

(Figure 2.5). Comparing Figures 2.4 and 2.5 shows how ECR has developed to accommodate changes in the market environment. It is not surprising that the Global Commerce Initiative (GCI) has been the instigator of the global scorecard in that one of its key objectives is to advocate the promulgation of common data and communications standards, including those pertaining to global web exchanges.

Aastrup *et al* (2008) have proposed a model which integrates the prerequisites for success to ECR activities and outcomes (Figure 2.6). The prerequisites are either industry level or specific company based. The industry level prerequisites include the availability of applicable standards and tools, the existence of critical mass within the sector and consensus on norms. Firm-specific prerequisites include attitudes towards the ECR concept, degree of collaboration necessary to share information and agreement on how costs/benefits are realized. Furthermore, the capability of companies to develop ECR initiatives is important, for example top management commitment to ECR and the technical capabilities to carry out such initiatives.

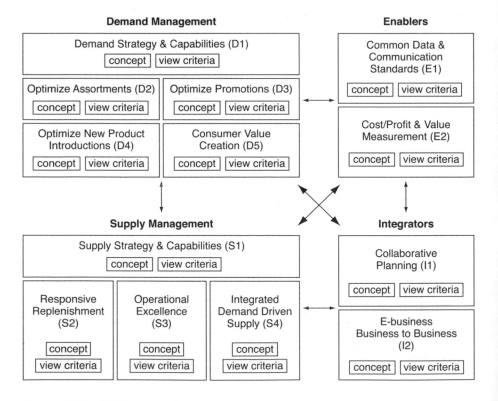

Figure 2.5   ECR concepts
Source: www.ecr-sa.co.za

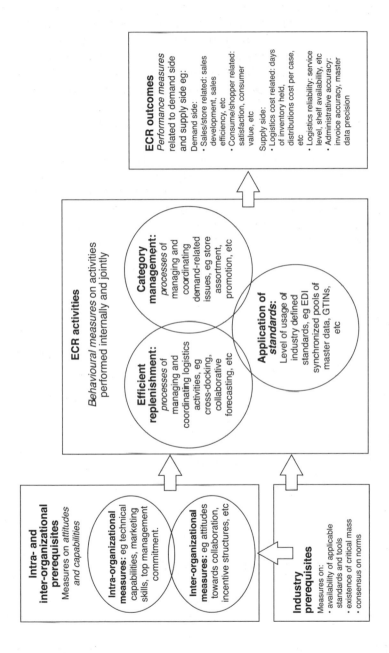

Figure 2.6 Structures of measures in efficient consumer response

On performing ECR activities, outcomes and performance measures can be evaluated through demand- and supply-related indicators. Demand-related factors are grouped into sales/store variables and consumer/shopping measures. The latter are strongly focused on consumer satisfaction, the former on 'hard' data such as category sales, sales per square metre, DPP or ABC indicators. Supply-related measures can be classified into three areas: logistics costs, logistics reliability (service levels, on-shelf availability) and administrative accuracy (invoice accuracy and master data precision).

Retailers are becoming more sophisticated in their approach to demand and supply management and there has been considerable progress in moving from a traditional organizational structure, the 'bow tie', to a multi-functional team structure (Figure 2.7) as relationships changed between retailers and their suppliers (Table 2.4). ECR conferences are replete with examples of how category performance has been improved through enhancing the consumer experience 'in store' by remerchandising traditional layouts. Such approaches are not only being adopted by major companies but also the small to medium-sized

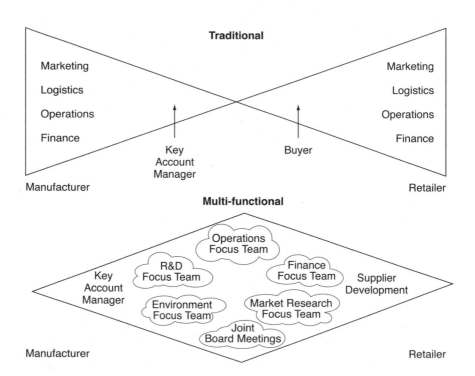

Figure 2.7 Transformation of the interface between manufacturer and retailer

Source: Fiddis, 1997

Table 2.4 Changing relationships between manufacturers and their suppliers

Current relationship	Target relationship
• Adversarial relationship	• Collaborative relationships
• Price	• Total cost management
• Many suppliers	• Few 'alliance' suppliers
• Functional silos	• Cross-functional
• Short-term buying	• Long-term buying
• High levels of just-in-case inventory	• Compressed cycle times
• Expediting due to problems	and improved demand
• Historical information	visibility
• Short shipments	• Anticipating due to
• Inefficient use of capacity	continuous improvement
	• 'Real-time' information (EDI)
	• Reliability focus
	• Run strategy and
	synchronization

Source: Coopers & Lybrand, 1996

retailers. Each year the Scottish Grocers Federation conference highlights the success of category planning between major snack and soft drink manufacturers and their convenience store customers. After all, these businesses have limited store space and depend heavily on impulse purchases.

Although logisticians would prefer a consistent flow of product through the supply chain, tactical promotions remain a feature in many retailers' marketing strategies. Research by Hoch and Pomerantz (2002) on 19 food product categories in 106 supermarket chains in the United States shows that price sensitivity and promotional responsiveness are much greater with high frequency 'staple' purchases. Compared with more specialist niche products, however, where greater variety and range built store traffic, staple products benefited from range reduction – a strategy that has been adopted by multinational FMCG manufacturers.

In order to integrate this demand-side planning with continuous replenishment, collaborative planning is necessary. The main catalyst to fostering integration has been the VICS initiative on CPFR, previously alluded to in the Quick Response section. VICS, a non-profit organization, drew its membership primarily from US non-food retailers and their suppliers until the late 1990s when the grocery sector embraced the CPFR model. For example, Wal-Mart and Warner-Lambert are usually cited as key partners in sales forecast collaboration in the early/mid-1990s. The shift into grocery is hardly surprising in view of Wal-Mart's move into

food through its supercentres in the United States and its overseas acquisitions of grocery businesses such as Asda in the United Kingdom.

By the late 1990s, VICS had produced a nine-step generic model
bringing together elements of ECR initiatives – the development of
collaborative arrangements, joint business plans, shared sales forecasts
and continuous replenishment from orders generated. GCI has been the
key player in globalizing this US initiative through collaboration
between VICS, ECR Europe, other ECR country associations and global
exchange groups.

Although the tenets of CPFR have been established, the implementation of the model remains patchy and like ECR initiatives will tend to
focus on 'quick wins' where measurable profit enhancement or cost
savings can be achieved. Most pilot schemes have involved a handful of
partners dealing with specific categories. Companies come from a variety
of technical platforms and 'cultures' of collaboration. Indeed, the likes of
Wal-Mart, Tesco and Sainsbury with their own intranet exchanges could
actually impede more universal adoption of common standards!

Overall, however, to implement CPFR it is a prerequisite that a close
working relationship has been fostered between trading partners in order
to invest the necessary human resources to develop joint plans to
generate real-time forecasts. In the discussion earlier on promotional
activity, it is clear that more volatility of demand is evident here with price
promotions, seasonal and event planning. CPFR would generate greater
benefits in these heavily promoted channels where overstocks or out-of-
stocks are more evident than in high volume, staple, frequently
purchased items where demand is more predictable.

Fernie *et al* (2004) undertook research into logistics practices and KPIs of
leading grocery retailers in Europe. One aspect of the research was to
establish the extent to which collaboration and information exchange
occurred within the context of supply chain structures in country markets.
Senior logistics directors/managers from 12 leading grocery retailers from
six European markets were interviewed. Although all companies engaged
in some degree of information sharing with suppliers, only two companies
had an IT infrastructure to conduct this efficiently.

The VICS process model was deemed to be too complex and laborious
for successful implementation. The companies that had most success
with CPFR claimed that 'keeping it simple' was the key to success. The
results show that certain preconditions are required to facilitate CPFR
implementation, namely:

- advanced IT systems;
- a centralized decision-making structure;
- scale to justify the costs incurred;
- an integrated supply chain from supplier to store.

As indicated in other research, most schemes in operation were at the pilot stage and tended to be related to specific product categories or promotional campaigns.

THE ROLE OF LOGISTICS SERVICE PROVIDERS

Third-party logistics providers are 'the missing piece in the ECR puzzle' (Rozemund, quoted in Mitchell, 1997, p 60). So much has been written on relationships throughout the supply chain, especially manufacturer–retailers relationships, but the actual physical process of getting the products to the stores has been largely ignored. Yet the decision on whether to outsource or not is very similar to that of the 'make or buy' decision in operations management. Although we will focus our attention on logistics outsourcing here, ECR draws a range of third-party activities into the equation. As companies move to become virtual organizations and concentrate upon their core competencies, relationships will be formed with IT providers, banks, advertising agencies and security companies in addition to logistics service firms. The theoretical work on outsourcing is based on the seminal work of Williamson (1979, 1990) on transaction cost analysis, which has been further developed by Reve (1990) to a contractual theory of the firm and applied by Cox (1996) and Aertsen (1993) to supply chain management. In essence, these authors have revised Williamson's ideas on high asset specificity and 'sunk costs' to the notion of 'core competencies' within the firm. Therefore, a company with core skills in logistics would have high asset specificity and would have internal contracts within the firm. Complementary skills of medium asset specificity skills would be outsourced on an 'arm's length' contract basis.

Conceptual research tends to establish the context within which the outsourcing decision is taken. Much of this work emphasized that long-term relationships or alliances are being formed between purchasers and suppliers of logistical services (Bowersox, 1990; Gardner and Cooper, 1994; McKinnon, 2003). Empirical work on the use of logistics service providers and their relationship with purchasing companies has tended to be biased towards surveys of US manufacturing companies with regard to both the provision of domestic and international outsourcing services (Gentry, 1996; Lieb and Randall, 1996; McGinnis et al, 1995; Sink et al, 1996). Throughout the latter half of the 1990s and the early years of the millennium, Langley et al (2002) have undertaken annual reviews of third-party logistics in the United States involving a range of industrial sectors, including the retail sector. In 2002 the geographical scope of the survey was widened to include western Europe and Asia.

UK research has been largely driven by surveys by consultants or contractors, for example CDC (1988) and Applied Distribution (1990) with the period surveys of PE International (1990, 1993, 1996) being the most comprehensive. Academic surveys have been limited to Fernie's exploratory work in the buying and marketing of distribution services in the retail market (Fernie, 1989, 1990) and two separate surveys on the role of dedicated distribution centres in the logistics network (Cooper and Johnston, 1990; Milburn and Murray, 1993).

These empirical surveys have shown that the contract logistics market has grown and the providers of these services have increased in status and professionalism. Logistics is no longer solely associated with trucking but warehousing, inventory control, systems and planning. However, the market is volatile and many of the reasons cited for contracting out such as cost, customer service and management expertise are also used to justify retention of the logistical service in-house. There is an impression that companies enter some form of partnership but in many cases lip-service is being paid to the idea.

In a survey of British retailers by the author in the mid-1990s it was shown that outsourcing was of marginal significance to many British retailers, which have a tendency to retain logistics services in-house (Fernie, 1999). Indeed, retail management were much more positive about the factors for continuing to do so than for contracting out such services. Clearly retailers not only wished to maintain control over the logistics functions but feel that their staff could provide customer service at a lower cost. As with other industrial sectors, transport was the most likely logistics activity to be contracted out. Despite the growth of the third-party market in the 1980s and 1990s, at that time a degree of saturation appeared to have been reached in that few companies expected to increase their proportion of contracting out in the future.

This has been borne out by the annual retail logistics surveys by the IGD, which have indicated a levelling off in expenditure in outsourcing of transport and warehousing by supermarket chains. Nevertheless, since the Fernie (1999) survey, trends in retail logistics have changed the nature of third-party support to focus more upon the primary network rather than the traditional RDC to store business. Retailers, seeking to reduce inventory at RDCs, have incorporated primary consolidation centres in their logistics network to increase vehicle fill and frequency of deliveries. The notion of 'dedicated distribution' is less relevant now than when RDCs were initially rolled out in the 1980s and 1990s. Vehicles no longer return empty to RDCs after delivering to stores but either pick up loads from suppliers or return packaging waste for recycling. Finally, factory gate pricing takes these initiatives a step further through the coordination of vehicle planning to minimize vehicle movements throughout the primary and secondary network.

All of these changes will offer opportunities to LSPs although there will be winners and losers in this new contractual environment with a rationalization of transport provision. Similar trends are evident in the clothing sector, which has come under intense price competition. In the early 2000s, the demerger of Arcadia led to outsourcing the logistics support to stores; Matalan outsourced its logistics operation in 2003 and, in order to save £20 million from its UK operation, Marks & Spencer continues to outsource but has rationalized its LSPs from five to two. The fast growing e-tailing company, ASOS, experienced difficulties in meeting customers' needs with an evolving distribution network and eventually contracted out the operation to Unipart.

Much of this discussion has focused on managing the logistics operation within the United Kingdom; however, global sourcing has become the norm for fashion retailers and their grocery counterparts have increased sourcing from overseas as they internationalize their store operations and establish buying centres around the world. This means that the 'factory gate' in factory gate pricing can be at the consolidation centre or port of entry of the country where the goods are exported. The 'core competences' of retailers do not extend to coordinating an international supply chain with involvement in tasks such as freight forwarding and customs clearance. With the evolution of global players in logistics service provision through mergers and acquisitions, the primary international network leads to increased collaboration between retailers, buying centres, intermediaries and LSPs. This discussion will be developed in the next chapter.

The outsourcing decision is a complex one related to the size and historical evolution of the network. Companies with a long history of in-house logistics have 'sunk costs' within the organizations, equating with Williamson's (1990) view on asset specificity; the contract relationship will be intra-organizational, that is between the retail and logistics departments in a company. Retail businesses with large, complex networks, however, have invariably developed relationships with logistics providers as they have moved into new geographical markets or new retail sectors. This has necessitated the use of complementary skills of medium asset specificity and the development of a range of contractual relationships of an inter-organizational nature (Cox, 1996).

This research showed that the transport function was most commonly outsourced, primarily because the core competencies required are of a residual nature with low asset specificity. Contracts are generally shorter and the relationship is more 'arm's length' in nature or what Cox (1996) classified as an adversarial leverage type of relationship.

The role of the outsourcing decision has to be seen within the context of a retailer's corporate strategy at discrete moments in a company's history. Acquisitions or demergers, expansion or withdrawal from markets can all influence logistical decisions. No two companies are the same and invariably a third-party provider is utilized to solve a particular logistical problem pertaining to a retailer's investment strategy. This 'horses for courses' argument tends to support the work undertaken in the United States by Sink *et al* (1996).

CONCLUSIONS

This chapter has illustrated the considerable research that has been undertaken into relationships through the supply chain.

A background to the theoretical constructs underpinning buyer–seller relationships was given, drawing on research from the marketing and logistics literature. The concepts of power and dependence, trust and commitment, cooperation and co-opetition were critically reviewed in the context of the retail sector. Much of the research on retailer–manufacturer relationships has focused on the concept of quick response and efficient consumer response. The development of QR from its US origins to applications in the clothing sector in Japan was discussed to illustrate that QR has less relevance in the 'fast fashion' Japanese market. ECR, by contrast, has been embraced in numerous markets throughout the world. The harmonization of the VICS model of collaborative planning forecasting and replenishment (CPFR) with ECR Europe initiatives bodes well for future collaborative initiatives in the grocery supply chain. Finally, the role of third-party logistics providers to instigate these strategic objectives was discussed. As the retail logistics environment changes – greater internationalization, integration of primary and secondary networks and reverse logistics – LSPs can capitalize on these marketing opportunities.

References

Aastrup, J, Kotzab, H, Grant, D B, Teller, C and Bjerre, M (2008) A model for structuring efficient consumer response measures, *International Journal of Retail & Distribution Management*, **36**, (8), pp 590–606

Aertsen, F (1993) Contracting out the physical distribution function: a trade-off between asset specificity and performance measurement, *International Journal of Physical Distribution and Logistics Management*, **23**, (1), pp 26–28

Applied Distribution (1990) *Third Party Contract Distribution*, Applied Distribution Ltd, Maidstone

Azuma, N (2001) The reality of Quick Response (QR) in the Japanese fashion sector and the strategy ahead for the domestic SME apparel manufacturers, *Logistics Research Network Conference Proceedings,* Heriot-Watt University, Edinburgh, pp 11–20

Birtwistle, G, Siddiqui, N and Fiorito, S S (2003) Quick response: perceptions of UK fashion retailers, *International Journal of Retail & Distribution Management,* **31,** (2), pp 118–28

Bowersox, P J (1990) The strategic benefits of logistics alliances, *Harvard Business Review,* **68,** (4) pp 36–45

Brandenburger, A and Naleboff, B (1996*) Co-opetition,* Doubleday, New York

Brown, T and Buttross, T E (2008) An empirical analysis of the financial impact of quick response, *International Journal of Retail & Distribution Management,* **36,** (8), pp 607–626

Christopher, M (1997) *Marketing Logistics,* Butterworth-Heinemann, Oxford

Christopher, M (1998) *Logistics and Supply Chain Management,* 2nd edn, Financial Times, London

Christopher, M and Juttner, U (2000) Achieving supply chain excellence: the role of relationship management, *International Journal of Logistics: Research & Application,* **3,** (1), pp 5–23

Christopher, M and Peck, H (1998) Fashion logistics, in (eds) J Fernie and L Sparks, L *Logistics and Retail Management,* Kogan Page, London

Christopher, M and Peck, H (2003) *Marketing Logistics,* Butterworth-Heinemann, Oxford

Competition Commission (2000) *Supermarkets. A report on the supply of groceries from multiple stores in the United Kingdom,* Competition Commission, London

Competition Commission (2008) *Grocery Market Investigation – Provisional Decision on Remedies,* Competition Commission, London

Cooper, J and Johnston, M (1990) Dedicated contract distribution: an assessment of the UK marketplace, *International Journal of Physical Distribution & Logistics Management,* **20,** (1), pp 25–31

Coopers & Lybrand (1996) *European Value Chain Analysis Study – Final Report,* ECR Europe, Utrecht

Corporate Development Consultants (CDC) (1988) *The UK Market for Contract Distribution,* CDC, London

Cox, A (1996) Relationship competence and strategic procurement management. Towards an entrepreneurial and contractual theory of the firm, *European Journal of Purchasing & Supply Management,* **2,** (1), pp 57–70

Dapiran, G P and Hogarth-Scott, S (2003) Are cooperation and trust being confused with power? An analysis of food retailing in Australia and the UK, *International Journal of Retail & Distribution Management,* **31,** (5), pp 256–67

Fearne, A, Duffy, R and Hornibrook, S (2005) Justice in UK supermarket buyer-supplier relationships: an empirical analysis, *International Journal of Retail & Distribution Management*, **33**, (8), pp 570–82

Fernie, J (1989) Contract distribution in multiple retailing, *International Journal of Physical Distribution & Materials Management*, **20**, (1), pp 1–35

Fernie, J (1990) Third party or own account – trends in retail distribution, Chapter 5 in Fernie, J (1990) *Retail Distribution Management*, Kogan Page, London

Fernie, J (1994) Quick Response: An international perspective, *International Journal of Physical Distribution & Logistics Management*, **24**, (6), pp 38–46

Fernie, J (1998) Relationships in the supply chain, in (eds) J Fernie and L Sparks, *Logistics and Retail Management*, Kogan Page, London

Fernie, J (1999) Outsourcing distribution in UK retailing, *Journal of Business Logistics*, **21**, (2), pp 83–95

Fernie, J, Smaros, J, Angerer, A, Torkay, B and Zotteri, G (2004) Collaborative Planning, Forecasting and Replenishment (CPFR): implementation by major grocery retailers in Europe', paper presented at EIRASS conference, Budapest, July

Fiddis, C (1997) *Manufacturer–Retailer Relationships in the Food and Drink Industry: Strategies and tactics in the battle for power*, FT Retail & Consumer Publishing, Pearson Professional, London

Finnie, T A (1992) *Textiles and apparel in the USA: Restructuring for the 1990s*, Special Report No 2632, Economist Intelligence Unit, London

Forza, C and Vinelli, A (1996) An analytical scheme for the change of the apparel design process towards quick response, *International Journal of Clothing Science and Technology*, **8**, (4), pp 28–43

Forza, C and Vinelli, A (1997) Quick Response in the textile–apparel industry and the support of information technologies, *Integrated Manufacturing Systems*, **8**, (3), pp 125–36

Forza, C, and Vinelli, A (2000) Time compression in production and distribution within the textile–apparel chain, *Integrated Manufacturing Systems*, **11**, (2), pp 138–46

French, J R P and Raven, B H (1959) The basis of social power in (ed) P Cartwright, *Studies in Social Power*, Institute for Social Research, University of Michigan, Ann Arbor, Michigan

Gardner, J and Cooper, M (1994) Partnerships: a natural evolution in logistics, *Journal of Business Logistics*, **13**, (2) pp 121–44

Gentry, J J (1996) Carrier involvement in buyer–seller supplier strategic partnerships, *International Journal of Physical Distribution & Logistics Management*, **26**, (3), pp 14–25

Giunipero, L C, Fiorito, S S, Pearcy, D H and Dandeo, L (2001) The impact of vendor incentives on Quick Response, *The International Review of Retail, Distribution and Consumer Research*, **11**, (4), pp 359–76

Hart, S (2003) *Marketing Changes*, Thomson Learning, London

Hines, T (2001) From analogue to digital supply chain: implications for fashion marketing, in (eds) P Hines and M Bruce, *Fashion Marketing, Contemporary Issues*, Butterworth-Heinemann, Oxford

Hingley, M K (2005) Power imbalanced relationships: cases from UK fresh food supply, *International Journal of Retail & Distribution Management*, **33**, (5), pp 551–69

Hoch, S J and Pomerantz, J J (2002) How effective is category management?, *ECR Journal*, **2**, (1), pp 26–32

Hogarth-Scott, S and Parkinson, S T (1993) Retailer–supplier relationships in the food channel – a supplier perspective, *International Journal of Retail & Distribution Management*, **21**, (8), pp 12–19

Hunter, A (1990) *Quick Response in apparel manufacturing: A survey of the American scene*, The Textile Institute, Manchester

Ko, E, Kincade, D and Brown, J R (2000) Impact of business type upon the adoption of quick response technologies: The apparel industry experience, *International Journal of Operations & Production Management*, **20**, (9), pp 1,093–111

Kumar, N (1996) The power of trust in manufacturer–retailer relationships, *Harvard Business Review*, **74**, (6), pp 92–106

Kurt Salmon Associates (KSA) (1997) *Quick Response: Meeting customer needs*, KSA, Atlanta, GA

Langley, C J, Allen, G R and Tyndal, G R (2002) *Third-Party Logistics Study*, Georgia Institute of Technology, Atlanta, GA

Lieb, R and Randall, M (1996) A comparison of third party logistics services by large American manufacturers, 1991, 1994 and 1995, *Journal of Business Logistics*, **17**, (1), pp 303–20

Lowson, B (1998) *Quick Response for small and medium-sized enterprises: A feasibility study*, The Textile Institute, Manchester

Lowson, B, King, R and Hunter, A (1999) *Quick Response: Managing supply chain to meet consumer demand*, John Wiley & Sons Ltd, New York

McGinnis, M A, Kochunny, C M and Ackerman, K B (1995) Third party logistics choice, *The International Journal of Logistics Management*, **6**, (2), pp 93–102

McGrath, M (1997) *A Guide to Category Management*, IGD, Letchmore Heath

McKinnon, A C (2003) Outsourcing the logistics function, in (ed) D Waters, *Global Logistics and Distribution Planning*, Kogan Page, London

METI (2002) *Seni Sangyo no Genjo to Seisaku Taiou (The Current Status of the Japanese Textile Industry and the Political Responses)*, METI (The Japanese Ministry of Economy, Trade, and Industry; formerly MITI), Tokyo

Milburn, J and Murray, W (1993) Saturation in the market for dedicated contract distribution, *Logistics Focus*, **1**, (5), pp 6–9

Mitchell, A (1997) *Efficient Consumer Response: a new paradigm for the European FMCG sector*, FT Retail & Consumer Publishing, Pearson Professional, London

MITI (1993) *Seni Vision (Textile Vision)*, MITI (The Japanese Ministry of International Trades and Industries), Tokyo

MITI (1995) *Sekai Seni Sangyo Jijo (MITI World Textile Report)*, MITI, Tokyo

MITI (1999) *Seni Vision (Textile Vision)*, MITI, Tokyo

Office of Fair Trading (2004) *The Supermarket Code of Practice*, OFT, London

Ogbonna, E and Wilkinson, B (1996) Inter-organizational power relations in the UK grocery industry: contradictions and developments, *The International Review of Retail, Distribution and Consumer Research*, **6**, (4), pp 395–414

O'Malley, L (2003) Relationship marketing, in S Hart, *Marketing Changes*, Thomson, London

PE International (1990) *Contract Distribution in the UK – What the customers really think*, PE International, Egham

PE International (1993) *Contracting-out or Selling out?*, PE International, Egham

PE International (1996) *The Changing Role of Third Party Logistics – Can the customer ever be satisfied?*, PE International, Egham

Piore, M, J and Sable, C F (1984) *The Second Industrial Divide: Possibilities for prosperity*, Basic Books, New York

Quick Response Services (1995) *Quick Response Services for Retailers and Manufacturers*, Quick Response Services, Richmond, CA

Reve, T (1990) The firm as a means of internal and external contracts, in (eds) M Aoki *et al*, *The Firm as a Nexus of Treaties*, Sage, London

Riddle, E J, Bradbard, D A, Thomas, J B and Kincade, D H (1999) The role of electronic data interchange in Quick Response, *Journal of Fashion Marketing and Management*, **3**, (2), pp 133–46

Scarso, E (1997) Beyond fashion: Emerging strategies in the Italian clothing industry, *Journal of Fashion Marketing and Management*, **1**, (4), pp 359–71

Sink, H L, Langley, C J and Gibson, B J (1996) Buyer observations of the US third-party logistics market, *International Journal of Physical Distribution & Logistics Management*, **26**, (3), pp 38–46

Taplin, I M and Ordovensky, J F (1995) Changes in buyer–supplier relationships and labor market structure: Evidence from the United States, *The Journal of Clothing Technology and Management*, **12**, pp 1–18

VICS (1998) *Collaborative Planning, Forecasting, and Replenishment Voluntary Guidelines*, Voluntary Interindustry Commerce Standards Association, Lawrenceville, NJ

Waters, D (ed) (2007) *Global Logistics and Distribution Planning*, Kogan Page, London

Williamson, O E (1979) Transaction-cost economics: the governance of contractual relations, *Journal of Law and Economics*, **22**, pp 232–61

Williamson, O E (1990) The firm as a nexus of treaties: an introduction, in (eds) M Aoki *et al*, *The Firm as a Nexus of Treaties*, Swedish Collegium for Advanced Study in the Social Sciences

3

The internationalization of the retail supply chain

John Fernie

The internationalization of retailing has attracted considerable academic attention in recent years. Although the retail industry is generally considered to be more 'culturally grounded' and therefore its foreign to total assets is lower than other manufacturing sectors, the last decade has witnessed a major restructuring of the retail marketplace. The meteoric rise of Wal-Mart to become the largest corporation in the world with sales of around US$345 billion for the fiscal year ending January 2007 has reshaped global competition in the food and general merchandise sectors. In the late 1990s/early 2000s, 'mega groups' began to dominate the global stage to compete with Wal-Mart, most notably Carrefour, Tesco, Ahold and Metro (Fernie and Arnold, 2002; Wrigley, 2002). At the same time, other retailers such as Marks & Spencer and J Sainsbury began to retract from international markets in order to compete more successfully in their own domestic market (Ayman and Burt, 2008; Burt *et al*, 2003). During the rest of the decade considerable research has been undertaken on the divestment activities of retailers (Alexander and Quinn, 2002; Burt *et al*, 2003, 2004) with considerable focus on the financial crisis of the Royal Ahold group and their phased withdrawal from Latin America, Asia and parts of Europe (Palmer and Quinn, 2007; Wrigley and Currah, 2003). Palmer (2004) has also discussed restructuring and divestment of Tesco's portfolio. However, recent years have witnessed numerous 'swaps' of stores between groups as each major player begins to focus upon specific markets to concentrate investment as saturation of foreign entrants takes place. For example, in late 2005 Tesco sold its Taiwanese operations to Carrefour for €132 million in return for Carrefour's operations in the Czech Republic and Slovakia for €189.4 million.

Despite all of the hype about international retailing, little has been written about the supply chain implications of the internationalization process. Sparks (1995) acknowledges that there are three main threads to understanding retail internationalization: international sourcing, international retail operations and internationalization of management ideas. Of these, most researchers have concentrated on retail operations but by that they mean store, not logistics, operations. Nevertheless, with the internationalization of key logistics concepts such as Quick Response (QR) and ECR, it quickly became apparent that countries were at very different stages of the adoption process of these concepts. Distribution 'cultures' vary within and between countries; hence companies seeking to expand into new markets need to be cognizant of the macro-environmental factors they will face in these markets. This chapter will seek to explore how retail logistics has evolved in different market environments and how companies are transferring world-class logistics practices from market to market. Prior to discussing these issues, however, it is appropriate to comment upon international sourcing.

INTERNATIONAL SOURCING

Although the current debate on global strategies of retailers takes the form of entry to new geographical markets, most retailers are already familiar with the internationalization process through their sourcing policies. In much the same way as manufacturers have sought 'offshore' production to reduce the costs of the manufactured product, retailers have looked beyond their domestic markets to source products of acceptable quality at competitive prices. It has been the apparel sector which has led in international sourcing policies with US, Japanese and European companies targeting low-cost labour areas in the Far East, North Africa, eastern Europe and Latin America for finished and semi-finished product. The lengthening of the supply chain clearly has given logistics managers of these companies a set of challenges in terms of the cost trade-offs with regard to better buying terms but increased distribution costs. The US company, The Limited, revolutionized the fashion retail market in the United States through its global procurement strategy, which is underpinned by state-of-the-art technology from computer-aided design to EDI links with suppliers. Those suppliers in south-east

Asia have their goods consolidated in Hong Kong from where chartered jumbo jets fly direct to their Columbus, Ohio distribution centre for onward distribution to their stores. This enabled the company to turn its inventory twice as quickly as the average for a US speciality store.

It was shown in the previous chapter that QR initiatives were initially introduced to give domestic suppliers an opportunity to compete with low-cost offshore suppliers. The enormous labour cost advantages that many of these countries have over their 'developed' counterparts, however, has meant that offshore QR has been implemented, for example fashion retailers in Japan sourcing from the Dongdaemun Market in Seoul, Korea (Azuma, 2002).

In the United Kingdom the problem of making buying decisions too far in advance from Far East suppliers has been partially solved by using a combination of manufacturers from different sourcing locations. Thus basic lines from the Far East can be ordered three months in advance, seasonal lines are augmented by East European and North African suppliers in three weeks, and shorter runs of re-makes are manufactured by British companies (Birtwistle *et al*, 2003). Through a series of case studies, Bruce *et al* (2004) show how a combination of lean, agile and 'leagile' approaches have been taken by UK companies to reduce production costs from offshore sourcing whilst at the same time retaining capacity closer to home in order to be able to respond flexibly to an increasingly volatile fashion market.

It is not only the textile markets that have witnessed an increased globalization of sourcing; similar trends are evident in the grocery sector. As consumers acquire more cosmopolitan tastes and grocery retailers have developed their product ranges over the last 10 to 15 years, it is inevitable that many products cannot be sourced from the domestic market. Nonetheless grocery retailers in the United Kingdom invariably source some products from other parts of the EU, not because of geographical or climatic reasons but because of the ability of non-UK suppliers to provide products in the volume, quality, variety and price to meet the demands of buyers.

Furthermore, the increasingly cosmopolitan tastes of a new generation of consumers have led to the creation of buying centres throughout the world by the 'mega groups' discussed earlier. The global expansion of these companies has fostered regional sourcing networks to introduce successful products into the chain's operations in new markets. In the mass 'supermarket' clothing sector Wal-Mart has been able to build upon the relationships fostered by George at Asda in Turkey (GATT – George and Atila Turkmen), to Latin American markets (*Retail Week*, 8 December 2006).

The internationalization of sourcing has been facilitated by the liberal-ization of markets in the EU in the 1990s. This has been replicated in North

America with the North American Free Trade Agreement (NAFTA) and the overall policies of the UN's World Trade Organization at liberalizing trade on a global scale. In the EU, for example, a natural consequence of the harmonization of markets in Europe has been for more manufacturing companies to treat the EU as one market, rather than a host of individual national markets. Thus the removal of trade barriers, the deregulation of transport, especially road transport, and the acceptance of uniform standards in information systems, have all promoted the re-engineering of manufacturers' supply chains.

With the advent of factory gate pricing (FGP) by UK major grocery retailers, it is likely that the costs of product and transportation will be driven down as retailers exert more control further back down the supply chain. This is not to say that FGP is not being applied in the non-food sector; it is only that the non-food supply chain is longer and more complex than in the food sector. Thus both sectors are moving to the point of origin and therefore sourcing 'ex-works'. In non-food, however, 80 per cent of product is sourced from a non-UK supplier base, and 90 per cent is moved by sea and therefore product lead times are longer with a larger margin of error in matching demand with supply than in the more 'local' food market (Jones, 2003).

In essence, the principles of logistics are the same. In food we have moved from direct deliveries from UK manufacturers' factories to stores to FGP and the efficient transportation of product from factory through consolidation centre, RDC to store. In non-food, the change has been from delivery directly paid to FOB, where the vendor was still responsible for shipping from country of origin, to ex-works where the retailer controls the whole supply chain (Figure 3.1).

This approach is exemplified by Toys R Us's relationship with Exel, the logistics service provider. Since 1996 Exel has been developing an end-to-end value-based solution to Toys R Us sourcing and logistics in China. Exel deals with 800 suppliers across South China collecting goods and consolidating them at its Yantian distribution facility. Labelling and packing are carried out there prior to maximizing container fill for onward distribution to customers' DCs (Jones, 2003). Complementing this physical flow is product visibility through the use of Log Net, which allows the transmission of orders and a tracking facility to monitor shipments throughout the supply chain cycle.

While accepting that a degree of internationalization is inevitable as trade barriers are removed, the international development of a retailer's store network poses another set of problems pertaining to sourcing decisions. In the same way as Japanese automobile companies have reconfigured their supply chain by creating a new network of suppliers in Europe and North America, retailers going global have to decide whether

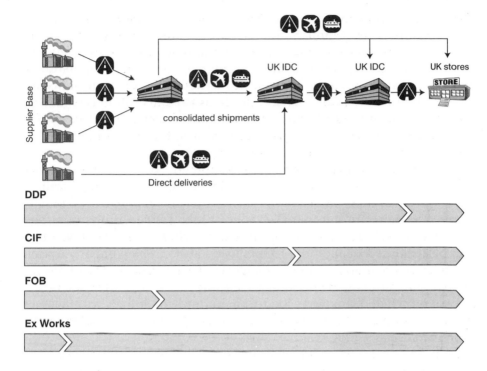

Figure 3.1 The end-to-end supply chain
Source: Jones, 2003

to source from traditional suppliers or seek new ones. Much will depend on the nature of the entry strategy. If entry is through organic growth, it may be possible to supply from the existing network; if a joint venture or an acquisition occurs, the retailer has to decide whether to retain or change the supply base it inherited. If we take the case of J Sainsbury, nearer home it entered the Northern Ireland market with an organic growth strategy, reassuring representatives of the province that it would generate considerable business for Irish suppliers. In developing economies, it has often been necessary to instil a sense of discipline into the supply chain relationship that was similar to the British model 40 years earlier.

In the case of Tesco's acquisition of ABF in Ireland a transformation of a distribution culture took place to move to a centralized logistics network. Hence, it can be argued that foreign competition or even the threat of competition has produced changes in supply chain practices. Indeed, the advent of ECR and QR can be attributed to traditional players in the US apparel and grocery sectors facing competition from new formats. Most of the success stories pertaining to the internationalization of the retail supply chain tend to relate to companies that have exerted strong control over their supply chain activities. This means the development of strong relationships with suppliers, the implementation of integrated technology systems and the willingness to be flexible in a changing marketplace. Zara, the Spanish fashion retailer, is renowned for its quick response to street fashion. With over 1,000 designers and a cost-effective production process it can take new products to stores within two to three weeks. This high product churn 'live fashion' is fuelled by an integrated supply chain operated from its production hub at La Coruña and its networks of SMEs in Galicia and northern Portugal.

It is also no coincidence that some companies such as Benetton have narrow product assortments. It should be noted that The Limited, although it is not an international firm in terms of store development, derived its name from its narrow range of high fashion sportswear. This streamlines and simplifies the logistical network. The success of Benetton can be attributed to all of the factors listed above. The company always has been at the forefront of technological efficiency from garment design, production, automated warehouses and the invoicing and transmission of orders by EDI. 'Benetton's long-term investment in logistics efficiency has been repaid with the fastest cycle times in the industry, no excess work in progress, little residual stock to be liquidated at the end of the season, and near perfect customer service' (Christopher, 1997, pp 127–8). More recently Benetton is beginning to transform its business by retaining its network structure but changing the nature of the network. Unlike most of its competitors, it is increasing vertical integration within the business (Camuffo *et al*, 2001). As volumes have increased, Benetton set up a production pole at Castrette near its headquarters. This large complex is responsible for producing around 120 million items per year. To take advantage of lower labour costs, Benetton has located foreign production poles, based on the Castrette model, in Spain, Portugal, Hungary, Croatia, Tunisia, Korea, Egypt and India. These production centres focus on one type of product utilizing the skills of the region, so T-shirts are made in Spain and jackets in eastern Europe. More recently these European platforms have been supplemented by hubs in Hong Kong, Taiwan and Shanghai.

To reduce time throughout the supply chain, Benetton has increased upstream vertical integration by consolidating its textile and thread supplies so that 85 per cent is controlled by the company. This means that Benetton can speed up the flow of materials from raw material suppliers through its production poles to ultimate distribution from Italy to its global retail network.

The retail network and the product on offer have also experienced changes. Benetton had offered a standard range in most markets but allowed for 20 per cent of its range to be customized for country markets.

Now, to communicate a single global image, Benetton is only allowing 5–10 per cent of differentiation in each collection. Furthermore, it has streamlined its brand range to focus on the United Colors of Benetton and Sisley brands.

The company has changed its store network to enable it to compete more effectively with its international competitors. It has enlarged its existing stores, where possible, to accommodate its full range of these key brands. Where this is not possible, it will focus on a specific segment or product. Finally, it is opening more than 100 megastores worldwide to sell the full range, focusing on garments with a high styling content. These stores are owned and managed solely by Benetton to ensure that the company can maintain control downstream and be able to respond quickly to market changes.

By contrast another vertically integrated company with a strong international brand name, Laura Ashley, has shown how a disastrous logistics operation can lead to the near demise of a company. In the early 1990s, the company began to incur losses, primarily because it could not deliver to its stores in time to meet a season's collection. It developed a series of uncoordinated management information systems which meant that orders invariably were not met despite its five major warehouses having over 55,000 lines of inventory (of which 15,000 were current stock). In addition, relationships with clothing suppliers, freight forwarders and transport companies were piecemeal and transactional in nature (Peck and Christopher, 1994). In 1992 Laura Ashley contracted out its entire logistics operation to Federal Express with a view to upgrading its systems and utilizing Federal Express's global network to minimize stock levels. Although Laura Ashley's logistics performance improved markedly in the following years, it terminated the contract in 1996, less than halfway through the 10-year deal. Whilst logistics can give companies competitive advantage, in this case non-availability of product in stores and catalogues lost Laura Ashley goodwill and market share in what was becoming an increasingly competitive clothing market.

In contrast to these vertically integrated companies, many international clothing retailers have either developed strong partnerships with key suppliers or allowed 'intermediaries' to carry out the sourcing, coordination and logistics to their stores from overseas markets. The example mentioned earlier of GATT (George and Atila Turkmen) illustrates how a Turkish company developed its business by working in partnership with George Davies, then of Asda, to develop the business through sharing ideas on design, production and service. The Turkmen business has now grown to the extent that it produces not only for George but also for other clothing retailers and coordinates production from 75 factories in Turkey, Romania, Egypt and China.

In their paper on global fashion supply chains, Masson *et al* (2007) discuss how UK clothing retailers manage offshore production and distribution to the United Kingdom from two markets, China and Romania. In their research they 'found that the common norm, and of course, a practice that could eliminate complexities at a stroke, was simply for the retailers to make use of third party indirect sourcing import/export agencies or what many choose to call intermediaries' (pp 244–5). These intermediaries act as agents through coordinating a network of suppliers to produce to retailer demand from around the globe. Masson *et al* (2007) also classify some of these companies as integrated service providers in that they provide in-house services from product design through manufacture to logistics provision to customers' (retailers') distribution centres.

According to this definition, Li & Fung, the Hong Kong-based multinational, is an integrated service provider. One of its main clients, The Limited, was discussed earlier in the chapter because of its innovative approach to reducing lead time to the US market. It was Li & Fung who were able to respond to The Limited's demand for yarns, specified by quantity, colour, etc for the next season (Magretta, 1998). Li & Fung started as a Chinese export company in 1906 when China was dominated by foreign commercial houses. Now it is a quoted public company with 25,000 staff in 40 countries generating revenues of US$10.4 billion. Traditionally a sourcing business, it has two other divisions – retailing and distribution – that offer a range of facilities from sourcing, manufacturing, marketing and logistics to retailing.

DIFFERENCES IN DISTRIBUTION 'CULTURE' IN INTERNATIONAL MARKETS

It was shown in the last chapter how ECR principles have been adopted at different stages by different companies in international markets; also, in the previous section it was noted that new entrants to a market can change the distribution culture of that market. Differences in such markets are more likely to exist in the context of FMCG products, especially groceries, because of the greater variations in tastes that occur in not only national but regional markets. The catalyst for much of the interest in these international comparisons was the revealing statistic from the KSA report in 1993 that it took 104 days for dry grocery products to pass through the US supply chain from the suppliers' picking lines to the checkout. With the advent of ECR, it was hoped to reduce this time to 61 days, a figure that was still behind the lead times encountered in Europe, especially in the United Kingdom where inventory in the supply chain averages around 25 days (see the GEA Consultia, 1994 report for further details).

In 1997 Mitchell explained the differences between the United States and Europe in terms of trading conditions:

- The US grocery retail trade is fragmented, not concentrated as in parts of Europe.
- US private label development is limited compared with many European countries.
- The balance of power in the manufacturer–retailer relationship is very different in the United States compared with Europe.
- The trade structure is different in that wholesalers play a more important role in the United States.
- Trade practices such as forward buying were more deeply rooted in the United States than Europe.
- Trade promotional deals and the use of coupons in consumer promotions are unique to the United States.
- Legislation, especially anti-trust legislation, can inhibit supply chain collaboration.

Many of these factors remain today. Around the same time Fernie (1994, 1995), cited the following factors to explain these variations in supply chain networks:

- the extent of retail power;
- the penetration of store brands in the market;
- the degree of supply chain control;
- types of trading format;
- geographical spread of stores;
- relative logistics costs;
- level of IT development;
- relative sophistication of the distribution industry.

The first three factors can be classified as being of a relationship nature, the others as operational factors. Clearly there has been a significant shift in the balance of power between manufacturer and retailer during the last 20 to 30 years as retailers increasingly take over responsibility for aspects of the value-added chain, namely product development, branding, packaging and marketing. As merger activity continues in Europe, retailers have grown in economic power to dominate their international branded manufacturer suppliers. While there are different levels of retail concentration at the country level, the trend is for increased concentration including the southern and eastern European nations, which have experienced an influx of French, German, British and Dutch retailers.

Although Ohbora et al (1992) argued that this power struggle is more evenly poised in the US where the grocery market is more regional in character enabling manufacturers to wield their power in the marketplace, this began to change when Wal-Mart developed its supercenters and acted as a catalyst for the 'consolidation wave' throughout the 1990s and early 21st century (Wrigley, 2001). Nevertheless, the immense size of the United States has meant that there has never been a true national grocery retailer.

Commensurate with the growth of these powerful retailers has been the development of distributor labels. This is particularly relevant in Britain whereby supermarket chains have followed the Marks & Spencer strategy of strong value-added brands that can compete with manufacturers' brands. In Britain a levelling out of own-brand penetration has been realized, whereas growth has occurred in the rest of European and other markets. It is expected that by 2020, own label will account for 30 per cent of global food sales compared with 20 per cent in 2004. In the United States, Wal-Mart's supercenter growth in the 1990s / early 2000s increased its private label share to 40 per cent and Target, one of its main competitors, reached 45 per cent (Planet Retail, 2004).

The net result of this shift to retail power and own label development has meant that manufacturers have been either abdicating or losing their responsibility for controlling the supply chain. In the United Kingdom the transition from a supplier-driven system to one of retail control is complete compared with some parts of Europe and the United States.

Of the operational factors identified by Fernie (1994), the nature of trading format has been a key driver in shaping the type of logistics support to stores. For example, in the United Kingdom the predominant trading format has been the superstore in both food and specialist household products and appliances. This has led to the development of large RDCs for the centralization of stock from suppliers. In the grocery sector, supermarket operations have introduced composite warehousing and trucking whereby products of various temperature ranges can be stored in one warehouse and transported in one vehicle. This has been possible because of the scale of the logistics operation, namely large RDCs supplying large superstores. Further upstream, primary consolidation centres have been created to minimize inventory held between factory and store. The implementation of factory gate pricing further reinforces the trend to retail supply chain control.

The size and spread of stores will therefore determine the form of logistical support to retail outlets. Geography is also an important consideration in terms of the physical distances products have to be moved in countries such as the United Kingdom, the Netherlands and Belgium compared with the United States and, to a lesser extent, France and Spain. Centralization of distribution into RDCs was more appropriate to urbanized environments where stores could be replenished regularly. By contrast, in France and Spain some hypermarket operators have few widely dispersed stores, often making it more cost-effective to hold stock in store rather than at an RDC.

The question of a trade-off of costs within the logistics mix is therefore appropriate at a country level. Labour costs permeate most aspects of the logistics mix – transport, warehousing, inventory and administration costs. Not surprisingly dependence on automation and mechanization increases as labour costs rise (the Scandinavian countries have been in the vanguard of innovation here because of high labour costs). Similarly, it can be argued that UK retailers, especially grocery retailers, have been innovators in ECR principles because of high inventory costs due to high interest rates in the 1970s and 1980s. This also is true of land and property costs. In Japan, the United States and the Benelux countries the high cost of retail property acts as an incentive to maximize sales space and minimize the carrying of stock in store. In France and the United States the relatively lower land cost leads to the development of rudimentary warehousing to house forward-buy and promotional stock.

To achieve cost savings throughout the retail supply chain, it will be necessary for collaboration between parties to implement the ECR and CPFR principles discussed in the previous chapter. Research by Aastrup *et al* (2008) on the relative success of ECR concepts in Austria and Denmark showed that a lack of collaboration, especially on sharing forecasts and plans, was a barrier to successful ECR implementation. Similarly, the work of Fernie *et al* (2004) highlighted the importance of advanced IT systems and a centralized decision-making structure in realizing CPFR objectives in European markets.

As mentioned in the previous chapter, one area of collaboration that is often overlooked is that between retailer and professional logistics contractors. The provision of third-party services to retailers varies markedly by country according to the regulatory environment, the competitiveness of the sector and other distribution 'culture' factors. For example, in the United Kingdom the deregulation of transport markets occurred in 1968 and many of the companies that provide dedicated distribution of RDCs today were the same companies that acted on behalf of suppliers when they controlled the supply chain 30 years ago. Retailers contracted out because of the opportunity cost of opening stores rather than RDCs; the cost was 'off balance sheet' and there was a cluster of well-established professional companies available to offer the service. The situation is different in other geographical markets. In the United States, in particular, third-party logistics is much less developed and warehousing is primarily run by the retailer whilst transportation is invariably contracted out to local hauliers. Deregulation of transport markets has been relatively late in the United States, leading to more competitive pricing. In China, the market has moved from a command economy and a state-controlled logistics network to a mixed economy approach and the gradual encouragement of foreign entrants. This has led to the incorporation of best practice principles (Liu, 2008). Similarly the progressive deregulation of EU markets is breaking down some nationally protected markets. Nevertheless, most European retailers, like their US counterparts, tend to only contract out the transport function. Compared with the United Kingdom, the economics of outsourcing are less attractive. Indeed, in some markets a strong balance sheet and the investment in distribution assets are viewed more positively than in the United Kingdom.

Although LSPs have their origins in national markets often with particular specialisms (Christian Salvesen with frozen food, Tibbet and Britten in clothing) most famous names of UK logistics have disappeared since the beginning of the new millennium. The internationalization of business has led to the internationalization of LSPs. Mergers and acquisitions have been a feature of the LSP sector in order to achieve scale economies in a global market. Excel Logistics bid for Tibbet and Britten in 2004 only to be taken over by DHL Logistics (Deutsche Post) in 2005. Many of the LSPs in the United Kingdom are now in foreign ownership.

THE INTERNATIONALIZATION OF LOGISTICS PRACTICES

The transfer of 'know-how', originally proposed by Kacker (1988) in reference to trading formats and concepts, can be applied to logistics practices. Indeed, we have shown already that Tesco's acquisition strategy has led to a transformation of the logistics culture in these host markets. Alternatively, companies can pursue an organic growth strategy by building up a retail presence in target markets before rolling out an RDC support function. Prior to withdrawing from the European market, Marks & Spencer's European retail strategy initially was supported from distribution centres in southern Britain. As French and Spanish markets were developed, warehouses were built to support the stores in Paris and Madrid respectively. Another dimension to the internationalization of retail logistics is the internationalization of logistics service providers, many of whom were commissioned to operate sites on the basis of their relationship with retailers in the United Kingdom. In the above Marks & Spencer example, Exel was the contractor operating the DCs in France and Spain.

Another method of transferring 'know-how' is through retail alliances. Throughout Europe, a large number of alliances exist, most of which are buying groups (Robinson and Clarke-Hill, 1995). In the 1990s some of these alliances promoted the cross-fertilization of logistics ideas and practices such as the Safeway, Casino and Ahold alliance at that time.

Composite distribution was developed by Safeway's European partners and as these companies moved into new international markets best practice principles were applied to the new geographical areas. Again LSPs tended to follow the market with Tibbett and Britten providing support to retailers in Europe and North America.

The expansion of the retail giants with their 'big box' formats into new geographical markets is leading to internationalization of logistics practice. The approach to knowledge transfer is largely dependent upon the different models of globalized retail operations utilized by these mega groups. Wrigley (2002) classified these retailers into two groups, one following the 'aggressively industrial' model, the other the 'intelligently federal' model (Table 3.1). In the former model, in which Wal-Mart and to a lesser extent Tesco can be classified, the focus is upon economies of scale in purchasing and strong implementation of the corporate culture and management practices. Hence, Tesco's implementation of centralized distribution in Ireland, the incorporation of a chilled 'composite' facility and the use of best practice ECR principles developed in the United Kingdom to Ireland. In developing markets such as in eastern Europe and Asia, Tesco has had to instil discipline with regard to quality assurance for a very fragmented supplier base. Development programmes for a large number of small suppliers were necessary prior to the implementation of centralized distribution in these markets.

Wal-Mart, however, is the best example of the aggressively industrial model. In Europe, for example, it tried to integrate buying across the acquired chains in Germany and the United Kingdom. The problem here for Wal-Mart was its size in the German market. It did not bring in sufficient

Table 3.1 Alternative corporate models of globalized retail operation

'Aggressively industrial'	vs	'Intelligently federal'
Low format adaptation	–	Multiple/flexible formats
Lack of partnerships/ alliances in emerging markets	–	Parnerships/alliances in emerging markets
Focus on economies of scale in purchasing, marketing, logistics	–	Focus on back-end integration, accessing economies of skills as much as scale, and best practice knowledge transfer
Centralized bureaucracy, export of key management and corporate culture from core	–	Absorb, utilize/transfer, best local management acquired
The global 'category killer' model	–	The umbrella organization/corporate parent model

Source: Wrigley, 2002

volumes to warrant significant discounts from suppliers to justify central distribution (Fernie *et al*, 2006). Clearly Wal-Mart had intended to acquire further stores in Germany to achieve such scale economies but its acquisition efforts came to nothing. The initial two acquired chains had a widely dispersed store network leading to high transport costs from the two distribution centres (see Figure 3.2). Eventually, after eight years without breaking even, Wal-Mart withdrew from Germany selling to Metro in 2006.

Figure 3.2   Wal-Mart's stores and DCs in Germany
Source: Fernie et al, 2006

In the United Kingdom, Wal-Mart's impact on Asda's logistics has been mainly in enhancing IT infrastructure and reconfiguring its distribution network to supply the increase in non-food lines. Its plan to create 20 supercenters by 2005 was realized with 50 per cent of its space devoted to non-food (general merchandise, clothing, electricals, etc). Furthermore, existing stores have released more space for such lines because of enhanced IT systems. Wal-Mart has revolutionized Asda's EPOS and stock data systems in Project Breakthrough, which commenced in 2000 and was rolled out to stores, depots and finally Asda House by late 2002. The incorporation of Wal-Mart's Retail Link system has allowed greater coordination of information from till to supplier, reducing costs and enhancing product availability.

Ahold, by contrast, adheres to the intelligently federal model. It has transformed logistics practices through its relationships in retail alliances and through synergies developed with its web of subsidiaries. In the United States, for example, it has retained the local store names post-acquisition and adopted best practice across subsidiaries. Furthermore, it shares distribution facilities for its own label and non-grocery lines.

References

Aastrup, J, Kotzab, H, Grant, D B, Teller, C and Bjerre, M (2008) A model for structuring efficient consumer response measures, *International Journal of Retail & Distribution Management*, **36**, (8), pp 590–606

Alexander, N and Quinn, B (2002) International retail investment, *International Journal of Retail & Distribution Management*, **30**, (2), pp 112–25

Ayman, El-Amir and Burt, S (2008) Sainsbury's in Egypt: the strange case of Dr Jekyll and Mr Hyde, *International Journal of Retail & Distribution Management*, **36**, (4), pp 300–322

Azuma, N (2002) Pronto moda Tokyo-style – emergence of collection-free street fashion in Tokyo and the Seoul-Tokyo fashion connection, *International Journal of Retail & Distribution Management*, **30**, (2), pp 137–44

Birtwhistle, G, Siddiqui N and Fiorito, S S (2003) Quick response: perceptions of UK fashion retailers, *International Journal of Retail & Distribution Management*, **31**, (2), pp 118–28

Bruce, M, Daly, L and Towers, N (2004) Lean or agile: a solution for supply chain management in the textiles and clothing industry?, *International Journal of Operations and Production Management*, **24**, (2), pp 151–70

Burt, S L, Dawson, J and Sparks, L (2003) Failure in international retailing: research propositions, *International Review of Retail, Distribution and Consumer Research*, **13**, pp 355–73

Burt, S L, Dawson, J and Sparks, L (2004) The international divestment activities of European grocery retailers, *European Management Journal*, **22**, pp 483–92

Burt, S, Mellahi, K, Jackson, T P and Sparks, L (2002) Retail internationalization and retail failure: issues from the case of Marks & Spencer, *The International Review of Retail, Distribution and Consumer Research*, **12**, (2), pp 191–219

Camuffo, A, Romano, P and Vinelli, A (2001) Back to the future: Benetton transforms its global network, *MIT Sloan Management Review*, Fall, pp 46–52

Christopher, M (1997) *Marketing Logistics*, Butterworth-Heinemann, Oxford

Fernie, J (1994) Quick Response: an international perspective, *International Journal of Physical Distribution and Logistics Management*, **24**, (6), pp 38–46

Fernie, J (1995) International comparisons of supply chain management in grocery retailing, *Service Industries Journal*, **15**, (4), pp 134–47

Fernie, J and Arnold, S J (2002) Wal-Mart in Europe: prospects for Germany, the UK and France, *International Journal of Retail & Distribution Management*, **30**, (2), pp 93–102

Fernie, J, Hahn, B, Gerhard, U, Pioch, E, and Arnold, S (2006) The impact of Wal-Mart's entry into the German and UK grocery markets, *Agribusiness*, **22**, (2), pp 247–66

GEA Consultia (1994) *Supplier–Retailer Collaboration in Supply Chain Management*, Coca-Cola Retailing Research Group Europe, London

Harvey, J (1997) International Contract Logistics, *Logistics Focus*, April, pp 2–6

Jones, M (2003) An international perspective, paper presented at the IGD Conference, Factory Gate, Open Book and Beyond, London

Kacker, M (1988) International flows of retail know-how: bridging the technology gap in distribution, *Journal of Retailing*, **64**, (1), pp 41–67

Kurt Salmon Associates (1993) *Efficient Consumer Response: Enhancing Consumer Value in the Supply Chain*, Kurt Salmon, Washington DC

Liu, X (2008) The competitiveness of logistics service providers: an investigation in China and the UK, PhD thesis, Heriot-Watt University, Edinburgh

Magretta, J (1998) Fast, global and entrepreneurial supply chain management, Hong Kong style, *Harvard Business Review*, September/October

Masson, R, Iosif, L, MacKerron, G and Fernie, J (2007) Managing complexity in agile global fashion industry supply chains, *The International Journal of Logistics Management*, **18**, (2), pp 238–54

Mitchell, A (1997) *Efficient Consumer Response: A new paradigm for the European FMCG sector*, FT Retail & Consumer Publishing, Pearson Professional, London

Ohbora, T, Parsons, A and Riesenbeck, H (1992) Alternative routes to global marketing, *The McKinsey Quarterly*, **3**, pp 52–74

Palmer, M (2004) International retail restructuring and divestment: the experience of Tesco, *Journal of Marketing Management*, **20**, pp 1075–105

Palmer, M and Quinn, B (2007) The nature of international retail divestment: insights from Ahold, *International Marketing Review*, **24**, (1), pp 26–45

Peck, H and Christopher, M (1994) Laura Ashley: the logistics challenge, in (ed) P McGoldrick, *Cases in Retail Management*, Pitman, London

Planet Retail (2004) Private Label Trends Worldwide, Press Release, London, December

Robinson, T and Clarke-Hill, C M (1995) International alliances in European retailing, in (eds) P J McGoldrick and G Davies, *International Retailing Trade and Strategies*, Pitman, London

Sparks, L (1995) Reciprocal retail internationalization: the Southend Corporation, Ito-Yokado and 7-Eleven convenience stores, *Service Industries Journal*, **15**, (4), pp 57–96

Wrigley, N (2001) The consolidation wave in US food retailing: a European perspective, *Agribusiness*, **17**, pp 489–513

Wrigley, N (2002) The landscape of pan-European food retail consolidation, *International Journal of Retail & Distribution Management*, **30**, (2), pp 81–91

Wrigley, N and Currah, A D (2003) The stresses of retail internationalization: lessons from Royal Ahold's experience in Latin America, *International Review of Retail, Distribution and Consumer Research*, **13**, pp 221–43

Part 2

Non-food (fashion) logistics

4

Market orientation and supply chain management in the fashion industry

Nobukaza J Azuma, John Fernie and Toshikazu Higashi

INTRODUCTION

The apparel industry has always been at the mercy of whims of styles and fickle customers who want the latest designs while they are still in fashion (Abernathy *et al*, 1999), along with uncontrollable parameters such as weather and economic conditions. The fashion market today is marked by ever-changing characteristics of consumers, competition and technologies. On the one hand, sophisticated consumers call for a relentless changeover of choices in products, brands and even retail trading formats. A global spread of corporate activities in the textile and fashion industry, on the other hand, has accelerated the competition among fashion businesses at all levels. In addition to this, continuous improvement in the related technologies has created less room for a technology-driven differentiation and thus become a major barrier for a fashion firm to accomplish sustainable competitive advantage vis-à-vis its rivals (Porter, 1985; Tamura, 2003).

During the last few years, many apparel firms have forged their success by reshaping their supply chain and serving their customers in an increasingly timely manner. Quick Response (QR) within Supply Chain Management

(SCM) has gained much attention as a key managerial philosophy (Fernie, 1994, 1998) to realize a firm's market-oriented strategy. In this an organization seeks to understand and anticipate customers' expressed and latent needs and develop superior solutions to these (Slater and Narver, 1999). The fashion industry is characterized by a high level of competitive intensity and market turbulence. It consists of notoriously labour-intensive multi-faceted processes with relative technological simplicity (Dicken, 1998; Dickerson, 1995). A successful implementation of a market orientation approach will, in theory, have a considerable impact on improving a firm's business performance (Jaworski and Kohli, 1993; Kohli and Joworski, 1990) as well as augmenting its customer value.

Despite such a logical fit between the QR/SCM concept and the market orientation approach, it is indeed a challenge for a fashion firm to achieve a sustainable competitive advantage within the limited scope of innovation that is dictated by the fashion process (in which the trend is directed long before the start of each season at various stages, such as colour, fibre, yarn, fabric, print, silhouette, styling details and trims; Jackson, 2001). This systematic process considerably increases the competitive intensity in the marketplace, together with a short-term competitive horizon (Tamura, 1996) that is peculiar to fashion. The condition for a fashion firm to differentiate itself from the competition, therefore, is to create a subtle yet communicable value to customers in a seemingly homogenized and yet fast-moving environment. The economy of speed (Minami, 2003) can no longer be the single driver of a firm's competitive advantage, as time compression in the supply chain is increasingly becoming a de facto standard in the fashion industry.

This chapter investigates the factors that encompass fashion firms' competitive strategies in such a dynamic yet institutionally constrained homogenized system. First, this chapter reviews the theories behind the concept of market orientation including an extended view of marketing logistics (Christopher, 1997, 1998) and supply chain management. It is followed by a discussion on the role of imitation and innovation as part of the organizational learning process and hence the competitive strategy in the fashion industry. The concluding part proposes a research agenda for future studies on the basis of the conceptual framework that is presented in this study.

MARKET ORIENTATION APPROACH AND SUPPLY CHAIN MANAGEMENT – A FOCAL POINT

Competitive advantage is at the heart of a fashion firm's performance in a volatile business environment (Lewis and Hawkesley, 1990), characterized by fragmented markets with dynamic consumers, rapid technological changes and growing non-price competition (Tamura, 2003; Weerawardena, 2003). Market orientation is an approach in which a business seeks to understand and anticipate customers' expressed and latent needs, and develop superior solutions to these (Day, 1994; Kohli and Jaworski, 1990; Slater and Narver, 1995, 1999) in order to remain proactive as well as responsive to the changing nature of the marketplace.

Market orientation (Figure 4.1) is the organization-wide generation of market intelligence pertaining to current and future customer needs, dissemination of the intelligence across departments, and organization-wide coordination (Ogawa, 2000a, 2000b; Tamura, 2003) and responsiveness to it (Kohli and Jaworski, 1990) in an efficient and effectual manner. Tamura (2003), building upon a series of conceptual frameworks of market-oriented strategy (Day, 1994; Deshpande, 1999; Deshpande *et al*, 1993; Jaworski and Kohli, 1993; Kohli and Jaworski, 1990; Narver and Slater, 1990), proposes an operationalization model of market orientation.

Much of this earlier literature is centred around the market orientation approach within the scope of a single firm's internal organization, mainly in the manufacturing sector. Kohli and Jaworski (1990) extrapolate the role of the supply-side and demand-side moderators and the environmental factors (eg market turbulence, competitive intensity and technological turbulence) (Jaworski and Kohli, 1993) as the external medium between a firm's market orientation practice and its business performance. The former stands for the nature of the competition among suppliers and the technology employed within a firm's value-adding behavioural system,

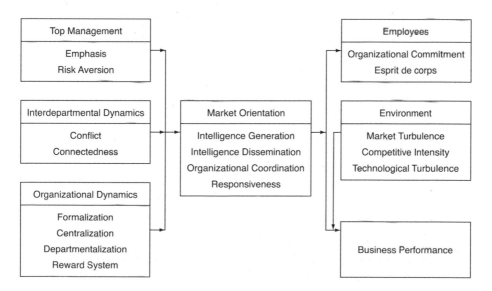

Figure 4.1 Antecedents and consequences of market orientation

and the latter represents the characteristics of demands in the industry, such as customer preferences and value consciousness.

While such references to the roles of external factors imply the potential benefit of incorporating marketing logistics (Christopher, 1997, 1998; Christopher and Juttner, 2000; Christopher and Peck, 1998) into the market orientation approach, it is Elg (2003) who explicitly emphasizes the impacts of market orientation at an inter- as well as an intra-organizational level by defining it as a joint process by retailers, suppliers, and other supply chain members (Figure 4.2). This proposition is inspired by Siguaw *et al's* (1998, 1999) studies on the influence of a firm's market orientation programme over other supply chain players in the network. Looking at the boundary between retailers and suppliers, Elg (2003) demonstrates the latent benefit that lies in this integrated market orientation approach.

Dissemination and exchange of data about consumers among the members in a retail system (retailer's supply chain) are likely to encourage each player in the network to better understand and anticipate customer needs and expectations. This also contributes to minimizing the 'Bullwhip effect' by synchronizing the flow of information and inventories in the supply chain. Joint investment in sharing a common platform in delivering quick and effective market responses facilitates the supply chain players with opportunities to develop an interdependent (De Toni and Nassimbeni, 1995) long-term partnership. Trust that is created through a transaction-specific investment (Yahagi, 1994; Yahagi *et al*, 1993) is recognized as a critical factor in maintaining an efficient and effectual inter-organizational virtual integration (Fiorito *et al*, 1999) in a long-term perspective.

In addition to these official settings in supply chain relationships, Elg (2003) singles out the salience of informal occasions where representatives

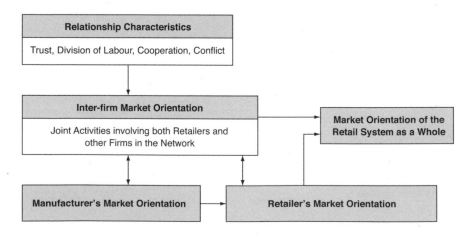

Figure 4.2 A framework for analysing a retailer's market orientation

of different members of a distribution network may meet and exchange information (Stern *et al*, 1996) and insights. This viewpoint shares much in common with the notion of 'shared space and atmosphere' (*Ba*) that is first introduced by Itami (1999) in the context of the product innovation process at a Japanese automotive company. It has often been applied to explain the agglomeration effects in the industrial districts on a number of studies in Japan (Nukata, 1998; Yamashita, 1993, 1998, 2001) and in Italy (Inagaki, 2003; Ogawa, 1998; Okamoto, 1994). The concept of *Ba* sheds light on the ambiguous effect of supply chain members' sharing of a common platform and encoding procedure towards a particular issue, upon directing the common goals and hence collaborative behaviours and a loop of organizational learning at both intra- and inter-organizational interfaces.

This last adds an important element or 'missing piece' to the classic view on supply chain management, which places an emphasis on a rather IT investment-driven systematic approach (Forza and Vinelli, 1996, 1997, 2000; Hunter, 1990; Riddle *et al*, 1999) to achieve efficiency from raw materials to retail sales floors. The traditional supply chain approach focuses on an orderly shift from a transaction-based buyer–supplier relationship to a network-based (Tamura, 2001) partnership (Figure 4.3), which is often explained by a dyadic node of communications between the two parties (Azuma and Fernie, 2003; Christopher, 1997, 1998; Fernie, 1994, 1998). The role of *Ba* is deemed to be a moderating factor in the supply chain in that it facilitates the involved parties with motivations to keep creating a unique value in a seemingly fixed and stabilized partnership environment, which otherwise can become a major inhibitor of continuous innovation. An intra- and inter-organizational learning loop in the supply chain deals not only with the ongoing and latent needs and expectations of the customers, but also serves as an implicit agent to monitor the competition's moves

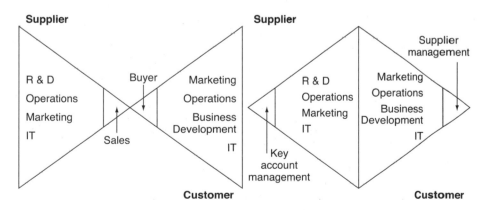

Figure 4.3 Traditional buyer–supplier relationship (left) and partnership buyer–supplier relationship (right)

and innovatively copy (Levitt, 1969, 1983; Takeishi, 2001) their operational excellence to gain advantage in the competitive league in the volatile world of fashion.

Figure 4.4 summarizes the relationship between a firm's market-oriented strategy and the role of the supply chain in organically coordinating a series of actions in the external as well as internal processes of

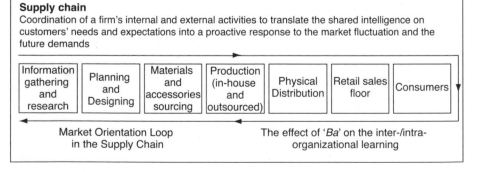

Operational Flow of Actions →

Intelligence Generation	Intelligence Dissemination & Organizational Response System	Response & Feedback Mechanism

← **Continuous Organizational Learning & Entrepreneurship** →

Customer focus	**Response system**	**Short-term response**
Industry & market information (External forces to affect customer expectations and preferences – eg competition, technologies & regulations)	Inter-functional dissemination of intelligence	Service augmentation
	Inter-functional integration and coordination at a corporate level to effectively respond to the captured intelligence	Minor style/product adjustment
		Price-based response to competition
Trend intelligence at various levels		Sales promotion and advertising
Current customer needs	Organizational design to implement the market-oriented programme	Store display and VMD adjustment
Future customer needs and expectations		**Long-term response**
Information from informal as well as formal sources	The senior management's commitment to the market-oriented approach	New product/brand/retail format development
(Speed of Intelligence generation is important.)	Inter-firm sharing of intelligence and collaborative response to the existing and latent customer needs	Style/product augmentation
		Channel/sourcing development and diversification

Supply chain
Coordination of a firm's internal and external activities to translate the shared intelligence on customers' needs and expectations into a proactive response to the market fluctuation and the future demands

Information gathering and research	Planning and Designing	Materials and accessories sourcing	Production (in-house and outsourced)	Physical Distribution	Retail sales floor	Consumers

← Market Orientation Loop in the Supply Chain ← The effect of 'Ba' on the inter-/intra-organizational learning

Figure 4.4 The conceptual model of the market orientation approach in the fashion industry

market orientation: 1) recognition of the market environment, 2) generation of intelligence on the customer's existing needs and latent/future expectations, 3) intra- and inter-organizational dissemination of the intelligence, and 4) responses to satisfy the needs and feedback of the actions (Pelham, 1997; Tamura, 2001, 2003).

The objectives of QR and supply chain management in the fashion industry are far simpler than trade-offs between the size of IT (SCM enablers) investment and the actual impact of SCM on improving the pipeline throughput and financial performance (Fiorito et al, 1999; Tamura, 2001). A supply chain, as Porter (1985) describes in the value system concept, is a network of independent firms' value chains that are involved in the production and marketing of particular products and services. This network of value chains targets customer satisfaction, while the traditional value chain approach intends to increase a firm's profit margin (McGee and Johnson, 1987). Supply chain, in this sense, is a fundamental behavioural architecture in which any market-oriented firm finds itself involved and therefore it is not a system to be configured from scratch, but an existing framework that needs refinement and restructuring in accordance with the degrees of a firm's market orientation. Particularly in the fashion industry where highly fragmented SME contractors commit many of the supply chain phases, the organizational aspect of supply chain management should be given more credibility than the IT investment vs economies of scale justification.

To put it simply, the goals of supply chain management in the fashion industry are, therefore, in delivering the in-vogue style at the right time in the right place (Fernie, 1994), with increased variety and affordability (Giunipero et al, 2001; Lowson, 1998; Lowson et al, 1999) and more room for customization (Pine, 1993), thus satisfying both the existing and potential needs of the customers (Slater and Narver, 1999). In other words, QR/SCM, in theory, is a medium that induces an organization to create superior customer value, and hence achieve a competitive advantage in the volatile marketplace (Porter, 1985).

At an operational level, the concept of QR and SCM requires a firm and its supply chain partnerships to coordinate its internal and external activities (Chandra and Kumar, 2000) in order to translate their shared intelligence on customers' needs and expectations into a proactive response to the market fluctuation and the future demands. It aims at accurately forecasting the market trends and flexibly synchronizing these with the entire process in the supply chain, based upon an efficient and effectual sharing of key information, and the risks and benefits that are embedded in the long and complex pipeline (Christopher, 1997, 1998; Christopher and Juttner, 2000).

Thus, it would be reasonable, at least at a theoretical level, to integrate the action flow in the market orientation approach into an extended concept of marketing logistics and supply chain management (Christopher, 1997, 1998; Christopher and Juttner, 2000; Christopher and Peck, 1998), since it is consistent with the intra- and inter-firm coordination mechanism of the supply chain in delivering a flexible and rapid response to the current and foreseen needs of the customer.

MARKET ORIENTATION APPROACH AND SUPPLY CHAIN MANAGEMENT – THE REALITY

Despite such a strong potential for a market orientation being rooted in the SCM philosophy, it is hardly possible for a fashion firm to establish a sustainable competitive advantage solely through its market orientation and supply chain effectiveness. This is due partly to an institutional mechanism in which the fashion trend is set farther ahead of the beginning of each season by a variety of international bodies at various levels, such as colour directions, fibre, yarn, fabric, print and finish, silhouette, styling details and trims (Chimura, 2001; Jackson, 2001). Even the designs presented at the international catwalks mostly find their origins in the design movement, exotic costumes, styles on the street, and other sources that share a continuity from the past, although futuristic as well as contemporary components are always added on to the new collection.

This systematic fashion process of planned creation and obsolescence considerably limits the scope of innovation and thus increases the competitive intensity in the fashion industry towards the state of competitive myopia (Tamura, 1996). No one creation in the history of modern fashion is as epoch-making as the cornerstone innovations in other industries, such as James Watt's and Edison's or more recently the internet, in terms of impacts on the lifestyle of the people. Due to its relative simplicity in related technologies and uniformity in the usage of clothes, a breakthrough innovation (Shumpeter, 1934) is unlikely to take place in the fashion industry. Whilst production technologies and consumer preferences in the fashion industry are in a constant state of change and sophistication, their degree of mutation does not reach the extent that it invalidates or 'de-matures' (Abernathy et al, 1983) the existing technological and design paradigm (Dosi, 1982; Kuhn, 1970; Takeishi, 2001).

Fashion is, indeed, a unique phenomenon. It consistently transforms and fluctuates, reflecting the mood of the society. The degree of metamorphosis, however, is within a nominal but a discernable extent in the mind of the consumer. The condition for a fashion firm to differentiate from competition, therefore, is to create a subtle yet appealing difference to the customers in an apparently homogenized environment, where the economy of speed (Minami, 2003) can no longer deliver a sustainable competitive advantage. Compression in the three dimensions of time in marketing the fashion style, serving the customers and reacting to the market change (Christopher and Peck, 1998; Hines, 2001) within a supply chain has been becoming a de facto standard in the fashion industry.

If one assumes an entrepreneurial risk and explores ideas to achieve a higher level of intrinsic differentiation by increasing levels of product transformation, the ideal means would be by bringing the decoupling point at the material development stage back up the supply chain (Meijboom, 1999). It, nevertheless, involves a significant risk to commit too much to backward speculation (Yahagi, 2001), because a firm is then required to trade off the variety of its fashion offers with the post-ponement benefits. The order lot size is by far larger in the materials than in the finished apparel products, and lead times are lengthier in the upstream sector. To narrow down the variety in the materials not only deprives a firm of its organizational agility (Tamura, 1996) to effectively respond to the market fluctuation but also affects its financial performance, once the trend ceases to be up for the business. The Japanese women's clothing sector, for example, calls for a considerable variety in designs and hence diversity in the choice of materials (Azuma and Fernie, 2003). Some of the functions delivered by textile converters, such as assortment in a smaller lot size, risk avoidance, finance, conveyance of market information and the introduction of cutting-edge materials (Tamura, 1975), are indispensable to executing a market-oriented response to the ever-changing fragmented needs of the consumer. Thus, there still remains a question regarding this trade-off issue in the fashion supply chain.

Besides, the relationships among the supply chain members in reality tend not be motivated by common goals and objectives that are based upon an effective sharing of key information and an efficient flow of inventories in the entire supply chain. It is too often the case in the fashion industry that an extreme responsiveness of a firm's fashion supply chain is achieved through an unequal distribution of power. The players who command the creative shrewdness and the marketing function in the mid-to-down stream of the pipeline effectually impose a flexible response in the labour-intensive processes on their SME subcontractors who are mostly dependent upon their orders (Azuma, 2001; Azuma and Fernie, 2003). An effective sharing of *Ba*, in reality, is hard to realize in a power-game relationship (Fernie, 1998; Whiteoak, 1994). Therefore, collaborative creation of a unique value 'from the source' is normally hard to achieve for a fashion firm, coupled with the speculation/postponement issue (Alderson, 1957; Bucklin, 1965) above.

Thus, the competitive environment in the fashion industry is configured in a somewhat unique way, and this makes it difficult for a fashion firm to differentiate from competition simply via implementing a market-oriented supply chain approach. An integrated programme of market orientation and supply chain management certainly provides a fashion firm and its supply chain partnerships with better visibility of its market-orientation activities and helps them deliver a rapid and flexible response to the actual and latent needs in the marketplace. Nevertheless, it doesn't allow a firm to achieve a concrete differentiation and hence a sustainable competitive advantage. Being locked into a partnership with a smaller number of suppliers, based on a transaction-specific investment, a firm would gradually decrease its capability in satisfying the market needs for variety and in executing an effective organizational leaning at both official and unofficial settings.

It is indeed paradoxical that an inter- and intra-organizational approach to anticipate and better respond to the changing needs of the customers results in homogenizing firms' responses to the consumers within the restrained scope of innovation in the fashion industry. A rapid and flexible response is often just a prerequisite for a fashion firm to avoid being left out in the midst of harsh competition. So, what are the real drivers of differentiation in the fashion market?

THE ROLE OF IMITATION AND INNOVATION IN THE FASHION BUSINESS

The fashion industry is an institutional system in which firms' market-oriented commitment can very often result in an apparent homogenization in the fashion retail mix beyond the boundaries of companies as well as brand labels (Azuma and Fernie, 2003). In addition to the restraint on the scope of innovation and the degree of product transformation, due to the systematic mechanism of shaping trends and the difficulties in bringing up the decoupling point (Meijboom, 1999) in the supply chain, there is a complex set of factors that prohibits a clear-cut fashion differentiation in the marketplace.

While an increasing number of fashion firms have gained much of the time-based (Maximov and Gottschilich, 1993; Stalk and Hout, 1990) competitive capability via a flexible and responsive supply chain, their responses to the market change are predominantly short-term oriented. This is partially because there exists a power-game relationship within the inter-firm network in the pipeline (Azuma, 2001; Azuma and Fernie, 2003; Fernie, 1998; Whiteoak, 1994). It prevents the creative effect of sharing *Ba* among the supply chain members from being realized and reduces the degree of intrinsic differentiation from the materials stage. Stronger members in the supply chain are more prone to gleaning a short-term benefit than pursuing a long-term competitive edge. Their contracted suppliers, on the other hand, are historically highly dependent on their order placements and so have not developed their own innovative function. A truly collaborative market-oriented supply chain in a fast-moving environment is indeed hard to organize for a shared goal and objective.

The influence of fashion media is another factor that inhibits a fashion firm's sustainable competitive advantage. These media, especially the fashion press, persistently feature the upcoming trend and styles, and simultaneously invalidate the trend in the 'near past'. Thus, what is 'in' at present can possibly become 'out', even overnight, with the power of the media. The positioning of a fashion firm in the marketplace is, by the same token, susceptible to 'what the fashion press says' in addition to 'what the consumers expect'.

Finally, innovation spill-over (Porter, 1985; Takeishi, 2001) is a very conspicuous phenomenon in the fashion industry. Earlier studies identify a set of inhibitors of imitation (Besanko *et al*, 2000; Levin *et al*, 1998; Porter, 1996; Rumelt, 1984; Teece, 1986; White, 1982; Williams, 1992) – legal and regulatory protection, superior access to the materials, resources and customers, the size of the market and the economies of scale, company-specific intangible capabilities and strategic fit.

In the fashion industry, however, most of these barriers are less effective to prevent imitators, due to the nature of the industry. First of all, tangible aspects of the fashion retail mix, such as products and retail formats, can easily be copied through observation and reverse engineering (Von Hipper, 1988), and it is almost impossible to ban the 'me-toos' and the innovative imitators (Levitt, 1969, 1983). In fact, many of the so-called innovative high street retailers, such as The Limited, Zara and many of the Japanese players, have developed their capability to adapt the external fashion sources in their own style (Azuma, 2002; Burt *et al*, 2003; Fisher *et al*, 1999; Levitt, 1969, 1983; Minami, 2003) through their market-oriented supply chain approaches.

Even the know-how and expertise in the backyard of the retail mix are not secure from competitors' intelligence activities (Tamura, 2003). By sharing common suppliers, interior decorators, consulting firms, sales promotion companies, third-party logistics service providers, credit card operators and IT service providers, a fashion firm's operational secrets are sometimes passed on from one party to another, thus decimating the operational competence of a company. Higher occurrences of job-hopping in the fashion industry also stimulate the leakage of such 'tacit knowledge' from one company to another. This fluid movement of human resources across the industry encourages the formation of unofficial human contacts and thus a 'tacit knowledge' that works within the particular environment at a specific company is translated into a 'common knowledge' among a much larger group of the players in the industry.

Figure 4.5 summarizes the nature of the competition and innovation in the fashion industry, and describes why the market-oriented approach tends to take on a short-term competitive horizon. Taking the institutional and operational characteristics of the fashion industry into consideration, firms' short-termism in their market orientation would be logical, as there exist few opportunities to leverage from the fast-mover advantage and establish a sustainable competitive advantage (Levitt, 1969; Schnaars, 1994).

Fashion firms' market-oriented supply chain behaviours are, rather, sustained by an organizational learning loop of their market operation. As Weerawardena (2003) explains, it is not solely the heterogeneous firm-specific resources (Barney, 1991; Montgomery and Wernerfelt, 1988; Rumelt, 1984), such as all assets, capabilities, organizational processes, firm attributes, information and knowledge, that determine a firm's source of competitive advantages. Resources do not exclusively determine what the firm can do and how well it can do it (Grant, 1991; Weerawardena, 2003). It is a firm's capabilities to make better use of available resources (Mahoney and Pandian, 1992; Penrose, 1955; Weerawardena, 2003) that help a firm achieve real rents, although the corporate capability itself is counted as part of the resources.

In the context of the fashion industry, this capability-based approach fits well into the framework of firms' market-oriented supply chain activities. Fashion firms are consistently faced with a situation in which

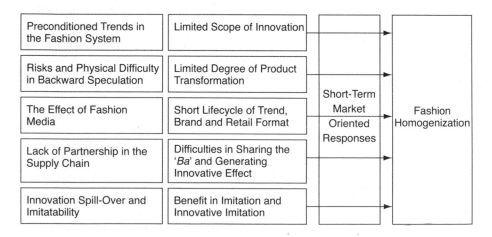

Figure 4.5 The process of fashion homogenization

their current competitive excellence is innovatively imitated or leapfrogged by their entrepreneurial competition at any point of time. Whilst this is a natural phenomenon in the volatile world of fashion, such a competitive intensity, coupled with the institutional factors, requires fashion firms to continuously monitor each other as well as their customers' needs and then create a subtle yet unique 'difference' that better satisfies the customers' expectations than its rivals. This continuous loop of imitation, ongoing subtle innovation, organizational learning, resultant accumulation of new resources and a firm's capability to utilize its internal and external resources, are deemed the determinant of a fashion firm's competitive advantage in the short-term volatile competitive horizon.

This sequence of imitation and innovation among the competitors is persistently taking place within the setting of their integrated market-oriented supply chain. The business that translates the understated needs of the customer can create a subtle yet effective difference in a seemingly homogenized market environment. In addition to this, the loop of the short-term market-oriented responses to the marketplace plays a crucial role in turning the wheel of innovation in the fashion industry, although the nature of the innovation is incremental due to the industry's specificity. Figure 4.6 depicts the organizational learning loop within a fashion firm's market-orientation approach.

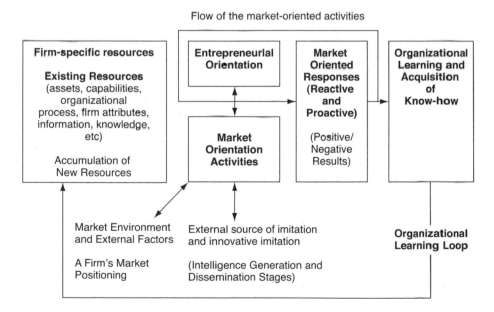

Figure 4.6 Organizational learning model in a fashion firm's market orientation

CONCLUSION AND THE RESEARCH AGENDA FOR FUTURE STUDIES

This chapter has explored the unique nature of competition in the fashion industry from the viewpoint of market orientation and supply chain management. An integrated approach of these two concepts is found, in theory, to create a great potential for a fashion firm (and its supply chain members) to enhance business performance and hence achieve a sustainable competitive advantage by effectively translating latent as well as existing customer needs and expectations into their market responses. The limited scope of innovation in the fashion industry, however, hinders an intrinsic fashion differentiation from taking place, and so fashion firms tend to build their market-oriented activities upon a short-term competitive horizon. Thus, a firm's capability to innovatively copy its competition in the process of its market-oriented supply chain is the determinant of its competitive advantage in the midst of ever-changing needs and expectations of the consumers in the marketplace. An implication is that a firm's long-term success in such an environment is thus dependent on its capability in organizationally learning from the past, present and future of its market-oriented activities in the restrained yet volatile environment.

Whilst this study has focused on a theoretical discussion and identified some of the key factors in the fashion industry that affect fashion firms' market-oriented supply chain strategy, there exists a strong need to empirically analyse the nature of the competition, the degree of homogenization of the fashion market, and the key retail mix components for differentiation in a seemingly homogenized marketplace. Particularly in the second and third issues, it will be worthwhile to compare and contrast firms' perception of their own retail mix with consumers' relative evaluation of different firms' retail mix. Since a fashion firm's retail mix is a major consequence of its market-oriented supply chain activities, an intensive analysis of the gap between the two parties will reveal the conditions for achieving a competitive advantage in the fast-moving yet restricted marketplace environment.

References

Abernathy, F H, Dunlop, J T, Hammond, J H and Weil, D (1999) *A Stitch in Time*, Oxford University Press, New York

Abernathy, W J, Clark, K and Kantrow, A (1983) *Industrial Renaissance: Producing a competitive future for America*, Basic Books, New York

Alderson, W (1957) *Marketing Behaviour and Executive Action*, Richard D Irwin, New York

Azuma, N (2001) The reality of Quick Response (QR) in the Japanese fashion sector and the strategy ahead for the domestic SME apparel manufacturers, *Logistics Research Network 2001 Conference Proceedings*, Heriot-Watt University, Edinburgh, pp 11–20

Azuma, N (2002) Pronto Moda Tokyo style – emergence of collection-free street fashion and the Tokyo–Seoul connection, *International Journal of Retail & Distribution Management*, **30**, (3), pp 137–44

Azuma, N and Fernie, J (2003) The changing nature of Japanese fashion: can Quick Response improve supply chain efficiency? *European Journal of Marketing*, **38** (7), pp 790–808

Barney, J (1991) Firm resources and sustained competitive advantage, *Journal of Management*, **17**, (1), pp 99–120

Besanko, D, Dranove, D and Shanley, M (2000) *Economics of Strategy*, 2nd edn, John Wiley and Sons Ltd, New York

Bucklin, L P (1965) Postponement, speculation, and structure of distribution channels, *Journal of Marketing Research*, **2**, (1)

Burt, S L, Dawson, J and Larke, R (2003) Inditex – Zara: Rewriting the rules in apparel retailing, Conference Proceedings, 2nd Asian Retail and Distribution Workshop, UMDS Kobe, Japan

Chandra, C and Kumar, S (2000) Supply chain management in theory and practice: a passing fad or a fundamental change?, *Industrial Management & Data Systems*, **100**, (3), pp 100–113

Chimura, N (2001) *Sengo Fashion Story (Post War Fashion Story)*, Heibonsha, Tokyo

Christopher, M (1997) *Marketing Logistics*, Butterworth-Heinemann, Oxford

Christopher, M (1998) *Logistics and Supply Chain Management*, 2nd edn, Financial Times, London

Christopher, M and Juttner, U (2000) Achieving supply chain excellence: the role of relationship management, *International Journal of Logistics: Research & Application*, **3**, (1), pp 5–23

Christopher, M and Peck, H (1998) Fashion logistics, in (eds) J Fernie and L Sparks, *Logistics and Retail Management*, Kogan Page, London

Day, G (1994) The capabilities of market-driven organizations, *Journal of Marketing*, **58**, pp 37–52

Deshpande, R (ed) (1999) *Developing a Market Orientation*, Sage Publishing, CA

Deshpande, R, Farley, J U and Webster Jr, F E (1993) corporate culture, customer orientation, and innovativeness in Japanese firms; a quadrad analysis, *Journal of Marketing*, **57**, pp 23–37

De Toni, A and Nassimbeni, G (1995) Supply networks: Genesis, stability and logistics implications. A comparative analysis of two districts, *International Journal of Management Science*, **23**, (4), pp 403–18

Dicken, P (1998) *Global Shift – Transforming the world economy*, 3rd edn, Paul Chapman Publishing, London

Dickerson, K (1995) *Textiles and Apparel in the Global Economy*, Prentice Hall, New Jersey

Dosi, G (1982) Technological paradigms and technological trajectories: a suggested interpretation of the determinants and directions of technical change, *Research Policy*, **11**, (3), pp 147–62

Elg, U (2003) Retail market orientation: a preliminary framework, *International Journal of Retail & Distribution Management*, **31**, (2), pp 107–17

Fernie, J (1994) Quick Response: an international perspective, *International Journal of Physical Distribution & Logistics Management*, **24**, (6), pp 38–46

Fernie, J (1998) Relationships in the supply chain, in (eds) J Fernie and L Sparks, *Logistics and Retail Management*, Kogan Page, London

Fiorito, S S, Giunipero, L C and Oh, J (1999) Channel relationships and Quick Response implementation, Conference Paper, 10th International Conference on Research in the Distributive Trades, Stirling University

Fisher, M L, Raman, A and McClelland, A S (1999) *Supply Chain Management at World Co., Ltd.*, World Co., Ltd., Tokyo

Forza, C and Vinelli, A (1996) An analytical scheme for the change of the apparel design process towards quick response, *International Journal of Clothing Science and Technology*, **8**, (4), pp 28–43

Forza, C and Vinelli, A (1997) Quick Response in the textile–apparel industry and the support of information technologies, *Integrated Manufacturing Systems*, **8**, (3), pp 125–36

Forza, C and Vinelli, A (2000) Time compression in production and distribution within the textile–apparel chain, *Integrated Manufacturing Systems*, **11**, (2), pp 138–46

Giunipero, L C, Fiorito, S S, Pearcy, D H and Dandeo, L (2001) The impact of vendor incentives on Quick Response, *The International Review of Retail, Distribution and Consumer Research*, **11**, (4), pp 359–76

Grant, R M (1991) Analysing resources and capabilities, in (ed) R M Grant, *Contemporary Strategic Analysis: Concepts, techniques and applications*, Basil Blackwell, Oxford

Hines, T (2001) From analogue to digital supply chain: implications for fashion marketing, in (eds) T Hines and M Bruce, *Fashion Marketing, Contemporary Issues*, Butterworth-Heinemann, Oxford

Hunter, A (1990) *Quick Response in Apparel Manufacturing: A survey of the American scene*, The Textile Institute, Manchester

Inagaki, K (2003) *Italia no Kigyouka Network (Entrepreneurs' Networking in Italy)*, Hakuto-Shobo, Tokyo

Itami, H (1999) *Ba no Dynamism (The Dynamics of Shared Space and Atmosphere)*, NTT Publishing, Tokyo

Jackson, T (2001) The process of fashion trend development leading to a season, in (eds) T Hines and M Bruce, *Fashion Marketing*, Butterworth-Heinemann, Oxford

Jaworski, B and Kohli, A (1993) Market orientation: antecedents and consequences, *Journal of Marketing,* **57,** pp 53–70

Kohli, A and Jaworski, B (1990) Market orientation: the construct, research propositions, and managerial implications, *Journal of Marketing,* **54,** pp 1–18

Kuhn, T (1970) *The Structure of Scientific Revolutions,* University of Chicago Press, Chicago

Levin, R C, Klevorick, A K, Nelson, R R and Winter, S G (1988) Appropriating the returns from industrial research and development, *Brooking Papers on Economic Activity,* **13,** (2) pp 839–916

Levitt, T (1969) *The Marketing Mode,* McGraw-Hill, New York

Levitt, T (1983) *The Marketing Imagination,* Free Press, New York

Lewis, B R and Hawkesley, A W (1990) Gaining a competitive advantage in fashion retailing, *International Journal of Retail & Distribution Management,* **18,** (4), pp 21–32

Lowson, B (1998) *Quick Response for Small and Medium-sized Enterprises: A feasibility study,* The Textile Institute, Manchester

Lowson, B, King, R and Hunter, A (1999) *Quick Response: Managing supply chain to meet consumer demand,* John Wiley & Sons, New York

Mahoney, J T and Pandian, J R (1992) The resource-based view within the conversation of strategic management, *Strategic Management Journal,* **13,** (5), pp 363–80

Maximov, J and Gottschilich, H (1993) Time-cost-quality leadership, *International Journal of Retail & Distribution Management,* **21,** (4), pp 3–12

Meijboom, B (1999) Production-to-order and international operations: a case study in the clothing industry, *International Journal of Operations & Production Management,* **19,** (5/6), pp 602–19

McGee, J and Johnson, G(eds) (1987) *Retail Strategies in the UK,* John Wiley & Sons, Chichester

Minami, C (2003) *Fashion Business no Ronri – ZARA ni Miru Speed no Keizai* (The logic in the fashion business – the impact of economies of speed from ZARA experiences), *Ryutsu Kenkyu,* June, pp 31–42

Montgomery, C A and Wernerfelt, J M (1988) Diversification, Ricardian rents and Tobins Q, *Rand Journal of Economics,* **19,** pp 623–32

Narver, J and Slater, S (1990) The effect of a market orientation on business profitability, *Journal of Marketing,* **54,** pp 20–35

Nukata, H (1998) *Sangyo Shuseki ni Okeru Bungyo no Jyunansa* (Flexible division of labour in industrial agglomerations), in (eds) H Itami, S Matushima and T Kitsukawa, *Sangyo Shuseki no Honshitsu (The Essence of the Industrial Agglomeration),* Yuhikaku, Tokyo

Ogawa, H (1998) *Italia no Chusho Kigyo (SMEs in Italy),* JETRO, Tokyo

Ogawa, S (2000a) *Innovation no Hassei Genri (The Process of Innovation),* Chikura Shobo, Tokyo

Ogawa, S (2000b) *Demand Chain Keiei (Demand Chain Management),* Nippon Keizai Shimbunsha, Tokyo

Okamoto, Y (1994) *Italia no Chusho Kigyo Senryaku (SMEs' Strategies in Italy),* Mita Shuppan Kai, Tokyo

Pelham, A J (1997) Market orientation and performance: the moderating effects of product and customer differentiation, *Journal of Business and Industrial Marketing,* **12,** (5), pp 276–96,

Penrose, E T (1955) *The Theory of the Growth of the Firm,* John Wiley and Sons, New York

Pine II, B J (1993) Mass customization, *Harvard Business School Press,* Boston, MA

Porter, M E (1985) *Competitive Advantage,* Free Press, New York

Porter, M E (1996) What is strategy?, *Harvard Business Review,* **74,** pp 61–78

Riddle, E J, Bradbard, D A, Thomas, J B and Kincade, D H (1999) The role of electronic data interchange in Quick Response, *Journal of Fashion Marketing and Management,* **3,** (2), pp 133–46

Rumelt, R P (1984) Towards a strategic theory of the firm, in (ed) R Lamb, *Competitive Strategic Management,* Prentice Hall, Englewood Cliffs, NJ

Schnaars, S P (1994) *Managing Imitation Strategies,* Free Press, New York

Schumpeter, J A (1934) *The Theory of Economic Development: An inquiry into profits, capital, credit, interest, and the business cycle,* Harvard University Press, Cambridge, MA

Siguaw, J S, Simpson, P and Baker, T (1998) Effects of supplier market orientation on distributor market orientation and the channel relationship, *Journal of Marketing,* **63,** pp 99–111

Siguaw, J S, Simpson, P and Baker, T (1999) The influence of market orientation on channel relationships: a dyadic examination, in (ed) R Deshpande, *Developing a Market Orientation,* Sage, London

Slater, S and Narver, J (1995) Market orientation and the learning organization, *Journal of Marketing,* **59,** pp 63–74

Slater, S and Narver, J (1999) Research notes and communications: market-oriented is more than being customer-led, *Strategic Management Journal,* **20,** pp 1165–68

Stalk, G. Jr and Hout, T M (1990) *Competing Against Time,* Free Press, New York

Stern, L, El-Ansary, A and Coughalan, A (1996) *Marketing Channels,* 5th edn, Prentice-Hall, Englewood Cliffs, NJ

Takeishi, A (2001) *Innovation no pattern* (patterns in innovation), in Hitotsubashi University Innovation Research Centre, *Innovation Management Nyumon (Fundamentals of Innovation Management),* Nihon Keizai Shimbunsha, Tokyo

Tamura, M (1975) *Seni Oroshiuri-Sho no Keiei Kouritsuka no Houkou – Seni Oroshiuri-Sho no Kinou Bunseki Houkoku (The Direction towards Textiles and Apparel Wholesalers' Efficient Management – An analysis of the function of textiles and apparel wholesale merchants)*, Osaka Chartered Institute of Commerce, Osaka

Tamura M (1996) *Marketing Ryoku (The Power of Marketing)*, Chikura Shobo, Tokyo

Tamura M (2001) *Ryutsu Genri (Principles of Marketing and Distribution)*, Chikura Shobo, Tokyo

Tamura M (2003) *Shijoushikou no Jissen Riron wo Mezashite (Towards an Operationalization of the Market Orientation Approach)*, University of Marketing and Distribution Science Monograph, No 15

Teece, D (1986) Profiting from technological innovation: implications for integration, collaboration, licensing and public policy, *Research Policy,* **15,** pp 285–305

Von Hipper, E A (1988) *The Sources of Innovation,* Oxford University Press, New York

Weerawardena, J (2003) Exploring the role of market learning capability in competitive advantage, *European Journal of Marketing,* **37,** (3/4), pp 407–29

White, L (1982) The automobile industry, in (ed) W Adams, *The Structure of American Industry,* 6th edn, MacMillan, New York

Whiteoak, P (1994) The realities of quick response in the grocery sector: a supplier viewpoint, *International Journal of Physical Distribution and Logistics Management,* **29,** (7/8), pp 508–19

Williams, J (1992) How sustainable is your advantage?, *California Management Review,* **34,** pp 1–23

Yahagi, T (1994) *Convenience Store System no Kakushin-sei (Innovativeness of the Convenience Store System)*, Nihon Keizai shimbunsha, Tokyo

Yahagi, T (2001) *Chain Store no Seiki ha Owattanoka* (Has the chain store age ended?), *Hitotsubashi Business Review,* August, pp 30–43

Yahagi T, Ogawa, K and Yoshida, K (1993) *Sei-Han Tougo Marketing (Supplier–Retailer Integrated Marketing Approach)*, Hakuto Shobo, Tokyo

Yamashita, Y (1993) *Shijo ni Okeru Ba no Kino* (The role of *Ba* in the market-place), *Soshiki Kagaku,* **27,** (1), pp 75–87

Yamashita, Y (1998) *Discounter no Seisui* (The rise and fall of discount stores), in (eds) H Itami, T Kagono, M Miyamoto and S Yonekura, *Innovation to Gijutsu Chikuseki (Innovation and Technology Accumulation)*, Yuhikaku, Tokyo

Yamashita, Y (2001) *Shogyo Shuseki no Dynamism* (The dynamics of commercial accumulation), *Hitotsubashi Business Review,* August, pp 74–94

5

Fashion logistics and Quick Response

Martin Christopher, Bob Lowson and Helen Peck

The ability to respond to customer requirements on a timely basis has always been a fundamental element of the marketing concept. However, there has perhaps never been as much pressure as exists today to accelerate further the responsiveness of marketing systems. 'Time-based competition' has become the norm in many markets, from banking to automobiles. The challenge to marketing and logistics in the current environment is to find ways in which product development times can be reduced, feedback from the marketplace made more rapid and replenishment times compressed.

Nowhere is this pressure more evident than in markets governed by fashion. 'Fashion' is a broad term that typically encompasses any product or market where there is an element of style that is likely to be short-lived. We have defined fashion markets as typically exhibiting the following characteristics:

1. Short lifecycles – the product is often ephemeral, designed to capture the mood of the moment; consequently the period in which it is saleable is likely to be very short and seasonal, measured in months or even weeks.
2. High volatility – demand for these products is rarely stable or linear. It may be influenced by the vagaries of weather, hit films, TV shows or even by pop stars and footballers.

3. Low predictability – because of the volatility of demand it is extremely difficult to forecast with any accuracy even total demand during a period, let alone week-by-week or item-by-item demand.
4. High impulse purchase – many buying decisions for these products are made at the point of purchase. In other words, the shopper when confronted with the product is stimulated to buy it, hence the critical role of 'availability' and, in particular, availability of sizes, colours, etc.

The combined effect of these pressures clearly provides a challenge to logistics management. Traditional ways of responding to customer demand have been forecast-based, with the resultant risk of overstocked or under-stocked situations.

More recently there has emerged another trend that has added further complexity and difficulty to the management of fashion logistics. The growing tendency to source product and materials offshore has led in many cases to significantly longer lead times. Whilst there is usually a substantial cost advantage to be gained, particularly in manufacturing, through sourcing in low-labour-cost areas, the effect on lead times can be severe. It is not only distance that causes replenishment lead times to lengthen in global sourcing, it is the delays and variability caused by internal processes at both ends of the chain as well as the import/export procedures in between. The end result is longer 'pipelines' with more inventory in them with consequent risks of obsolescence.

Much of the pressure for seeking low-cost manufacturing solutions has come from retailers. At the same time there have been moves by many retailers in the apparel business to reduce significantly the number of suppliers they do business with. This supply-base rational-ization has been driven by a number of considerations, but in particular by the need to develop more responsive replenishment systems – some-thing that is not possible when sourcing is spread over hundreds, if not thousands, of suppliers.

MANAGING THE FASHION LOGISTICS PIPELINE

Conventional wisdom holds that the way to cope with uncertainty is to improve the quality of the forecast. Yet, by definition, the volatility of demand and the short lifecycles found in many fashion markets make it highly unlikely that forecasting methods will ever be developed that can consistently and accurately predict sales at the item level. Instead, ways must be found of reducing the reliance that organizations place upon the forecast and to focus on lead-time reduction. Shorter lead times mean, by definition, that the forecasting horizon is shorter – hence the risk of error is lower. In the same way that the captain of a supertanker has a planning horizon that is determined by the vessel's stopping distance (many miles) so too in business the forecast period is determined by the time it takes to design, make and ship the product – lead times in other words.

There are three critical lead times that must be managed by organizations that seek to compete successfully in fashion markets:

1. Time-to-market – how long does it take the business to recognize a market opportunity and to translate this into a product or service and to bring it to the market?
2. Time-to-serve – how long does it take to capture a customer's order and to deliver the product to the retail customer's satisfaction?
3. Time-to-react – how long does it take to adjust the output of the business in response to volatile demand? Can the 'tap' be turned on or off quickly?

1. Time-to-market

In these short lifecycle markets, being able to spot trends quickly and to translate them into products in the shop in the shortest possible time has become a prerequisite for success. Companies that are slow to market can suffer in two ways. First, they miss a significant sales opportunity that probably will not be repeated. Second, the supplier is likely to find that when the product finally arrives in the marketplace, demand is starting to fall away, leading to the likelihood of markdowns. Figure 5.1 illustrates the double jeopardy confronting those organizations that are slow to market. New thinking in manufacturing strategy that has focused on flexibility and batch-size reduction has clearly helped organizations in their search for quick response. The use of highly automated processes such as computer aided design (CAD) and computer aided manufacturing (CAM) have revolutionized the ability to make product changes as the season or the lifecycle progresses.

2. Time-to-serve

Traditionally in fashion industries orders from retailers have had to be placed on suppliers many months ahead of the season; nine months was not unusual as a typical leadtime. Clearly, in such an environment the risk of both obsolescence and stock-outs is high as well as the significant inventory-carrying cost that inevitably is incurred somewhere in the supply chain as a result of the lengthy pipeline.

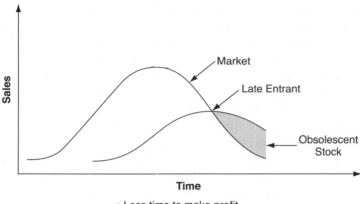

Figure 5.1 Shorter lifecycles making timing crucial

Why should the order to delivery cycle be so long? It is not the time it takes to make or ship the product. More often the problem lies in the multiple steps that occur from the point at which a decision is taken to place an order, through the generation of the accompanying documentation (particularly in overseas transactions involving quota approvals, letters of credit and so forth), into the suppliers' processes – which themselves are likely to be equally lengthy. Often the total time in manufacture is considerable because of the traditional, batch-based production methods. In other words each step in the total manufacturing cycle is managed separately and the quantities processed at each step are determined by so-called economic batch quantities. Furthermore, when manufacture takes place offshore, considerable time is consumed in preparing documentation, in consolidating full container loads and inbound customs clearance after lengthy surface transportation.

The underpinning philosophy that has led to this way of doing things is cost minimization. Primarily the costs that are minimized are the costs of manufacture and secondly the costs of shipping. In fact, this view of cost is too narrow and ultimately self-defeating. The real issue is the total supply chain cost including the costs of obsolescence, forced markdowns and inventory-carrying costs.

3. Time-to-react

Ideally, in any market, an organization would want to be able to meet any customer requirement for the products on offer at the time and place the customer needs them.

Clearly, some of the major barriers to this are those highlighted in the previous paragraphs, ie time-to-market and time-to-serve. However, a further problem that organizations face as they seek to become more responsive to demand is that they are typically slow to recognize changes in real demand in the final marketplace. The challenge to any business in a fashion market is to be able to see 'real' demand. Real demand is what consumers are buying or requesting hour by hour, day by day. Because most supply chains are driven by orders (ie batched demand), which themselves are driven by forecasts and inventory replenishment, individual parties in the chain will have no real visibility of the final marketplace. As Figure 5.2 suggests, inventory hides demand. In other words, the fact that there will usually be multiple inventories from the retail shelf back through wholesalers to suppliers means that upstream parties in the chain are unable to anticipate the changing needs of the customers other than through a forecast based as much upon judgement and guess-work as it is upon actual consumer demand.

THE LEAD-TIME GAP

The fundamental problem that faces many companies – not just those in fashion industries – is that the time it takes to source materials, convert them into products and move them into the marketplace is invariably longer than the time the customer is prepared to wait. This difference between what might be called the 'logistics pipeline' and the customer's order cycle time is termed the 'lead-time gap'. Conventionally, this gap was filled with a forecast-based inventory – there was no other way of attempting to ensure that there would be product available as and when customers demanded it.

The problem was that often it would be the 'wrong' inventory, for example sizes, colours or styles that were not those actually demanded. Figure 5.3 highlights the problems of the lead-time gap which, in the fashion industry, was traditionally measured in months rather than weeks.

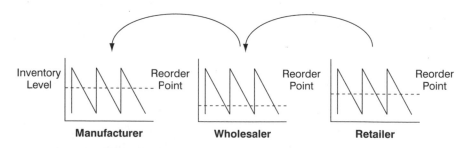

Figure 5.2 Inventory hides demand

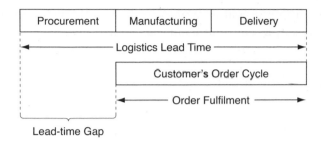

Figure 5.3 Lead times

These lengthy supply pipelines often result in revenue losses in the final market. Table 5.1 provides an indication of the size of these losses; of note is the cost of carrying inventory. The biggest item is forced markdowns – mainly at retail – with the total losses amounting to over 14 per cent of retail sales. A distinction is made between promotional markdowns, eg special sales, and the marking down that occurs out of necessity when a season ends and unwanted goods must be moved to make way for new merchandise – forced markdowns.

It is against this background that the Quick Response (QR) movement originated in 1984 from a textile industry research programme in the United States. Studies at the time revealed a clothing industry pipeline in which inventories and work-in-progress had reached alarming levels (see Table 5.2) and it is a situation that can still be seen in many industries. More information concerning the history of QR can be found in Hunter (1990) and Gunston and Harding (1986). Today, QR is a recognized operations strategy (Lowson, 2002) and as such it continues to attract considerable interest for two additional yet closely related reasons: the ability of this strategy to cope with the complexity of fashion logistics; and as a method to combat the relentless shift toward offshore sourcing from low-wage economies.

In all fast moving consumer goods (FMCG) industries, demand is now more fragmented and the consumer more discerning about quality and

Table 5.1 Revenue losses in the apparel pipeline (% retail sales)

	Fibre and textile	Apparel	Retail	Total
Forced markdowns	0.6	4.0	10.0	14.6
Stock-outs	0.1	0.4	3.5	4.0
Inventory @ 15% carrying cost	1.0	2.5	2.9	6.4
Total	1.7	6.9	16.4%	25.0

Source : Lowson et al, *1999*

Table 5.2 Clothing pipeline inventories and work in progress (weeks)

		Inventory	WIP
Fibre			
Raw material		1.6	
WIP			0.9
Finished fibre @ fibre		4.6	
Fibre @ textile		1.0	
	Total	*8.1*	*0.9*
Fabric			
WIP – Greige			3.9
Greige goods @ greige		1.2	
Greige goods @ finish		1.4	
Finishing			1.2
Finished fabric @ textile		7.4	
Fabric @ apparel		6.8	
	Total	*16.8*	*5.1*
Apparel			
WIP			5.0
Finished apparel @ Apparel		12.0	
Ship to retail		2.7	
Apparel @ retail Distribution centre		6.3	
Apparel @ store		10.0	
	Total	*31.0*	*5.0*
	Total	**55.0**	**11.0**

Source: Lowson et al, 1999

choice. There is also an increasing fashion influence; no single style or fashion has dominated for any length of time. For many consumer sectors, demand is approaching the chaotic in its insatiable appetite for diverse services and goods. 'Mass-customization' and individualized products with shorter season lengths; micro merchandizing and markets segmented at the individual level; large numbers of products chasing a diminishing market share – all are evidence of the inexorable movement toward a 'sea change' and mark the folly of firms expecting to operate as they have in the past. One of the most important findings from the early studies was the ability of QR to compress time in the supply system. If the pipeline were condensed to about a third of its traditional length, not only did the design of goods better reflect more accurate consumer information, it was possible for the retailer to reassess the demand for products while the season was under way and receive small, frequent reorders from the supplier, provided reorder lead times are short enough (of the order of two to four weeks) (Gunston and Harding, 1986).

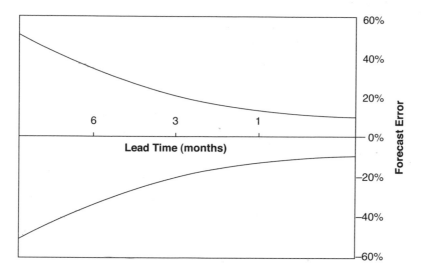

Figure 5.4   Lead time and forecast error

The effect on sales forecast errors of compressing the supply system is shown in Figure 5.4. Here, the central horizontal axis shows the number of months ahead of the season that predictions are made and the upper and lower curves show estimates of the forecast error. Twelve-month lead times are common in many FMCG sectors but significant improvements are available if these times can be reduced.

QUICK RESPONSE STRATEGIES

Quick Response (QR) can be defined as:

> A state of responsiveness and flexibility in which an organization seeks to provide a highly diverse range of products and services to a customer/consumer in the exact quantity, variety and quality, and at the right time, place and price as dictated by real-time customer/consumer demand. QR provides the ability to make demand-information driven decisions at the last possible moment in time ensuring that diversity of offering is maximized and lead times, expenditure, cost and inventory minimized. QR places an emphasis upon flexibility and product velocity in order to meet the changing requirements of a highly competitive, volatile and dynamic marketplace. QR encompasses an operations strategy, structure, culture and set of operational procedures aimed at integrating enterprises in a mutual network through rapid information transfer and profitable exchange of activity. (Lowson et al, 1999)

> QR has a number of strategic implications for the organization. Research has shown that mere implementation of technology or particular procedures without the strategic underpinning leads to sub-optimal performance. (Lowson, 2002)

The alignment of organizational activity to demand

This is a fundamental principle of QR. All activities within an enterprise should be paced to demand and customer behaviour. Products and services are produced and delivered in the variety and volume that match demand. The activity within a company moves to the beat of this drum. Swings in demand are closely monitored: too little or too much leads to waste and inefficiency. Whether it is marketing, purchasing, new product development or operations, all endeavours follow the market tempo and the realization that this alignment may necessitate a change in corporate culture. Consequently, it is important that senior management recognize and understand these demand patterns. Resources need to be deployed that can undertake this vital externally focused role.

Linkages between demand and supply

Given the importance of the alignment activity above, a strategic under-standing of the drivers of demand and its synchronized connection with supply is imperative for QR. In the past, much attention has, quite rightly, been placed upon improvements in supply. However, demand is the target – no matter how sophisticated the supply weaponry, it is ineffectual if the target is not understood. Only when the value and benefits sought by the customer/consumer are appreciated in all their complexity, can a strategy to supply them be developed. This involves detailed assessment of supply and demand processes and sub-processes by customer or consumer grouping. Together with the supply of a tangible product, there will be a myriad of other dimensions peculiar to the customer/consumer. These will include varying information content, time frames, physical arrangement for logistics, service support, marketing campaigns, infor-mation systems, etc.

Demand relationships

QR recognizes that both customers/consumers and products are dynamic and place unique demands on the organization. Identical products, jeans for example, will have unique product flows depending upon customer/consumer buying behaviour and QR needs (whether a department store, speciality store, supermarket, wholesaler, independent corner store, etc). Similarly, product attributes will vary by product, for example volume and flow characteristics, demand patterns, seasonality, promotional strategy, cyclical needs, information content, credit terms and customer incentives, repeat purchase patterns, etc. These attributes can be aligned with the QR product categories of 'basic', 'seasonal', 'fashion or short-season' and 'ultra-short-season'. These different customer/consumer and product behaviours will customize and tailor QR channels in line with the requirements. Once this assessment is done, it is possible to apply specific QR components or systems that can be tied into the unique supply pipeline.

Resource configuration

Conventional strategy looks long term for some form of advantage by configuration of activities and resources to the environment of operation; a strategic fit between strengths and weaknesses and opportunities and threats. In the QR world, this strategic architecture is inter-organizational. Strategy and strategic thinking are at a network level, encompassing many external interconnections. In addition, within this configuration must fit the mapping of customer/consumer values and perceived benefits onto operations, in order to underpin the link between demand and activity (as above).

Time

Time as a strategic weapon is vital to QR operation, but like any weapon its effectiveness depends upon the circumstances of its use. Strategies of time compression have gained much popularity of late. Unfortunately, as with many such movements, the application has been widespread but often ill considered. A time-based strategy is subtle and, above all else, must be well thought-out. Mere slashing of time for the sake of it misses the point. As with demand, time-based competition requires careful assessment as to where best it can serve customers/consumers. Fast and accurate adaptation to market change is perhaps the most important element of the QR strategy. The adroitness and dexterity to move to satisfy unplanned demand or previously unrecognized market niches requires any organization to be strategically configured for such a response. However, this architecture will only be effective if the operational environment is understood and the opportunities for time compression assessed. Accuracy and flexibility will reduce time delays, and postponement strategies will enable products, indeed all activity, to be tailored to known and exact needs rather than those forecast. It should also be remembered that the use of time for advantage will be inter-organizational; gains made internally will be rapidly lost if not carried through by network partners.

Primacy of information

Data and information are the foundation of QR – every business is an information business. Here, we are not dealing with information technology (IT), but a strategy for information systems (IS). Technology is merely the vehicle used to carry vital data resources. The link between demand and successful, accurate and flexible supply is data and the resulting information. For any operation in the 21st century, the prime strategic consideration will be the use of information as a resource. Timely and accurate flows will enable fast and accurate responses without waste and unnecessary cost.

Partnerships and alliances

Perhaps one of the most significant developments in recent management and business thinking has been externalization: the recognition that performance relies increasingly upon a series of alliances and relationships with other enterprises in the environment as the most effective way to deal with constantly changing market conditions. Competition is now between networks rather than individual firms. The coordination and relationships between these various entities are a matter for strategic consideration. From a QR perspective, the web of relationships and mutual networks upon which the organization depends requires a professional management approach, and increasingly firms are devoting staff and other resources to this task. The use of outsourcing, the concept of virtuality, and a focus on core value-adding processes have heightened this pressure for proper external organization and management with commercial partners. This requires a greater understanding of organizational behaviour and communication beyond traditional boundaries, particularly power and culture, in order to manage the growing number of strategically significant relationships that impact on the modern firm.

GLOBAL SOURCING AND QR

As highlighted earlier, consumer demand is becoming more volatile. QR is designed for such an environment. The clothing industry is, perhaps, one of the most demanding challenges for logistics management with hundreds of colours, thousands of styles and millions of SKUs on the retail shelves at any one time. Further, the average shelf-lives of these merchandise items shorten with each passing year.

A key factor in the value of QR is its ability to deal with uncertainty or variance. There are numerous sources of uncertainty in a supply pipeline, starting with demand through to the reliability on the part of suppliers and shippers, etc, and Quick Response offers the ability to counter the negative impacts of uncertainty. Speed and flexibility are the key, but it is important to realize that the level of uncertainty associated with the product dictates the optimal level of speed and flexibility required. The type of supply chain needs to fit the characteristics of the product as well as the uncertainty associated with it.

Many fashion or fast moving goods sell in distinct seasons and are on the shelf for just one season and almost totally replaced in the following year. Figure 5.5 represents sales of a typical product subject to pronounced seasonal fluctuation.

The normal practice is to manufacture as much as possible of the finished goods inventory required before the season starts and then deliver half to two-thirds of the necessary products before the beginning of the season (point A) and ship the balance of the inventory at pre-agreed times (eg point B), or await reorders (points B to C). QR takes a different route. Although it may pose manufacturing capacity problems, as little as possible is made or shipped before the season. From day one, PoS data are gathered, analysed and used to understand demand preferences. Manufacturing is then guided by the continuing (daily or weekly) PoS data. Reorder and re-estimation and replenishment approaches are then used for frequent reorders (points A to B). This QR approach can be better appreciated when applied to a particular demand situation such as global or offshore sourcing.

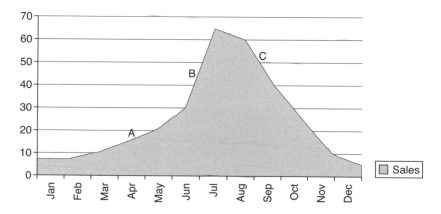

Figure 5.5   Seasonality profile

The costs of offshore sourcing

As discussed earlier, a quick response operations strategy offers a high degree of speed, flexibility and responsiveness in supply pipelines. This has substantial implications for sourcing decisions, particularly offshore sourcing. Empirical research has established that sourcing offshore to secure lower cost inputs (typically from low-wage, underdeveloped regions) can have negative consequences once the hidden and inflexibility costs are quantified (Lowson, 2001).

Hidden costs are those that are not typically anticipated by the buying organization, but almost always occur. Some examples include the various initial investments to establish the new source of supply, control of quality and delivery variables; high initial training costs, coupled with a high staff turnover affecting both throughput and quality; significantly lower operator efficiency offshore; irrevocable letters of credit charges; delays at the port of entry, last minute use of air freight and other logistics costs; expensive administrative travel to correct problems; process inefficiencies and quality problems; long lead times and the need for large buffer inventories; and finally, the not insubstantial human cost involved in the conditions endured in many foreign factory environments often employing child labour and overusing natural resources.

Inflexibility costs are the costs of using suppliers that are inflexible and unresponsive to changes in demand (before, during and after a product selling season), leading to disproportionate levels of demand amplification across a longer supply network and a number of considerable cost implications.

It is only when these two cost categories can be properly quantified that the advantages and disadvantages of low-wage, foreign purchasing can be fully understood and a method for their true representation becomes apparent. Once the hidden costs are categorized, sourcing from sources on the basis of low cost alone becomes far less attractive. Further, when the costs of inflexibility are added, it becomes clear that using a domestic quick response supplier may be a far better option due to the added velocity and flexibility that are provided.

The QR alternative

Collapsing the product pipeline can reduce time and provide a more efficient response to rapidly changing consumer demand. In this way, a QR operations strategy will encourage the cross-enterprise re-engineering of business processes, from product development to replenishment, with resulting improved stocking points, lower inventory, lower costs and increased sales. The value chain is reconfigured to reflect speed of response, flexibility and differentiation. Table 5.3 compares two different sourcing alternatives: the quick response domestic supplier and the offshore counterpart.

In this initial scenario two possible buying decisions are reviewed using QR and then offshore sources of supply. First, end-consumer purchases, whether bought from a retailer or manufacturer, are assumed to be £100,000. It is then assumed that the customer (a manufacturer or retailer) has bought the goods for the same price (£60,000). An averaged gross margin is also assumed of 40 per cent on these sales. The only difference between the two sourcing alternatives is the flexibility and speed of response. The ability of the QR supplier to rapidly replenish the stock of the customer (manufacturer or retailer) to real-time consumer demand allows the customer to turn inventory of the product six as opposed to two and a half times a year. This faster turnover rapidly increases the customer's gross margin return on each pound invested in inventory from £1.67 to £4.00, more than twice that of the offshore competition. (GMROI is calculated as gross margin/average inventory.) Because of this inventory turnover advantage the manufacturer or retailer could afford to pay a premium for the product and still get a better return (Table 5.4).

Table 5.3 QR and faster turnover

	QR supplier	Offshore supplier
Consumer purchase price (£)	100,000	100,000
Customer purchase price (£)	60,000	60,000
Gross margin (£)	40,000	40,000
Average inventory (£)	10,000	24,000
Gross margin (%)	40.00	40.00
Inventory turns (pa)	6.02	2.5
GMROI (%)	400	167

Table 5.4 QR and a higher cost of goods

	QR supplier	Offshore supplier	Cost advantage applicable
Consumer purchase price (£)	100,000	100,000	
Customer purchase price (£)	78,000	60,000	30.33%
Gross margin (£)	22,000	40,000	
Average inventory (£)	13,033	24,000	
Gross margin (%)	22.00	40.00	
Inventory turns (pa)	6.02	2.5	
GMROI (%)	169	167	

In the table the price paid for goods by the customer has increased by a third, but because of the flexibility and responsiveness of the supplier, the return on inventory has increased by 1.2 per cent or from £1.67 to £1.69.

Table 5.5 views the sourcing decision from another perspective: the decision to move sourcing offshore to a competitor with lower unit cost but a slower response.

In this situation the foreign supplier would need to reduce the purchase price by nearly 35 per cent to retain a comparative GMROI to that of the QR supplier. The more flexible and higher velocity supplier proves more competitive than the lower-cost one, even without taking into account the other hidden and inflexibility costs.

Product velocity also produces other benefits. Replenishing stock in response to real-time demand ensures that the right goods are available reflecting what is being demanded. Revenue will rise as products in demand are sold at the expected price rather than marked down as unwanted. Table 5.6 shows the combined effect of velocity, faster inventory turns and reduced markdowns.

As product velocity increases so too will revenue as there is less need to sell goods below optimum price points. The customer's (manufacturer or retailer) return on investment grows to over three times that of a competitor.

Finally, Quick Response also has an impact upon strategic pricing decisions. Velocity and flexibility in the supply system will allow an original equipment manufacturer (OEM) or retailer to reduce the price of the finished good below that of the competition and capture greater market share (Table 5.7).

Because of QR flexibility and responsiveness, the retailer or manufacturer can reduce the purchase price to the consumer by 32 per cent and still earn a slightly better return in terms of GMROI than competitors.

Table 5.5   A move to offshore supply

	QR supplier	Offshore supplier	Cost reduction applicable
Consumer purchase price (£)	100,000	100,000	
Customer purchase price (£)	60,000	38,448	35.92%
Gross margin (£)	40,000	61,552	
Average inventory (£)	10,000	15,379	
Gross margin (%)	40.00	61.55	
Inventory turns (pa)	6.02	2.5	
GMROI (%)	400	400	

Table 5.6 The effect of QR velocity

	QR supplier	Offshore supplier
Consumer purchase price (£)	113,000	100,000
Customer purchase price (£)	60,000	60,000
Gross margin (£)	53,000	40,000
Average inventory (£)	10,000	24,000
Gross margin (%)	40.00	40.00
Inventory turns (pa)	6.02	2.5
GMROI (%)	530	167

Table 5.7 QR and strategic pricing

	QR supplier	Offshore supplier	Possible price reduction %*
Consumer purchase price (£)	76,840	100,000	−32.00
Customer purchase price (£)	60,000	60,000	
Gross margin (£)	16,840	40,000	
Average inventory (£)	10,000	24,000	
Gross margin (%)	21.91	40.00	
Inventory turns (pa)	6.0	2.5	
GMROI (%)	168	167	

* Based upon purchase price of £113,000 as seen in Table 5.6

THE IMPORTANCE OF AGILITY

Successful companies in fashion markets seem to be not just able to capture the imagination of the consumer with their products but are often characterized by their agility. In other words, by their ability to move quickly, uninhibited by cumbersome processes and lengthy supply chains. Many organizations are finding that it is possible to make significant improvements by adopting a twin strategy of simultaneously reducing the logistics lead time and capturing information sooner on actual customer demand.

The Spanish-based apparel company Zara provides a good example of how an integrated design, manufacturing and retail group is successfully managing its international supply chains. The first Zara shop opened in La Coruña, northern Spain in 1975. In under 30 years the business had grown to become one of Spain's leading textile and apparel companies, with sizable production facilities in Spain, purchasing operations in south-east Asia and the Caribbean, a finance holding company in the Netherlands and around 200 retail outlets (owned by the company) in Europe and the Americas. Like Italian fashion giant Benetton, Zara produces a single global product range, designed to appeal to an international target market, in this case fashion-conscious 18- to 35-year-olds (the same market segment as targeted by The Limited and Gap in the United States and Next in the United Kingdom).

The whole process of supplying goods to the stores begins with cross-functional teams – comprising fashion, commercial and retail specialists – working within Zara's Design Department at the company's headquarters in La Coruña. The designs reflect the latest in international fashion trends, with inspiration gleaned through visits to fashion shows, competitors' stores, university campuses, pubs, cafés and clubs, plus any other venues or events deemed to be relevant to the lifestyles of the target customers. The team's knowledge of fashion trends is supplemented further by regular inflows of EPOS data and other information from all of the company's stores and sites around the world.

Fashion specialists within the Design Department are responsible for the initial designs, fabric selection and choice of prints and colours. It is then up to the team's commercial management specialists to ascertain the likely commercial viability of the items proposed. If the design is accepted, the commercial specialists proceed to negotiate with suppliers, agree purchase prices, analyse costs and margins, and fix a standard cross-currency price position for the garment. The size of the production run – ie the number of garments required – and launch dates (the latter vary between countries in accordance with custom and climate) are also determined at this point.

Raw materials are procured through the company's buying offices in the United Kingdom, China and the Netherlands, with most of the materials themselves coming in from Mauritius, New Zealand, Australia, Morocco, China, India, Turkey, Korea, Italy and Germany. This global sourcing policy using a broad supplier base provides the widest possible selection of fashion fabrics, while reducing the risk of dependence on any source or supplier. Approximately 40 per cent of garments – those with the broadest and least transient appeal – are imported as finished goods from low-cost manufacturing centres in the Far East. The rest are produced in Spain, using Zara's own highly automated factories and a network of smaller contractors. Two guiding principles underlie all of its operations: quick response to market needs and working without inventory. Here lies the company's principal source of competitive advantage.

Zara's manufacturing systems are in many ways similar to those developed and employed so successfully by Benetton in northern Italy, but refined using ideas developed in conjunction with Toyota. Only those operations that enhance cost-efficiency through economies of scale are conducted in-house (such as dyeing, cutting, labelling and packaging). All other manufacturing activities, including the labour-intensive finishing stages, are completed by networks of more than 300 small subcontractors, each specializing in one particular part of the production process or garment type. These subcontractors work exclusively for Zara's parent, Inditex SA. In return they receive the necessary technological, financial and logistical support required to achieve stringent time and quality targets. Inventory costs are kept to a minimum because Zara pays only for the completed garments. The system is flexible enough to cope with sudden changes in demand, though production is always kept at a level slightly below expected sales, to keep stock moving. Zara has opted for undersupply, viewing it as a lesser evil than holding slow-moving or obsolete stock.

Finished goods are forwarded to the company's huge distribution centre in La Coruña, where they are labelled, price-tagged (all items carry international price tags showing the price in all relevant currencies) and packed. From there they travel by third-party contractors by road and/or air to their penultimate destinations. The shops themselves receive deliveries of new stock on a twice-weekly basis, according to shop-by-shop stock allocations calculated by the Design Department. The whole production cycle takes only three or four weeks. In an industry where lead times of many months are still the norm, Zara has reduced its lead-time gap for more than half of the garments it sells to a level unmatched by any of its European or North American competitors.

CONCLUSION

Fashion retailing, and the manufacturing sector that supports it, is clearly highly dependent upon an agile logistics capability. The ability to capture new design ideas, to convert these into products and to bring them to market in the shortest possible time scale has become a prerequisite for success in the fashion business. Paradoxically many retailers in this sector have actually seen their design-to-store lead times increase as a result of so-called low-cost sourcing strategies.

To compete successfully in short lifecycle and volatile markets requires that a wider definition of cost be adopted. The real cost is the total end-to-end pipeline cost, which includes not only the manufacturing cost of the product, but also the inventory carrying cost, the cost of markdowns as well as the cost of loss of sales through stock-outs. The key to the minimization of this total supply chain cost is the adoption of agile strategies that focus on time compression and quick response.

Retailers and manufacturers who recognize the importance of agility will outperform those who do not.

References

Gunston, R and Harding, P (1986) Quick Response: US and UK experiences, *Textile Outlook International*, **10**, pp 43–51

Hunter, N A (1990) *Quick Response for Apparel Manufacturing*, Textile Institute, Manchester

Lowson, R H (2001) Retail sourcing strategies: are they cost-effective?, *International Journal of Logistics*, **4**, (3), pp 271–96

Lowson, R H (2002) *Strategic Operations Management: The new competitive advantage*, Routledge, London

Lowson, R H, King, R and Hunter, N A (1999) *Quick Response: Managing the supply chain to meet consumer demand*, John Wiley and Sons, Chichester

6

Agile merchandizing in the European textile fashion industry

Neil Towers and Johanna Bergvall-Forsberg

INTRODUCTION

An increasing number of firms are combining international and global sourcing to achieve sustainable competitive advantages such as lower prices, better quality, access to new markets and shorter product lifecycles (Bozarth *et al*, 1998). Globalization has become an inevitable trend in recent years as garment retailers have to deal with change more quickly and more frequently than ever before. Leading retailers in developed countries depend heavily on overseas manufacturers for their source of garments. Some brands such as Nike cooperate through alliances with overseas partners to produce branded clothing and footwear (Lee *et al*, 2004). According to a 2003 Accenture report, about 91 per cent of the respondents planned to increase their purchases from low-cost countries and regions. With the large volume garment producers of China and India gradually opening up to foreign companies, there is an increasing trend of multinational companies that regard a global procurement strategy as an important part of the new business strategy. Global sourcing can generate cost savings from 10 to 40 per cent, which makes it an attractive strategy to pursue for garment retailers (Frear *et al*, 1992). Some popular European fashion brands have progressively moved their supply regions from Europe to Asia as these countries are very competitive with their low product prices and increasing quality levels (Towers and Peng, 2006). For example, 33 per cent of the garments from the fashion brand H&M are supplied from China.

To follow the trend of globalization, garment retailers choose global sourcing as their approach to procurement, accomplishing the process of production and distribution in different regions throughout the world. During this process, developed countries such as China dominate exports in the textiles sector. China was the world's largest exporter of both textiles and clothing in 1995 as well as 2002 and its world market share (excluding intra-EU trade) increased from 22.5 per cent to 30 per cent over this period in the clothing sector and from 16 to 22 per cent in the textile sector (Nordas, 2004).

The supply chain management process in the textiles industry is complex, generally with a large number of partners involved and a supply chain that is geographically relatively long. For instance the process of producing a mid-range cotton shirt sold at a typical high street retailer starts with harvesting the cotton buds in regions where there is a warm temperate climate such as western China or the southern states of the United States and finishing with final production in low-cost labour countries such as China, India or Sri Lanka. The processes involved are shown in Figure 6.1; the whole process can take approximately 12 months from harvesting to arrival in the European store.

Management of the supply chain is required to reduce lead times and improve efficiency, highlighting the need to use a responsive approach (Bruce *et al*, 2004). Some supply issues from China, for example, present a challenge, such as unforeseen risks in the delivery process, rigid negotiability, language barriers and Chinese-style business customs. However, the most important challenges are process improvement, sourcing location, language barriers, unforeseen delivery risks and customer service provision.

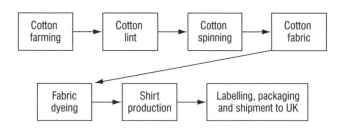

Figure 6.1 A typical garment supply chain

GLOBAL SOURCING CHALLENGES

Globalization is an inevitable trend and global sourcing is one of the methods widely used by European garment retailers to achieve cost reductions or profit improvement, managing vendors and comparing the suppliers more closely. Manufacturers have sought to collaborate with their customers and suppliers to upgrade their purchasing functions as an integral part of the supply chain. Retailers also exploited suppliers' common strengths and technology for the support of new product development. They have also tried to integrate their physical distribution and logistics functions into supply chain management as a strategic approach to operations, materials and logistics management (Croom *et al*, 2000).

The textile industry in the United Kingdom and comparable high cost economies has been in long-term decline for many years (TCSG, 2000). The rapid development of technology and communications has reduced the distance between nations and improved the time from order to delivery. Well-established textile businesses have been transferring their technology and knowledge into less developed countries so as to benefit from the abundant access of low cost labour (Towers and Peng, 2006). With an increase in world trade, European textile manufacturers have to work hard to sustain profitability, leaving little time and money for product development and innovation. However, to survive in the long run European manufacturers need to find competitive advantage in factors other than cost. Such a business strategy was suggested by Porter (1985) as part of the value chain. The proposition is to create a defendable position in the industry where firms can either compete on cost or differentiation advantages. Rather than providing competitiveness through delivering value equal to their competitors including a lower cost, customers can be won by exceeding the benefits of competing firms.

The traditional sourcing decisions based on manufacturing and shipping costs have been replaced by a more holistic approach to determining cost where additional requirements of lead time, inventory management, supplier performance and customer service level have to be considered (Lowson, 2003). Product characteristics also have demand patterns, which facilitates a more efficient lean supply chain, while seasonal products such as fashion garments require a more responsive agile supply chain to cope with demand uncertainty and short product lifecycles. Here, agility means responsive to market knowledge and a virtual corporation to exploit profitable opportunities in a volatile marketplace while leanness means developing a value stream to eliminate all waste, including time to enable a predictable

Table 6.1 The distinguishing attributes of lean and agile supply

Distinguishing attributes	Lean supply	Agile supply
Typical products	Commodities	Fashion goods
Marketplace demand	Predictable	Volatile
Product variety	Low	High
Product lifecycle	Long	Short
Customer driver	Cost	Availability
Profit margins	Low	High
Dominant costs	Physical costs	Marketability costs
Stock-out penalties	Long-term contractual	Immediate costs and volatile
Purchasing policy	Buy goods	Assign capacity
Information enrichment	Highly desirable	Obligatory
Forecasting mechanism	Algorithmic	Consultative

Source: Mason-Jones et al, 2000

supply profile. Table 6.1 summarizes the distinguishing attributes of lean and agile supply.

Retailers, particularly those selling garments and accessories, which are unable to respond to sudden market changes will experience losses due to final markdowns and missed sales opportunities. Being slow to market will result in unsatisfied customers with a consequential reduction in sales and residual stock. Consequently, a new business framework for European manufacturers has been developed with the production of garments through an agile merchandise approach. By providing smaller batches on the basis of real-time demand domestic manufacturers can be used to supply those parts of the merchandise range that are difficult to predict. The practical application of different outsourcing strategies in the textile and clothing industry was investigated by Bruce *et al* (2004). Their study confirmed that overseas manufacturers are widely used for companies to meet cost requirements whereas local manufacturers are used to provide quick replenishment orders and smaller batches to respond to unpredicted surges in demand. The mixed mode approach to supply, shown in Figure 6.2, allows basic products, where cost is the most important purchasing factor, to be sourced from overseas suppliers whilst fashion products, where in-store availability is much more important, to be sourced from within Europe.

FASHION MERCHANDIZING

To explain the impact of the supply response for different products Lowson (2003) divided the fashion merchandise range into three major

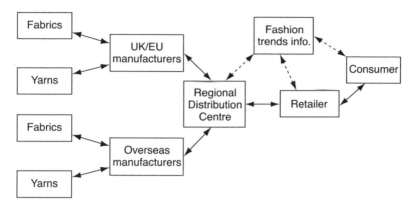

Figure 6.2 Mixed mode of supply model
Source: adapted from Bruce et al, *2004*

segments: basic products, seasonal products and short-season products. Basic products (eg T-shirts, socks and underwear) are the products sold during the whole year with a minimal variation in demand. Seasonal products and short-season products on the other hand have shorter shelf-lives and a greater design variety, which make the forecasting process more complex. The final manufacturing decision for basic products is mainly based on physical cost reduction, productivity and high production volumes. Not surprisingly basic products are more likely to benefit from overseas low-cost suppliers than short-season products and seasonal products.

To compete in today's marketplace supply chains must be engineered to match lifecycle attributes as well as product characteristics. As products proceed through their lifecycle these characteristics dramatically change (Aitken *et al*, 2003). In a study of a UK lighting company careful matching between product lifecycle character, demand attributes and supply alternatives was proven to maximize overall competitiveness (Childerhouse *et al*, 2002). The actual application of a mixed mode supply approach has been established in the fashion garment industry. Thus, rather than contracting either cost-effective overseas manufacturers or responsive domestic suppliers the mixed supply base approach can be applied to optimize the supply requirements. As seasonal products have a selling season of 9–12 weeks and sometimes less, they are likely to experience a quick passage through all four stages of the generic lifecycle. Many varieties of jeans, for example, have a relatively stable demand despite recurring updates of styles and colours. Prior to the introduction of a new design the response from the extensive clientele can be hard to predict. To distinguish the market response before the final production decision is taken, responsive manufacturers that can provide small batches quickly are more attractive. If the design proves successful the product will move into the growth stage followed by the maturity stage before moving into the final decline phase. Consequently, the introduction and decline phases of the seasonal product's lifecycle correspond with the demand for higher value manufacturers providing the quick responses, flexibility and reliability required for design, sample, pre-production and top-up volumes. Overseas suppliers are often not able to respond within the time frame necessary to provide the high delivery service required for volatile fashion markets. The use of air freight is often considered as an alternative but the additional costs are very high compared to conventional sea freight.

The characteristic lifecycle of different products varies greatly. When analysing the market trends within the electronics manufacturing industry Helo (2004) found that the approach to managing ever-shorter technological lifecycles is of critical importance. Whereas some industrial electronics such as automation control modules are produced with minor modifications for 10–20 years, products such as DVD players, personal computers and mobile phones only have lifecycles of months. In addition to volume and product mix, flexibility – described as the ability to take a product out of the market before its actual decline phase – was perceived as essential (Helo, 2004). Hence, not all products will follow the general product lifecycle. Instead the lifecycle pattern for fast-moving electronics is characterized by an s-shape curve where products are rapidly taken off the market and replaced by new and more innovative technology when they reach their maturity point. Similar lifecycle characteristics have been found in the fashion industry. Due to their extremely short shelf-life of merely six to 10 weeks, short-season products appear never to reach the maturity and decline phases of the product lifecycle. Hence, responsive domestic suppliers capable of responding within the short time frame necessary are preferred. The mixed supply approach applied to fashion merchandizing is illustrated in Table 6.2.

Due to the dynamic character of today's fashion retail market, recent attention has mainly been directed to the development of the agile

Table 6.2 The mixed supply approach applied to fashion merchandizing

Merchandise	Introduction	Growth	Maturity	Decline
Basic products	Lean	Lean	Lean	Lean
Seasonal products	Agile/Leagile	Lean/Leagile	Lean/Leagile	Agile/Leagile
Short-season products	Agile/Leagile	Agile/Leagile	Agile/Leagile	Agile/Leagile

paradigm that has been further extended to include entire textile supply chains rather than internal manufacturing activities (Christopher and Towill, 2001; Naylor *et al*, 1999). Taking the agile paradigm to a broader perspective, lean textile manufacturers still play an important part in satisfying complex needs in a volatile marketplace even though the overall strategy must be agile in nature.

THE AGILE SUPPLY NETWORK

There are four dimensions of agility: enriching the customer, cooperating to enhance competitiveness, organizing to manage change and uncertainty, and leveraging the impact of people and information (Goldman *et al*, 1991). To fulfil these requirements lean and agile capacities must be combined to construct a network of effective and efficient long-term strategic solutions (Towers and Ashford, 2003). Despite the agile character of the textile fashion market a plain focus on effectiveness is not enough to ensure customer satisfaction. Various customers will have different requirements on supply efficiency and effectiveness and thus the view of markets as either innovative or functional is too simplistic to ensure customer satisfaction. As the term 'mixed supply base approach' suggests, different supply strategies will be needed depending on the product segment to supply and the customer they serve. To assist companies in aligning their design, production and delivery with defined product characteristics and acknowledged customer expectations, Vonderembse *et al* (2004) developed a typology for designing supply chains. Their supply chain classification based on product type is illustrated in Table 6.3 and in addition to the mixed supply approach incorporates postponement. Postponement theories can be applied when a mix of both standard and innovative components are involved in the production activity.

Table 6.3 The supply chain classification based on product type

Product lifecycle	Standard products	Innovative products	Hybrid products
Introduction	Lean supply chain	Agile supply chain	Hybrid supply chain
Growth			
Maturity		Hybrid/Lean supply chain	
Decline			

Source: Vonderembse et al, *2004*

The computer industry was one of the first to use the postponement approach with 'leagile' strategies to overcome the problem with variability in the global market (Feitzinger and Lee, 1997). Generic products were delivered to national distribution centres and then customized in accordance with local requirements. Similar techniques have been used in the fashion industry to import plain garments, such as a single colour basic T-shirt from low labour cost countries and then print dyed locally when demand for customized requirements is known, driven by changing fashion and seasonal trends. The cost benefits are drawn from volume discounts of the base garment together with limited stock holding of the final fashion garment where the risk of obsolescence is greatest.

To maintain profitability and enhance customer satisfaction the supply chain design must reflect the distinct characteristics of the product, ie whether standard, innovative or hybrid, as it proceeds through its lifecycle. Market mediation, through transferring demand information between members of the supply chain, occurs when production is adjusted to match actual demand (de Treville *et al*, 2004). Normally this will facilitate greater responsiveness to changing customer needs but often results in lower production efficiencies. Fisher (1997) proposed that the choice between efficient physical supply and market mediation as a supply chain strategy depended primarily on whether the product had functional or innovative demand. Functional demand calls for a supply chain emphasizing efficient physical supply, and innovative demand calls for market mediation.

A combination of market mediation levels and supply chain designs defines the generic supply network required to increase overall supply chain agility in the textile and clothing industry, illustrated in Table 6.4.

'Market mediation' is the term used to describe a company's ability to adjust to changes in customer demand. For standard products that are

Table 6.4 A generic approach to the agile supply network

	The agile supply network			
Level of market mediation:	Full market mediation	Partial market mediation		No market mediation
Strategic supply focus:	Demand fulfilment	Postponement	Mixed supply base	Waste reduction
Supply chain/chains required:	Agile	Leagile	Agile/Lean	Lean

Source: adapted from de Treville et al, 2004

characterized by a focus on cost and where design variance is low, lean supply chain practices predominate. No market mediation is required and a focus on waste minimization is more likely to speed up the time from order to delivery and enhance performance levels. The important supply consideration is to ensure a high accuracy of forecast information so that deliveries can be allocated to meet customer volume requirements. Partial market mediation is applied when demand is visible to a certain extent. Such a leagile approach to supply chain tactics can be applied when a mix of standard and innovative components is involved in the production. However, for some seasonal products hybrid supply strategies might be more beneficial. In contrast to the leagile supply chain concept the mixed supply base approach was introduced to employ lean and agile suppliers independently, but within the same product lifecycle. To achieve full market mediation companies must ensure that demand variability is met more effectively. Not all of the supply chains listed in Table 6.4 may be necessary for every company but it is likely that the agile supply network will embody many of them. The more apparent the agile character of the business the more supply alternatives will be required to meet the complex needs of the marketplace (Sharp et al, 1999).

AGILE MERCHANDIZING

Unfortunately agile supply chain practices imply demand fulfilment rather than market mediation, so the agile supply network previously discussed is mainly directed towards planning the supply base rather than actively and accurately managing such a complex planning and control activity. Focus on customer demand has to be replaced by value to optimize the level of efficiency and effectiveness of the product offer provided and consumed. The view of the demand chain as a downstream flow of customer information that controls a premeditated supply network limits the supply network's ability to provide full market mediation. A plain focus on demand often misses out determining what customer demand actually is and how it evolves over time. Instead, the demand chain and the supply chain must work in synergy to optimize final value (de Treville et al, 2004).

Walters and Rainbird (2004) make an attempt to clarify the demand chain's and the supply chain's individual contribution to enhanced business performance by using practical examples from the UK retail and fast food industry. Following the distinct separation between efficient capacity planning and effective demand information transmission seen in Table 6.5, the supply chain is described as an internal component of the

Table 6.5 Comparison of the supply chain and the demand chain

Supply chain	Demand chain
Efficiency focus; cost per item	Effectiveness focus; product market fit
Processes are focused on execution	Processes are focused more on planning
Cost is the key driver	Revenue is the key driver
Short-term oriented, within the immediate and controllable future	Long-term oriented, within the next planning cycles
Typically the domain of tactical manufacturing and logistics personnel	Typically the domain of marketing, sales and strategic supply chain managers
Focuses on immediate resource and capacity constraints	Focuses on long-term capabilities, not short-term constraints
Historical focus on manufacturing planning and controls	Historical focus on marketing and supply chain alignment

Source: Walters and Rainbird, 2004

more strategically focused demand chain concept. As the supply chain was perceived to be predominately process driven, the more market sensitive aspect of the demand chain was suggested to control the process capacity of the supply chain.

Agile merchandizing represents the incentive to simultaneously plan and control the supply network in such a way that the value chain is most likely to comply with that expected by customers, suppliers, consumers and stakeholders. Consequently, the dynamic framework for agile merchandizing contains both an element of control (management components) and planning (supply chain structure). The actual implementation of the lean, agile and leagile supply chains will then be determined by the downstream flow of demand information and its business processes as an integrated supply chain management strategy. The supply chain and the demand chain are indirectly related to each other through the value chain they create. Whereas the control components are aimed at ensuring the responsiveness of the value creation, the dynamic arrangement of the business structure will provide the competencies on which the network is able to compete.

Customer integration is the main driver of the business network providing the information required to manage the value chain more effectively. Companies need to ensure that the value proposition offered to the customers conforms to the value they are expecting to receive. As the marketplace changes, adjustments to the value proposition need to be carried out accordingly. Moreover, once in the state of actual production the end-consumer demand will pull the production in the agile sections of the business plan and provide the signals that control the lean production plans.

Process integration can be described as uniting the dependent value-adding activities within the network. Driven by customer demand the aim is to amplify the competitive advantages held by participating business partners. Production skills such as inventory management, operations excellence and performance management will positively contribute to achievements in the areas of time to supply, flexibility and competency. Quickness is the ability to fulfil demand before competitors and flexibility the ability to cope with changes in customer demand (Lin et al, 2006). Once combined with customer integration a greater level of responsiveness will be achieved. Supply chain responsiveness can be described as the network's ability to respond to concurrent customer demand.

Despite customer integration being the fundamental driver for success in an agile marketplace the actual value of the process integration could not be achieved without a competent supply chain structure and the information to support it. Network integration symbolized the strategic segmentation of all components involved in the planning, creation and delivery of customer, supplier and stakeholder value. The impact of product and service attributes, internal competences and potential collaborative advantages derived from the external chains needs to be taken into consideration to ensure synergy between the demand chain and the supply chain. Customer segments as well as supplier segments will positively contribute to competence in process integration.

Virtual integration is the most complex component of the dynamic framework referring to the information structure within the defined network. However, whereas its implementation is fairly easy to achieve (particularly with the internet and the continuing cost reduction of information technology) effective demand transmission has been harder to achieve. Studies have shown a positive relationship between the degree of demand information available within the chain and the effectiveness of business processes (Lin et al, 2006; Li et al, 2006). However, collaborative relationship issues such as trust and commitment have been seen to inhibit its success (deTreville et al, 2004). To increase the usefulness of the information structure further investment in the relationship building aspects of supply chain management will be required. According to Li et al (2006) companies that have been able to establish good collaborative relationships with their competitive business network (including both supplier and customers) are more likely to benefit from effective information sharing and enhanced organizational performance. The dynamic framework of agile merchandizing is shown in Figure 6.3.

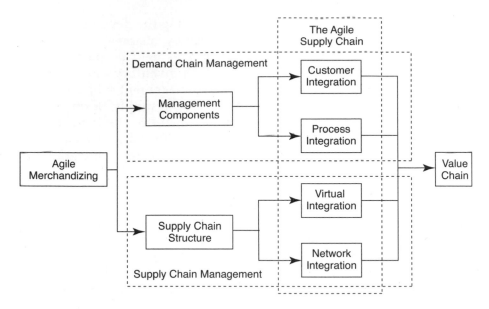

Figure 6.3 The dynamic framework for agile merchandizing
Source: Bergvall-Forsberg and Towers, 2006

Dynamic framework case study

Market mediation strategies that allow companies to continuously adjust the delivery process in response to actual customer demand are perceived as valuable business strategies for the majority of industries today. However, its practical implementation has been hard to achieve. To understand the practical relevance of the dynamic framework of agile merchandizing to the European textile and clothing manufacturers a descriptive case study investigation of 11 European manufacturing small and medium-sized enterprises (SMEs) was undertaken. Of the 11 manufacturers involved in the study, three were based in England, four in Italy and four in Sweden. All participating companies made and supplied textile products including knitted menswear and womenswear, knitted hats, tablecloths, sportswear and wedding dresses from their European factories. The focus of the study was the approach that these companies adopted to the increased pressures of cost and quality. The details of the participating companies are listed in Table 6.6, together with their competitive advantage.

Table 6.6 Participating company details

Company	Type of business	Product range	Number of employees	Location of production[1]	Competitive advantage	Customer base
1	Knitter	Menswear	>10	England	**Responsiveness:** *proximity to customer*	England
2	Coater	Book cloth material	>5	England	**Innovativeness:** *product development*	England
3	Knitter	Womenswear	11	England	**Responsiveness:** *proximity to customer*	England
4	Tailor	Wedding dresses	50	Italy	**Relationship Marketing:** *image, purchasing experience*	Worldwide
5	Manufacturer	Menswear	250	Italy	**Industry Leader:** *quality, reputation*	Worldwide
6	Knitter	Samples and First Production	42	Italy	**Responsiveness:** *proximity to customer, production expertise*	Europe
7	Weaver	Fabrics for men's shirts	90	Italy and Czech Republic	**Industry Leader:** *quality, responsiveness*	Worldwide
8	Manufacturer and Retailer	Womenswear	20–25 (Sweden) 54 (Estonia) 58 (shops)	Sweden and Estonia	**Design Excellence**	Europe (mainly Scandinavia)
9	Knitter	Hats	25 (Sweden) 30 (Estonia)	Sweden and Estonia	**Responsiveness and Marketing:** *production flexibility, brand name*	Worldwide
10	Weaver	Kitchen towels and tablecloth	43	Sweden	**Industry Leader:** *environment, design, quickness, quality*	Worldwide
11	Knitter	Sports wear	75	Sweden	**Marketing and Innovation:** *branding, product technology*	Worldwide

[1] Refers to the production facilities owned by the focal company

The case study results

The dynamic framework of agile merchandizing builds on the premise that competitive advantage is derived from an agile merchandizing approach linked to the segmentation of customers, product and suppliers by the European textile manufactures through network integration. Thus the first part of the descriptive study sought to measure the fundamental construct underlying the success of the dynamic framework's management components. The results are shown in Table 6.7 in order to understand the contribution of strategic planning to the creation of collaborative as opposed to competitive advantage. Collaborative advantages signify the value generated within the entire network of supply and demand.

Customer segmentation

It was immediately apparent that the customer segmentation of the three UK-based companies was at best unstructured and normally not present. This meant that there was no real attempt to differentiate between customer requirements; a common approach to customers was adopted by the UK-based companies. The Sweden- and Italy-based companies were more targeted in the approach to their customers. The basis of segmentation ranged between different product ranges and customer ethnographic groupings to geographical and commercial reasons. The fact that these approaches did exist meant that a more directed response could be made by the textile and clothing producer. The greatest advantages were achieved when the level of customer segmentation could be directly related to the value preposition (eg Company 4).

Product segmentation

There was limited product segmentation by the two UK-based garment manufacturers and some process-based approach by the UK-based textile fabric coater. The remaining companies from Italy and Sweden did have varying approaches to product segmentation, including end-consumer-based, yarn quality and product and lifestyle range. In these cases product segmentation was seen as an important contribution to responsiveness for fashion merchandise supply. There was a clear product focus within the companies based on accommodating their different technical and product attributes in the directed customer service.

Table 6.7 Research findings

| Company | NETWORK INTEGRATION | | | Collaborative advantage |
	Customer segmentation	Product segmentation	Supplier segmentation	
1	None	None	None	None
2	Unstructured	Processing based	None	Process technology
3	None	None	None	Informal feedback from agents/retailers Local yarn suppliers that deliver within hours
4	Product segmentation according to end-customers, direct customers selected accordingly Controls that the customers sell the 'right' concept	End-consumer based	Fabric based	Manufacturing support from local community
5	End-consumers are segmented according to collections, direct customers selected accordingly Direct customers are prioritised according to commercial importance	End-consumer based	Fabric based	Manufacturing support from 300 local (national) independents Innovation by help of fabric suppliers
6	Label based	None	Lead-time based (Asia, Turkey and Italy)	Mixed supply base
7	Managed by headquarters	Yarn quality, lead-time requirements	None	Vertically integrated business
8	Working women aged 30+	Garment type (knitted, sewn and imported)	Product based	None
9	Own brand and private labels	Adult, children and UK	None	Local dye house (uncoloured yarn dyed according to demand)
10	Geographical segmentation	Products are grouped according to warp	Yarn properties	Local dye house (uncoloured yarn dyed according to demand)
11	Own brand and private labels	Hats: functional and classic Socks: classic, soccer and functional	Product based	Innovative support from yarn suppliers

Supplier segmentation

The UK-based companies had no supplier segmentation. There was no attempt to relate the demand requirements to the suppliers' response capability. This was also the case for one Italian and one Swedish company. Only one company used lead time as the basis of segmentation and adopted a mixed mode of supply for different suppliers. In all other cases the supplier segmentation was based on a textile premise of either yarn, fabric or product capability of the supplier. For the segmentation of yarn and fabrics this indirectly resulted in the development of a mixed supply base as there was a prominent trend indicating that more innovative materials would be supplied from Europe and basic produce from low labour rate sources of production. For the two vertically integrated companies (Companies 7 and 8) manufacturing competencies had been clearly defined and divided into different product areas.

Collaborative advantage

The study revealed that there was a wide understanding by each business of its collaborative advantage, but generally they all thought it was based on some element of service provision. Within the sample of 11 companies there was a wide understanding of the core service components that gave them an internal competitive advantage. The findings indicated that those companies that did not understand the need for a structured segmentation and targeting of their customers were less likely to be able to gain leverage from their perceived collaborative advantage. For instance, in their search for low-cost alternatives the sample merchandise manufacturer (Company 9) had failed to recognize the potential benefits from selecting partners in accordance with the value-adding activities that they provided to their customers. This had an adverse effect on their capability to provide an agile response to their customers, leaving them with residual stock and other production inefficiencies, damaging the internal operations performance.

The use of supplier segmentation in practice had in general not been applied to the same extent as product segmentation and customer segmentation. Five out of the 11 companies had failed to segment their suppliers and instead applied a generic approach to managing them all. However, several companies (eg Companies 4 and 5) had shown great benefits when marketing strategies were combined with customer-based product segmentation. By identifying the service level required by a specific customer group the product offer could be designed accordingly. Given the close connection between customer and product segments the distinction between the two was often hard to define. But whereas the connection of customers and products was of significant importance and frequently applied in practice, the actual need for distinct supplier segmentation was not as obvious. The lack of focused supplier selection and management within the industry might signify that such a component has no impact on competitive integration in agile supply networks. Nevertheless, the majority of companies in this study using such a segmentation strategy were found to be more focused businesses with a precise understanding of how the supply chain would fulfil their customers' requirements, contributing to enhanced business performance. Consequently the absence of a segmentation strategy, within the context of the study, was seen to be significant. Textile manufacturing companies using suppliers capable of supplying them with not only products but also with competencies such as innovative support, quick response, customized deliveries or process technology were more likely to fulfil customer requirements than their competitors. Moreover, the use of a mixed supply base was found to be one of the most valuable strategies for supplying high fashion garments with sales turnover being increased by approximately 30 per cent from the previous year.

FUTURE DEVELOPMENTS

The findings from the descriptive case study supported the notion of agile merchandizing as a valuable business strategy for European textile and clothing manufacturers to achieve a higher degree of market mediation employing collaborative business practices and strategic segmentation within the company. By knowing where and when value is to be added, business processes can be integrated more effectively yet with minimum waste. However, to improve the practicability of the dynamic framework and its implementation to the industry, further research addressing the issues related to virtual integration and the suggested control need to be considered. Factors such as collaboration, commitment and trust may inhibit or drive practical success of the process integration.

For some parts of the organization vertical integration may be required, emphasizing a higher degree of process control than collaboration and outsourcing (eg Companies 7 and 8) whereas other activities are more likely to profit from the extended expertise of external suppliers (eg Companies 5 and 11). The literature related to trading relationships and collaboration drivers has until recently been fairly limited to the more operations-focused supply chain. Further research in this area will consequently be required to aid companies in satisfying an ever more demanding and fickle end-consumer.

In ensuring collaborative relationships, visibility is one of the main drivers (eg Companies 4, 5 and 6). Through being involved in the sample development and early production, Company 6 had managed to get an early understanding of customer demand and could effectively adjust its supply response accordingly. Similar advantages were gained by Companies 4 and 5 by strategic segmentation managed to clearly recognize the particular desires of the targeted end-consumers.

It appears that in respect of an industry characterized by changeable and unpredictable market demand, integration efforts need to be driven by demand visibility rather than traditional order information exchange. Future research will consequently have to address the implicit meaning of information sharing (virtual integration) to see how it reflects in value-adding supply chain decisions such as postponement strategy, stock management and supply chain relationships. Considering the rapid development of a global marketplace, agile merchandizing and its dynamic framework are believed to develop a valuable business strategy for companies to strive in an ever more competitive and demanding business environment.

References

Accenture (2003) *Outsourcing: Shared Risks and Shared Rewards*

Aitken, J, Childerhouse, P and Towill, D (2003) The impact of product life-cycle on supply chain strategy, *International Journal of Production Economics*, **85**, pp 127–40

Bergvall-Forsberg, J and Towers, N (2006) Creating agile supply networks in the fashion industry: A pilot study of the European textile and clothing industry, *Journal of the Textile Institute*, **98**, (4), pp 377–85

Bozarth, C, Handfield, R and Das, A (1998) Stages of global sourcing strategy evolution: an exploratory study, *Journal of Operations Management*, **16** (2/3), pp 241–55

Bruce, M, Daly, L and Towers, N (2004) Lean or agile: a solution for supply chain management in the textiles and clothing industry?, *International Journal of Operations & Production Management*, **24**, (2), pp 151–70

Childerhouse, P, Aitken, J and Towill, D (2002) Analysis and design of focused demand chains, *Journal of Operations Management*, **20**, pp 675–89

Christopher, M and Towill, D (2001) An integrated model for the design of agile supply chains, *International Journal of Physical Distribution and Logistics Management*, **31** (4), pp 235–46

Croom, S, Romano, P and Giannakis, M (2000) Supply chain management: an analytical framework for critical literature review, *European Journal of Purchasing & Supply Management*, **6**, (1), pp 67–83

de Treville, S, Shapiro, R D and Hameri, A-P (2004) From supply chain to demand chain: the role of lead-time reduction in improving demand chain performance, *Journal of Operations Management*, **21**, pp 613–27

Feitzinger, E and Lee, H L (1997) Mass customization at Hewlett Packard – the power of postponement, *Harvard Business Review*, January–February, pp 116–21

Fisher, M L (1997) The right supply chain for your products, *Harvard Business Review*, March–April, pp 105–16

Frear, C R, Metcalf, L E and Alguire, M S (1992) Offshore sourcing: its nature and scope, *International Journal of Purchasing and Materials Management*, **28**, (3), pp 2–11

Goldman, S L, Nagel, R N, Preiss, K and Dove, R (1991) *Iacocca Institute: 21st Century Manufacturing Enterprise Strategy, An industry led view, Vols 1 & 2*, Iacocca Institute, Bethlehem

Helo, P (2004) Managing agility and productivity in the electronics industry, *Industrial Management & Data Systems*, **104**, (7), pp 567–77

Lee, E-J, Lee, K-B and Moore, M (2004) Global sourcing and textile and apparel import value: a four-country study as an application of global commodity chains theory, *Journal of Textile and Apparel, Technology and Management*, **3**, (4), pp 1–10

Li, S, Ragu-Nathan, B, Ragu-Nathan, S and Rao, S (2006) The impact of supply chain management practices on competitive advantage and organizational performance, *Omega*, **34**, pp 1007–24

Lin, C-T, Chiu, H and Chu, P-Y (2006) Agility index in the supply chain, *International Journal of Production Economics*, **100**, pp 285–99

Lowson, R H (2003) Apparel sourcing: assessing the true operational cost, *International Journal of Clothing Science and Technology*, **15**, (5), pp 335–45

Mason-Jones, R, Naylor, B and Towill, D R (2000) Lean, agile or leagile? Matching your supply chain to the marketplace, *International Journal of Production Research*, **38**, (17), pp 4061–70

Naylor, J, Naim, M and Berry, D (1999) Leagility: integrating the lean and agile manufacturing paradigm in the total supply chain, *International Journal of Production Economics*, **62**, (1/2), pp 107–18

Nordas, H K (2004) *The Global Textile and Clothing Industry post the Agreement on Textiles and Clothing The World*, WTO, Vol 7, pp 1

Porter, M E (1985) *Competitive Advantage*, The Free Press, New York

Sharp, J M, Irani, Z and Desai, S (1999) Working towards agile manufacturing in the UK industry, *International Journal of Production Economics*, **62**, pp 155–69

TCSG (2000) *A National Strategy for the UK Textile & Clothing Industry,* DTI, June

Towers, N, and Ashford, R (2003) Supply chain production planning in manufacturing SMEs – a source of innovation for customer relationships, *International Journal of New Product Development and Innovation Management,* **5**, (1), pp 11–21

Towers, N and Peng, X (2006) An assessment of international strategic merchandizing from China, post quota elimination in January 2005 for the UK apparel market, *The Journal of the Textile Institute,* **97**, (6), pp 541–8

Vonderembse, M A, Uppal, M, Huang, S H and Dismukes, J P (2004) Designing supply chains: Towards theory development, *International Journal of Production Economics,* **100**, (2), pp 223–38

Walters, D and Rainbird, M (2004) The demand chain as an integral component of the value chain, *Journal of Consumer Marketing,* **21**, (7), pp 465–75

Part 3

Food logistics

7

Tesco's supply chain management

David Smith and Leigh Sparks

INTRODUCTION

The transformation of Tesco in the last 30 or so years is one of the more remarkable stories in British retailing. From being a comparatively limited 'pile it high, sell it cheap' downmarket retailer, the company has become one of the world's leading retail businesses, with retail operations in countries as dispersed as the United Kingdom, Poland, Malaysia, China, Japan and the United States. Tesco has become dominant in its home market (Burt and Sparks, 2003) and increasingly significant on the international stage. In the UK its loyalty card and its e-commerce operations are generally considered to be world-leading (Humby *et al*, 2003). More than 60 per cent of Tesco's store floor space is now located outside the UK, with the number of international stores (42 per cent), international sales (26 per cent) and international profit (25 per cent) growing very rapidly towards that percentage (Figure 7.1).

There are accounts available of this transformation by those involved (MacLaurin, 1999; Powell, 1991). Some aspects of the Tesco operations have been discussed in public by their executives (eg Child, 2002; Jones, 2001; Jones and Clarke, 2002; Kelly, 2000; Mason, 1998; *Retail Week*, 2007). Tesco is also the focus of much external attention (eg Bevan,

(a) Number of stores 1977–2008

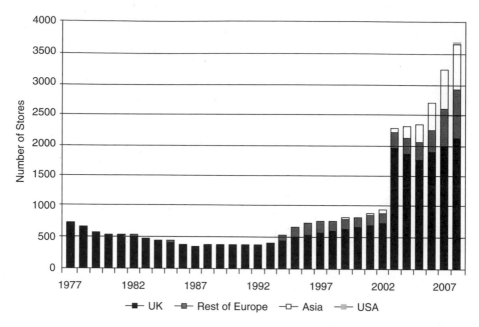

(b) Sales floorspace 1977–2008

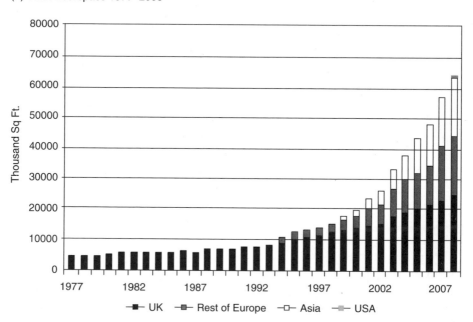

(c) Turnover 1977–2008

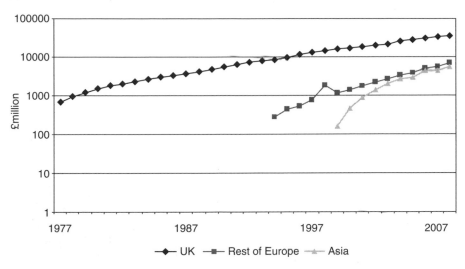

Figure 7.1 Tesco plc: an international business
Source: Tesco plc, annual reports

2005; Burt and Sparks, 2003; Coe and Lee, 2006; Dawson *et al*, 2006; Palmer, 2004; Reynolds, 2004; Seth and Randall, 1999, 2005; Sparks, 2008). This literature generally emphasizes the fundamental transformation of the retail business to meet changing consumer demands and global opportunities.

The visible component of this transformation is seen in the locations and formats of the retail outlets and in the range of products and services that the company offers. Customers are also aware of the changes through the constant reinforcement of the corporate brand. Less visible, however, is the supply chain transformation that has underpinned this retail success story. It should be obvious that the supply chain required to deliver comparatively simple products to lots of small, high street stores in the 1970s is vastly different to the supply chain delivering the extensive breadth of food and non-food products in a modern Tesco Extra hypermarket, the availability required to run modern Tesco Express convenience stores or the online and catalogue shopping on Tesco.com and Tesco Direct. This supply chain and logistics transformation has received less consideration, although some academic analysis is available (Gustafsson *et al*, 2006; Smith, 1998, 2006; Smith and Sparks, 1993, 2004; Sparks 1986).

This chapter presents a summary of this supply chain transformation in Tesco, and aims to describe, analyse and draw lessons from the journey it has undertaken.

THE CHANGING TESCO SUPPLY CHAIN: ESTABLISHING CONTROL AND DELIVERING EFFICIENCY

The current retail position of Tesco is far removed from the origins of the company. Tesco made its name by the operation of a 'pile it high, sell it cheap' approach to food retailing (Sparks, 2008). Price competitiveness was critical to this and fitted well with the consumer requirements of the time. The company and its store managers were essentially individual entrepreneurs. The growth of the company saw considerable expansion until by the early 1970s Tesco had 800 stores across England and Wales. This entrepreneurial approach to retailing, epitomized by the company founder Sir Jack Cohen, was put under pressure, however, as competition and consumer requirements evolved (Corina, 1971; Powell, 1991). Tesco had therefore to change.

The emblematic event signifying the beginning of this transformation was Operation Checkout in 1977 (Akehurst, 1984). Dramatically, trading stamps were removed from the business, prices were cut nationally as a grand event and the business received an immediate and considerable boost to volume. Stores were re-merchandized as part of Operation Checkout and consumers began to see a different approach to Tesco retailing. After this initial repositioning event and phase, Tesco began to better understand its customers, control its business and to move away from its downmarket image (Powell, 1991). This retail transformation, however, brought into sharp focus the quality and capability of Tesco supply systems and its relationships with suppliers.

Such concerns have remained fundamental during the subsequent almost irresistible rise of Tesco. By moving away from its origins, Tesco changed its business. Initially the focus was on 'conforming' out-of-town superstores, but since the early 1990s a multi-format approach has developed encompassing hypermarkets, superstores, supermarkets, city centre stores and convenience operations. Online retailing has become a major channel (Jones, 2001). The Tesco corporate brand has been strongly developed (Burt and Sparks, 2002) and international ambitions have accelerated (Dawson *et al*, 2006). In all this, the supply of appropriate products to the stores and customers has been fundamental.

Within the UK four main phases in distribution and supply chain strategy and operations can be identified. First, there was a period dominated by direct delivery by the supplier to the retail shops. Second, there was the move, starting in the late 1970s after Operation Checkout, to centralized regional distribution centres for ambient goods. Third, a composite distribution strategy emerged from the late 1980s. Fourth, from the late 1990s there has been a focus on vertical collaboration and integration in the supply chain through an emphasis on a 'lean' approach to supply chains, resulting amongst other things in 'stockless' distribution.

Direct to store delivery

Tesco in the mid-1970s operated a direct to store delivery (DSD) process. Suppliers and manufacturers delivered directly to stores, almost as and when they chose. Store managers often operated their own relationships (Powell's 1991 'private enterprise', p 185) which made central control and standardization difficult to achieve. Product ranges, availability, quality and even prices were inconsistent. This DSD system fell apart under the pressures of the volume increases of Operation Checkout. As Powell (1991, p 184) comments, quoting Sir Ian Maclaurin:

> Ultimately our business is about getting our goods to our stores in sufficient quantities to meet our customers' demands. Without being able to do that efficiently, we aren't in business, and Checkout stretched our resources to the limit. Eighty per cent of all our supplies were coming direct from manufacturers, and unless we'd sorted out our distribution problems there was a very real danger that we would have become a laughing stock for promoting cuts on lines that we couldn't even deliver. It was a close-run thing.

Powell continues:

> How close is now a matter of legend: outside suppliers having to wait for up to twenty-four hours to deliver at Tesco's centres; of stock checks being conducted in the open air; of Tesco's four obsolescent warehouses, and the company's transport fleet working to an around-the-clock, seven-day schedule. And as the problems lived off one another, and as customers waited for the emptied shelves to be refilled, so the tailback lengthened around the stores, delays of five to six hours becoming commonplace. Possibly for the first time in its history, the company recognized that it was as much in the business of distribution as of retailing.

The company survived the initial supply system consequences of the success of Operation Checkout by operational 'fire fighting'; whilst problems occurred, meltdown was avoided. It was clear, however, that a total change in approach to supply and distribution would be needed as the new corporate business strategy took hold.

Centralization

The decision was taken to move away from direct delivery to stores and to implement centralization. The basis of this decision (in 1980) was the realization of the critical nature of range control on the operations. Store managers could no longer be allowed to decide ranges and prices and to operate their own mini-empires. Concerns over the quality of product available to consumers in stores also suggested a need to relocate the power in the supply chain. If the company were to be transformed and modern customers better served, as the business strategy proposed, then head office needed control over ranging, pricing and stocking decisions. Centralization of distribution, to manage the supply of products into stores, was the tool to achieve this.

Tesco replaced DSD by a centrally controlled and physically centralized distribution network and service (Kirkwood, 1984a, 1984b) delivering the vast majority of stores' needs, utilizing common handling systems, with deliveries within a lead time of a maximum of 48 hours (Sparks, 1986). This involved a significant extension of the existing company distribution facilities and the building of new distribution centres, aligned more appropriately with the current and future store location profile. Investment in technology, handling systems and working practices allowed faster stock turn and better lead times. Components of the revised structure were outsourced, allowing comparisons amongst contractors and Tesco-operated centres, to compare practices and drive efficiency.

This strategy produced an organized network of centralized distribution centres, linked by computer to stores and head office. The proliferation of back-up stock-holding points and individual operations at store level was reduced. The introduction of centralization forced suppliers to meet Tesco's operational demands and gave Tesco control over the supply of products to stores. Suppliers were forced to deliver into the distribution network and not direct to stores. These centres were the hubs of the supply network, being larger, handling more stock, more vehicles and requiring a more efficient organization. Centralization produced the necessary control over the business and fitted with the changed retail store strategy of the 1980s (larger conforming out-of-town superstores). Figures 7.2 and 7.3 show the changing store profile and the impact of the distribution changes on corporate stock holding. The immediate impact of centralization on stock handling is seen clearly in Figure 7.3.

Centralization proceeded on a product line basis. By 1989 Tesco had 42 depots, of which 26 were temperature controlled. Whilst a massive improvement, it still had issues. Fresh foods were basically handled through single-temperature, single-product depots. These were comparatively small and inefficient and were subject to only tactical operational improvements, allowing, for example, more frequent store deliveries and a more accurate idea of the cost of product distribution.

While stores saw some improvements in supply in the mid-1980s, there remained disadvantages of the centralized network. For example, each product group had different ordering systems. Individual store volumes

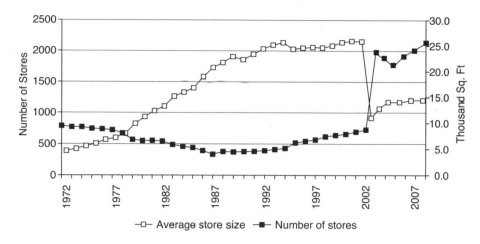

Figure 7.2 Number of stores and average size of stores, Tesco plc (UK only)
Source: Tesco plc, annual reports

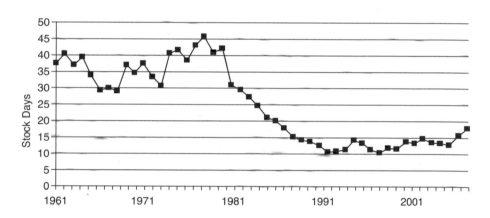

Figure 7.3 Inventory in Tesco plc
Source: Tesco plc, annual reports

were so low that delivery frequency was less than desired and quality
suffered. Delivery frequency was maintained, but at the price of high
vehicle empty-running costs and increased store receipt costs. It was
expensive to have on-site Tesco quality control inspection at each location,
which meant that the standards of quality desired could not be rigorously
controlled at the point of distribution. It was also realized that this
network would neither cope with the growth Tesco forecast in the 1990s
nor, as important, would it be ready to meet anticipated higher legal standards on temperature control in the chill chain.

The produce depot at Aztec West in Bristol opened in 1986 and represented the best of the centralized network. Tesco could have made further investment in single-product distribution systems, upgraded the depots and transport temperature control and put in new computer systems, but this would still have achieved overall a less than optimal use of resources across the company.

Composite distribution

It became recognized that an integrated approach to supply was required across the organization and that it could generate ongoing improvements. A strategy of composite distribution was thus planned in the 1980s to take full effect in the 1990s. A complication during this changeover was the need to ensure continuity of service to stores, made more difficult by the rapid growth of the business at this time. Composite distribution enabled temperature controlled product (chilled, fresh and frozen) to be distributed through one system of multi-temperature warehouses and vehicles. Composite distribution used specially designed vehicles with temperature controlled compartments to deliver any combination of these products. It provided daily deliveries of these products at the appropriate temperature so that they reached the customers at the stores in the peak of freshness. The insulated composite trailer could be sectioned into up to three independently controlled temperature chambers by means of movable bulkheads. The size of each chamber could be varied to match the volume to be transported at each temperature.

Composite distribution provided a number of benefits. Some derive from the original process of centralization and control, of which composite is an extension. Others are more directly attributable to the nature of composite. First, the move to daily deliveries of composite product groups to all stores in waves provided an opportunity to reduce the levels of stock held at the stores and indeed to reduce or obviate the need for storage facilities at store level. The result of this at store level is the better use of overall floor space (more selling space) and greater in-store availability. For the company a continuous reduction in stock levels resulted (see Figure 7.3).

The second benefit was the improvement of quality and its consequent reduction in wastage. Products reach the store in a more desirable condition. Better forecasting systems minimize lost sales due to out-of-stocks. The introduction of sales-based ordering produces more accurate store orders. More rigorous application of code control results in longer shelf-life on delivery, which in turn enables a reduction in wastage. This is of crucial importance to shoppers who demand better quality and fresher products. In addition, however, the tight control over the chain enabled Tesco to satisfy and exceed new legislation requirements on food safety.

Third, the introduction of composite provided an added benefit in productivity terms. The economies of scale and enhanced use of equipment provide greater efficiency and an improved distribution and supply service. Composite distribution required comparatively lower capital costs. Operationally, costs were also reduced through, for example, less congestion at the store. Throughout the system, an emphasis on maximizing productivity and efficiency of the operations, enabled by new computing and other technologies, also produced lower costs and better service levels.

The introduction of composite was not a simple procedure. Considerable problems were encountered requiring Tesco to work closely with suppliers and distribution operators to reorganize and develop new and altered practices (Smith, 2006). The move to composite led to the further centralization of more product groups, the reduction of stock holding, faster product movement along the channel, better information sharing, the reduction of order lead times and stronger code control for critical products. Such changes are easy to list but hard to implement and achieve, and required close working with, and changed behaviours of, a variety of supply partners (Smith, 2006).

Issues remained post-composite implementation. Composite provided control over one part of the supply chain, but other parts remained untouched. For example, the cost of primary distribution (from production to composite centre) remained within the buyer's gross margin and was not identified clearly and separately. This cost had to be substantiated indirectly by talking to suppliers and hauliers. In other words clarity and transparency were not achieved. As important, certain sectors of the supplier base were fragmented and not fully organized for the needs of retail distribution, despite the concomitant growth and development of Tesco retail brand products. Fragmentation made the task of securing further permanent improvements difficult. Whilst some suppliers could reorganize their procedures to meet the changed demands of composite, others could not. This had implications for the scale and scope of the supplier base. Tesco was interested in rationalizing the supplier base to improve efficiency and consistency of performance, amongst other benefits.

This composite structure became the backbone of the supply network, although it too continued to evolve. For example, to increase the volume capability of the composites, Tesco later implemented a change to its frozen distribution strategy by commissioning a new automated frozen distribution centre at Daventry. This national frozen centre delivered to Tesco stores by routing through the composite distribution centres. This enabled the composite frozen chambers to be converted to chill chambers, thus releasing extra volume capability to service Tesco's business growth. The 'true' composite nature of the centres has been replaced as the scale and balance of the business and operational policies and capabilities have altered. Essentially they have been affected by new methods of working and become regional distribution centres.

Vertical collaboration and 'lean' supply chains

Despite the successes of the reconfiguration of the Tesco supply chain in the 1980s and 1990s, analysis of the supply channel pointed to a number of areas where benefits could still be achieved (Jones and Clarke, 2002). In a much quoted example, a can of cola was followed in the supply chain from a mine (for the can) to the store. It was discovered that it took 319 days to go through the entire chain, during which time only two hours were spent making and filling the can. This process involved many locations, firms and trips (Jones, 2002; Jones and Clarke, 2002). As Jones and Clarke (2002, p 31) note 'even in the best-run value streams there are lots of opportunities for improvement'. The implications for, and changes in, aligning the supply chain consequent on the learning from the can example are summarized in Box 7.1.

Box 7.1　The Tesco cola can journey

The implications of the Tesco cola can journey

It was realized that practically all of Tesco's practices for getting goods from the supplier to the shelf would need to change.

The first step was to hook the point-of-sale data in the store directly to a shipping decision in Tesco's RDC. This made the end-customer at the checkout point the 'pacemaker', regulating the provision stream. Tesco then increased the frequency of deliveries to the retail stores. After several years of experimentation, Tesco's trucks now leave the RDCs for each store every few hours around the clock, carrying an amount of cola proportional to what was sold in the last few hours. At the RDC, cola is now received directly from the supplier's bottling plant in wheeled dollies. They are rolled directly from the supplier into the delivery truck to the stores. And once at the stores, the dollies are rolled directly to the point of sale, where they take the place of the usual sales racks. This innovation eliminates several 'touches', in which employees moved cola from large pallets to roll cages, to the stores,

---

and then onto dollies to reach the shelves, where they were handled one last time. (In drawing their provision-stream maps of the original process, Tesco discovered that half its costs in operating this provision stream was the labour required to fill the shelves in the store.)

For fast-moving products like cola, the Tesco RDC is now a cross-dock rather than a warehouse, with goods from suppliers spending only a few hours between their receipt and their dispatch to the stores. To guard against sudden spikes in demand, a buffer stock of full dollies is still held aside. But because of the frequency of replenishment, the buffer is very small. Back at the cola supplier, even larger changes have taken place. Britvic improved the flexibility of its filling lines so it can now make what the customer has just requested in small batches with very high reliability. This means that there are practically no finished goods awaiting shipment in Britvic's filling plant. The final logistics step is for Tesco's delivery truck to take the dollies several times a day from the RDC on a 'milk run' to a series of Tesco stores. At each store it collects the empty dollies and then visits several suppliers to return them. At each stop it also picks up full dollies and then returns to the Tesco RDC to restart the cycle. That may sound like a good way to increase truck miles and logistics costs, and many traditional managers, including those at Tesco and Britvic, have assumed it must. However, in practice, these methods substantially reduce the total miles driven along with freight costs, while also reducing total inventories in the system.

The consequence, in terms of performance, is remarkable. Total 'touches' on the product (each of which involves costly human effort) have been reduced from 150 to 50. The total throughput time, from the filling line at the supplier to the customer leaving the store with the cola, has declined from 20 days to five days. The number of inventory stocking points has been reduced from five to two (the small buffer in the RDC and the roller racks in the store), and the supplier's distribution centre for the items has disappeared.

Sources: Fortune, 14 November 2005; Womack and Jones, 2005, pp 110–17, 141–2

The can example is one illustration of a broader process undertaken by Tesco (Jones and Clarke, 2002; Womack and Jones, 2005). The first step involved the mapping of the traditional value stream. This mapping process demonstrated its stop-start-stop nature. Secondly and consequently therefore, value streams that 'flowed' were created/designed

(Figure 7.4 is a diagrammatic simplification of 'before and after'). Thirdly (and as Box 7.1 suggests) arising from flow principles, Tesco began to look at synchronization and aspects of lean manufacturing and supply. Finally, Tesco utilized its consumer knowledge from its loyalty card to rethink what products and services should be located where in the value stream (Humby *et al*, 2003). Jones and Clarke (2002) describe this process as the creation of a 'customer-driven supply chain'. Others might use the term 'demand chain'. The effect is to meet consumer demands in a timely fashion at a local level through whatever retail format the consumer requires.

Clarke (2002) summarized the supply chain projects of the early 2000s in Tesco that effectively comprised a movement to a 'lean' supply system (and are implicit in Box 7.1).

Continuous replenishment (CR)

CR was introduced in 1999 and has two key features. These are, first, a replacement of batch data processing with a flow system, and second,

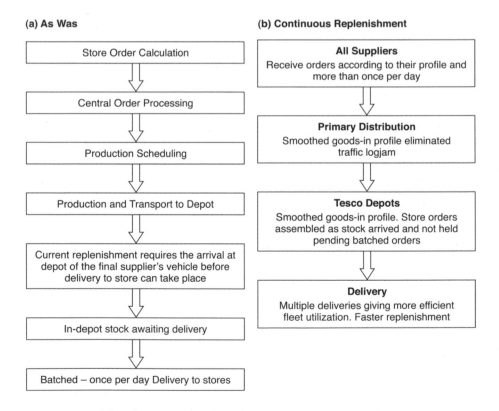

Figure 7.4 The change to replenishment
Source: after Clarke, 2002

using the flow system, multiple daily orders are sent to suppliers allowing for multiple deliveries, reducing stock holding through cross-docking and varying availability and quality.

In-store range management

Based on customer behaviour data and stock-holding capacity analysis at store, Tesco produces store-specific planograms and store-specific ranging. The system improves store presentation as well as stock replenishment and availability. Tesco provides the exact stock requirement for specific shelves in specific stores to its out-replenishment system.

Network management

Network management integrates and maintains the network assets and extends the life of the system. New sites add to the capacity of the system. The frozen element of the composite system had been centralized in a new frozen centre, allowing chill and ambient expansion in the released space. Cross-docking is used at regional centres for frozen and slow-moving lines. Consolidation centres provide fresh produce for cross-docking. These changes have produced a more integrated network that has made better use of the assets, extended the life of centres and improved performance by selecting the right 'value stream' for appropriate products.

Flow-through

Flow-through or cross-docking is now more extensive. Product storage is much reduced. Increasingly distribution centres have no racking and do not store product; they are essentially 'stockless'. Pick-by-store practices have been replaced by pick-by-line processes in many instances. A different but nonetheless important aspect of flow-through is the use of merchandizable-ready units to allow product to be put on sale in stores without extra handling. Such units (often called 'dollies') are increasingly common in fast-moving items, but can be used for many other items as well. More recently, retail-ready packaging and store-ready merchandizing have extended these principles and become increasingly important.

Primary distribution

'Primary distribution' is the term Tesco prefers for factory gate pricing (FGP), seeing the process as a 'strategic change in the way goods flow... (and about) achieving efficient flows and not a pricing process' (Wild, quoted in Rowat, 2003, p 48). However, cost reduction is a key driver behind the interest in primary distribution. Essentially, primary distribution is about control (and pricing) of the supply chain from the supplier despatch bay to the goods in the bay of the retail distribution centre. It separates out the cost of transportation from the purchase price of the product itself, and by putting it into a separate primary distribution budget, allows direct control and analysis by Tesco. Primary distribution requires the cooperation of the whole of the supply chain including the retail buyers. This was achieved by bringing together cross-functional teams and by the full endorsement of the policy from senior directors. Suppliers, and their transport service providers, went through quite major changes to their arrangements for the delivery of their goods to the retail distribution centres (Gustafsson *et al*, 2006; Smith, 2006). Simons and Taylor (2007) provide an example of how these elements come together and emphasize the benefits for the chain as a whole in thinking about value chain analysis, working with close partners and focusing on the chain rather than subsets of the chain. The process is complicated and requires commitment, but the benefits are clear. Tesco's vision for primary distribution is an inbound supply chain which is visible, low-cost, efficient and effective.

The combination of all these initiatives and the overriding lean approach produces a view of supply systems that is radically different from the DSD starting point some 30 years ago.

THE CURRENT NETWORK

The recent developments in terms of a 'lean' approach to the supply chain are focused on simplicity, transparency and efficiency of the entire supply chain. This, however, cannot hide the scale and indeed complexity of Tesco's UK supply chain network.

The Tesco supply chain network is well documented in IGD (2008). This report shows that in 2007 there were 29 distribution depots, with a warehouse area of 8.45 million square feet and annual total case volumes of 1.93 billion. Centralized distribution accounts for 95 per cent of the volume. Of these 29 depots, 23 are now run in-house by Tesco and the remainder are contracted to Wincanton (four) and DHL-Exel (two). National Distribution Centres (seven) are combined with Regional Distribution Centres (10), Composite Distribution Centres (one) and Temperature Controlled Depots (11). In addition there are five trunking or consolidation sites run by Tesco (managing non-food, slow-moving grocery and beers, wines and spirits lines) and a further 17 shared user consolidation centres operated by a variety of outsourced companies that feed into this system. The core network operates over 2,000 vehicle units and 4,000 trailer units, covering 659 million km per annum. The network utilizes an extensive set of transit handling (or flow) units including plastic crates (12 million), roll cages (1.06 million), dollies (382,000), soft drinks trays (210,000), half pallets (76,000) and banana merchandizing units (23,000). This is a large-scale network of supply which, if not utilized intensively, implies significant additional costs.

Developments in depot operation and location have been considerable in recent years as has the focus on achieving an effective and efficient operation. The components and the operations of this network have undergone significant change. The inter-linkage amongst these elements has been transformed by the lean and flow principles. Performance is rigorously monitored, including through the 'steering wheel' approach widespread throughout Tesco. The distribution centre steering wheel in 2005 focused on operations (safety and efficiency), people (appointment, development, commitment and values), finance (stock results, operating costs) and the customer (accuracy, delivery on time). The effect overall has been to build a supply chain system that is much admired worldwide.

Coping with complexity

As Jones and Clarke (2002) point out, the process of change outlined above made huge strides towards modernizing Tesco's supply chain, focusing in particular on the operations in the UK. As a consequence of this, lead times to stores and from suppliers have been cut radically and stock holding reduced enormously (Figure 7.3), particularly to the mid-1990s. The service to the consumer has improved immeasurably. Some argue (eg Burt and Sparks, 2003) that the supply revolution was an integral, if not essential, component of the rise to dominance of Tesco in the UK. The Tesco supply chain simply out-competed the competition, a fact implicitly recognized by subsequent major redevelopments of the supply systems of Asda and Sainsbury.

Massive progress had been made in reconfiguring the basic supply system. However, this progress had also been achieved at a time when Tesco had begun to move from being a standardized, conforming super-store-based, domestic-focused retailer, to a multi-format, multi-sector, international operator. Consequently, the retail and supply challenges were multiplying. In essence, Tesco set out to meet consumer demands wherever, whenever, however and for whatever it could. In 1997, Tesco outlined a strategy based on four pillars: Tesco UK, non-food, retail services and internationalization. At that time Tesco was essentially a UK-based food retailer. Ten years later this strategy has produced a dominant retailer in the home market, a strong and growing proportion of sales in non-food, with extensive financial and other service operations, and an organization with more international than UK floor space. In transforming the organization and operations to this degree, a number of challenges in the supply chain have had to be met. These challenges involved a fundamental change in the store format strategy in the UK, the development of successful internet and home shopping channels and rapid and extensive internationalization. Figures 7.1–3 show some of the dimensions and impacts of these changes and challenges. The business transformation is clear in Figures 7.1 and 7.2. Figure 7.3 shows the impact of rising complexity on group inventory levels, in particular through the move to non-food, international and multi-channel operations.

Multi-format development

The development of Tesco Metro and Tesco Express stores in the early 1990s was the first step towards a focus on the urban centre and convenience customers. The 1980s had been almost entirely focused on developing 'conforming' out-of-town superstores, but this approach was limiting in terms of the types of shopping trips that could be serviced. By re-entering high streets and locating Tesco Express stores as convenience outlets, often on petrol forecourts, Tesco began to capture those other shopping trips from both new and existing customers. As UK land-use planning tightened to reduce out-of-town opportunities so these different formats and locational types became more important. The convenience market in particular became a focus from 2002 when a major takeover dramatically increased the number of Tesco Express stores (Figure 7.2), presenting very different supply chain issues.

The present-day Tesco is a multi-format retailer with formats ranging from Extra hypermarkets to small Express convenience stores. This variation has been compounded by retail operational changes. Store hours have been extended in many locations to encompass 24-hour opening. Service levels and quality thresholds have been enhanced. Non-food has become a much greater proportion of even standard store offers than before. Product ranges, operating times and service standards all combine to pressurize a supply system that was essentially developed for a simpler, more standard situation. The movement from composite to 'stockless' was needed to enable an effective solution to this emerging complexity.

The format development in the United Kingdom in the 1990s is detailed in Table 7.1. Two components of the table are noteworthy in a supply chain context. First, the scale and location of the formats obviously vary, posing challenges in supplying products to stores. Second, this is compounded in some situations by the extension of the product range into non-food. Thus there has been an extensive development of hypermarkets, often by extending existing stores, with the new space occupied by non-food products. At the same time smaller stores have emerged in rather more problematic locations for supply systems, eg busy urban high streets. As such, if Tesco had not been developing flow and other handling systems, the potential for added complexity and cost would have been great. By using all the data and the network at its disposal, the variety of formats has been extended. The overall impact on the supply elements of the business has been managed, though inventory levels have risen.

The expansion into non-food products has required a complete overhaul of the clothing supply chain in the United Kingdom and elsewhere (*Retail Week*, 2007). In 2004 new facilities at Daventry were opened, managed by Tibbet and Britten and bringing together all the boxed clothing. Other new depots meet other non-food product supply demands.

Internet and home shopping

In 1995 Tesco conducted a home shopping pilot scheme at a single store. Customers could use a variety of methods to order, with these orders picked at the store by Tesco staff, and collected or delivered to the customer's home or drop-off point. This pilot was extended to 10 stores in 1997 and a store-based picking operation was expanded nationally from 1999. This store-based model was not the common approach adopted by competitors. Criticism of the approach was 'vitriolic' (Child, 2002). Jones (2001) in an interview with John Browett (then CEO of Tesco.com) points to three key elements of the decision to use store-picking. First, Tesco believed that warehouse picking schemes could not make money. Second, customers wanted the full range of products, and economics showed Tesco needed the wide range to drive basket size. Third, geographic coverage from warehouses was insufficient. A store-based picking model provided substantial benefits in terms of speed of implementation and national coverage. It also used existing resources more fully and allowed the supply network both to see the activity occurring and to capture this activity in existing processes of reordering and store delivery. At a local level the key components included ensuring picking processes were efficient based on store layouts and that home delivery by local vehicles was also efficient and effective.

The outcome of this has been the world's largest internet grocery operation, offering in the United Kingdom effectively national coverage through local stores but tying in to the national product supply network. In 2007, 294 stores were used for internet picking, with 1,860 local delivery

Table 7.1   Format development in the United Kingdom

Format/formula	Opening year	Description	Number of stores in 2008	Store floorspace in 2008 (000 sq.ft)
Hypermarket (Tesco Extra)	1996	Stores over c. 60,000 sq ft sales, offering food and non-food, often using mezzanine floors	166	11,736
Superstore (Tesco)	n/a	Specialist food stores with some non-food, varying from c. 20–45,000 sq ft	435	13,165
City supermarket (Tesco Metro)	1992	Food specialists with extensive ranges of convenience foods, mainly high street locations	164	1,892
Convenience store (Tesco Express)	1995	Convenience-focused stores in varying locations, but many on petrol station forecourts. Additionally has c. 500 One Stop convenience stores left over from takeover in 2002	836	1,808
E-retailing (Tesco.com)	1999	Internet ordering, store-based picking model covering most of the UK. Original trial from 1997		
Catalogue retailing (Tesco Direct)	2006	Catalogue available in store for ordering over the web, phone or in store, expanded in second issue to 10,000 products. Delivery direct to home or via collect at store		
Non-food stores (Tesco Homeplus)	2005	Stores of c. 30,000 sq ft offering wide range of non-food items	7	269

Note: This excludes stores not trading as Tesco, ie One Stop (507 stores, 679,000 sq ft) and Dobbies Garden Centres (22 stores, 908,000 sq ft)

vehicles. This is not to say that this is the only model in the future. In 2007 Tesco began to pick out of a dedicated (tesco.com only) store in Croydon, London for some internet supply orders. Demand in this area could not be met from local store picking and so a dedicated store was developed (not a warehouse pick). It may be that in some areas a dedicated facility makes economic sense.

Home delivery by internet ordering for food/grocery has subsequently been supplemented with an extensive internet site offering a huge range of food and non-food products. This site offers far more products than one carried in 'normal' stores and provides local customers access to an enhanced range. In 2006, Tesco launched a catalogue (Tesco Direct) aimed at non-food home shopping, which now runs to over 10,000 product lines, again focusing on providing products to customers as and when they wish to order them, and as and when they wish to receive them. Consumers can place orders by phone or online and have them delivered to the home or available for pick-up at the local store. In-store kiosks are also now being trialled.

Internationalization

Tesco's real strategic store internationalization began in 1994 with entry into Hungary but soon expanded into other central European countries. First steps were then made into the Asian market, both as a reaction to the Asian economic crisis of the 1990s, which meant assets were cheap, but also due to a more positive sense of the scale of the market opportunities in China and Japan, for example. Over time the countries in which Tesco operates have changed slightly. Withdrawals from some markets have been made (Palmer, 2004), recognizing the lack of scope to become the market leader and/or the desire to invest elsewhere (see Table 7.2). In some cases, these withdrawals have been made as part of asset-swaps with other leading global retailers, each recognizing their own strengths in particular markets. During this time Tesco also re-entered Ireland through a major acquisition, though it is still not represented in continental western Europe.

Internationalization has provided both additional sales and markets for Tesco, but it has also brought opportunities to develop new concepts and approaches (Coe and Lee, 2006; Dawson et al, 2006) and to learn from experiences (Palmer, 2005). In central Europe for example, variants of the hypermarket concept have been trialled and eventually transferred back to the United Kingdom in the form of the Tesco Extra concept. Experience in non-food gained in various countries, as well as the UK hypermarkets, has led to the non-food UK Tesco Homeplus stores. Versions of small format and discount-focused stores are operating in central Europe and Asia (especially Poland and Thailand) and these may yet offer potential in the United Kingdom or elsewhere in the world. The entry to Japan provided the opportunity to learn about convenience stores in a very competitive urban market. The learning from this experience has been used to help the convenience and urban chains in the United Kingdom, and has informed aspects of the 2007 entry into the United States.

Table 7.2 International store operations

Country	Year of entry/exit	Comments	Number of stores in 2008	Store floorspace in 2008 (million sq ft)
Ireland	(a) 1978/1986 (b) 1997	Tesco entered Ireland when it acquired stake in Albert Gubay's Three Guys, gaining 100% control in 1979. Sold to H Williams in 1986. Re-entry to Ireland came when Power Supermarkets and Quinnsworth were bought from ABF	100	2.4
France	1993/1998	Catteau's 92 stores were operated under their fascia before they were sold to Promodes. One Vin Plus alcohol store remains in France to capture British tourist spend	1	0.02
Hungary	1994	Entered by buying a stake in Global, now wholly owned	123	5.4
Poland	1995	The Savia chain was purchased initially. HIT hypermarkets were bought in 2003 and 220 Leader Price stores from Casino in 2006. Variety of formats now operated	301	6.7
Czech Republic	1996	When K-Mart pulled out of central Europe, Tesco took over the stores. Further stores were gained as part of an asset swap with Carrefour in 2005	96	4.3
Slovakia	1996	When K-Mart pulled out of central Europe, Tesco took over the stores. Further stores were gained as part of an asset swap with Carrefour in 2005	60	2.7
Thailand	1998	Tesco purchased a stake in Lotus (hypermarkets). Added Express format stores from 2002, followed by Value store and Talad (10k) formats. Now wholly owned	376	8.9
South Korea	1999	A joint venture with Samsung has been used to develop and operate stores, including Aram Mart chain bought in 2005. In May 2008 agreement to buy 36 Homever stores from E-Land (trading as Carrefour) was concluded, subject to regulatory approval	137	6.3
Taiwan	2000/2006	The Taiwan operation was sold to Carrefour as part of an asset swap in 2006, recognizing that it was not growing as desired	–	–
Malaysia	2002	A joint venture with Sime Darby was set up to develop the stores. Took over Makro stores in 2007. Tesco owns 70%	20	1.8
Japan	2003	A purchase of C–Two Network of Tokyo convenience stores marked entry, with Fre'c being added in 2004	125	0.4
Turkey	2003	A stake in Kipa stores marked entry; 93% owned by Tesco	66	1.7
China	2004	Entry came through Ting Hsin's Hymall hypermarket operation, which became 90% Tesco owned in 2006	56	5.2
United States	2007	The first stores opened as Fresh and Easy Neighbourhood Markets in California and Nevada in late 2007	53	0.5

The strategic approach to store internationalization has seen Tesco develop different solutions for diverse markets, using distinct formats and tailoring the product and service offer to the local market. In many countries it operates as a multi-format and even multi-channel retailer (home shopping is available in Ireland and Korea) and focuses on the core values and brands of the business. Behind the scenes people, processes and systems have been enhanced and rolled out initially as 'Tesco in a Box' and more recently as the Tesco Operating Model. This provides all the necessary systems to operate key Tesco processes in any country and is supported by its service centre in Bangalore, India. The impact of this strategic internationalization has been to turn Tesco from a company dominated by UK food superstore retailing to one where the sales floor space outside the United Kingdom is greater than that inside the United Kingdom, store number growth is focused internationally and profit and turnover growth is faster internationally than in the United Kingdom (Figure 7.1). Tesco has become an international retailer (Seth and Randall, 2005).

As can be readily understood, the internationalization of Tesco at store level brings supply chain issues as well. At the same time, Tesco buys products on a global basis and this also has to be 'fitted in' to the ever-changing pattern of supply and demand. With formats and products varying by country and with time, the need is for a supply system that can be adaptable. In some cases, eg Ireland and Hungary, the composite model has been effectively exported to these countries, often with the same logistics service partners. In other situations there is an attempt to rethink the supply system and the technology needed and use this as the platform moving forward.

For example, in 2003/4, based on the UK composite model, Tesco opened the largest distribution centre in Asia at Mokchon, Korea. It also opened major centres in Poland and the Czech Republic, extended a centre in Hungary (and added another fresh food distribution centre) and developed a new composite site in Ireland. As internationalization continues, so the infrastructure and the processes in the supply chain need to keep pace with or even lead the developments. The processes are now embedded in the Tesco Operating Model, but new facilities to meet expansion needs are required. In 2007/8 for example, Tesco opened new distribution centres in Thailand (for Express stores), and Malaysia and Japan (for fresh food products).

Retail internationalization itself can be controversial due to its impacts on the existing retail stores. Tesco has been criticized not only for its sourcing policies, but also for its impacts on small, local retailers in countries as far apart as Poland and Thailand. It also of course has an impact on the supply systems of the countries in which it sources and operates (see Humphrey, 2007 and Reardon *et al*, 2007 for a discussion of these issues).

When Tesco introduces a new supply system and approach by importing its western European style model, practices and standards, there are impacts on suppliers, manufacturers and other intermediaries. Coe and Hess (2005) in a study of such impacts in eastern Europe and east Asia identified five sets of ongoing restructuring dynamics: the centralization of procurement, logistical upgrading, supply network shortening and new intermediaries, the imposition of quasi-formal contracts and the development of private standards. They suggest that these processes are leading to an ongoing 'shakeout' of the supply base that is favouring relatively large, well-capitalized suppliers. There are thus also considerable 'winners' from Tesco's expansion.

Jones (2002) put forward a variety of scenarios for grocery supply chains. All have at their heart a move away from the current system of bigger, centralized and dispersed, to a model of faster, simpler and local. Such a system focuses on moving value creation towards consumers and eliminating non-value creation steps in supply. Information systems are simplified so as to avoid order amplification and distribution. The supply chain is thus compressed in space and time, producing and shipping closer to what is needed just in time. As Jones (2002) concludes: 'We cannot predict exactly what forms these developments will take... Nevertheless there are huge opportunities for improving the performance of the grocery supply chain, for those willing to think the unthinkable.'

Some of these proposed practices have informed Tesco supply chain management in the United Kingdom and elsewhere, but nowhere as much as in the newest market entry, the United States. Here, the opportunity has been taken to develop a new format and to think afresh about the supply chain, along some of the lines outlined by Jones (2002), but combined with other learning on environmental concerns and technology and process development. This is obviously easier in a new entry setup than in transforming an existing large-scale operation.

In November 2007, Tesco finally opened its much heralded Fresh and Easy stores in California and Nevada. Years in the planning, this US entry is intended to achieve 200 stores by February 2009 and to eventually develop into a major chain. Based on extensive consumer research with US families and a trial store built secretly, Fresh and Easy stores average about 10,000 sq ft and hold around 3,500 product lines. They focus on providing faster, easier neighbourhood retailing with an emphasis on fresh food and fresh prepared meals at affordable prices. Environmental, neighbourhood, employment and organic credentials are stressed. Fifty stores had opened by the end of February 2008, with expansion into Arizona, although a 'pause' in development was announced in April 2008 to reflect on the learning from these early developments.

It is too early to judge the success or otherwise of this US venture, but it has attracted considerable attention. The store format is different to Tesco stores elsewhere. Whilst the Tesco name is not used, its operations are based on the Tesco Operating Model, but with reduced complexity. The in-store processes are simplified, including extensive display-ready packaging, self-checkout and automated replenishment. The systems are advanced, linking processes to the service centre in India. This simplification has reduced payroll and other costs.

In supply terms, the Fresh and Easy operation is a little different to other Tesco operations, partly because the model of practices and processes has been built up from scratch, though it does rely on core processes from the Tesco Operating Model. For example, there has been a degree of co-location of production with distribution. UK suppliers with particular expertise have co-located production facilities at the head office and distribution hub (Riverside, CA), so as to react quickly to demand (a manifestation of the predicted developments in the Tesco supply system – Jones, 2002; Jones and Clarke, 2002). Whilst this is not unknown in, for example, Japan, the attempt here is to move towards a low-touch, lean operation and to rethink traditional approaches. There is extensive recycling of packaging, use of returnable crates and retail-ready merchandizing and packaging. The emphasis is on fully automated, one-touch replenishment supported by deep shelves. At Riverside, pick-by-line has been introduced and various environmental initiatives, eg solar power, developed (Stites, 2007). Store stock levels and availability were initially poor, however (Uwins, 2007) and the distribution systems performance has had to improve as the store development programme has moved on.

OTHER INITIATIVES: THE ENVIRONMENT

As can be predicted from the discussion above, the Tesco supply chain remains in a state of flux and change. As the business demands alter so the network has to be able to adapt and to continue to work effectively and efficiently. In the last two years, therefore, there have been major alterations to the network of facilities themselves, developments in the use of technology and changes to systems and a continued focus on aspects of lean and flow processes. There remain opportunities in network use intensity, vehicle usage and productivity (McIlwhee, 2006). In the case of technology, trials with RFID at pallet level have occurred and electronic notification of shipments amongst other changes has been introduced. Tesco Link has become the main interface for the management of supplier relationship articles, providing EPOS data, availability levels and performance information. Agreed performance indicators across suppliers are used to manage relationships and collaborations. As non-food and internationalization have occurred so technology and facilities have had to be developed to keep pace (eg *Focus,* 2007; *Retail Week,* 2008). IGD (2008) documents many of these recent developments in the British context.

An emerging overriding concern has been the environment and the environmental impact of the supply chain. Some of this concern has undoubtedly been externally created and may be motivated by many issues such as plastic bags, food miles and packaging waste, with food retailers acting as a 'lightning rod' for the topics. However, there is also internal business concern for the issues, as reducing waste and unnecessary elements in the supply chain provide commercial as well as ancillary other benefits. Thus, with the rising price of fuel, reducing miles travelled to distribute products and providing more fuel-efficient vehicles and driving practices make commercial as well as environmental sense. Broad issues in 'greening' the retail supply chain are discussed in Chapter 12, but the scale and significance of Tesco make some discussion of the steps and issues worthwhile here.

These aspects of environmental concern are manifest in Tesco in a variety of ways. At the consumer level there has been extensive development of recycling centres and initiatives. These produce 'waste' that needs to be managed and organized in reverse flows. At the store level, recycling of materials has been common for many years and Tesco was a pioneer in many respects of resource reduction in handling systems (Gustafsson *et al*, 2006). Retail-ready packaging, dollies, plastic trays, etc all reduce the need for single-use systems and focus on sustainability of supply approaches. In 2006 the plastic trays made 224 million journeys in the United Kingdom, replacing 132,000 tonnes of cardboard. Corporately, the company has looked at improving efficiency in supply generally. Specific initiatives in the United Kingdom have included the development of a rail freight service with Eddie Stobart running between Daventry (England) and Grangemouth (Scotland), and the use of the Manchester Ship Canal to move New World bulk wine containers from Liverpool to a Manchester bottling plant. In 2008 a new rail service between Grangemouth and Inverness commenced, with Stobart providing local store delivery around Inverness. In the Tesco.com business, trials with fully electric, zero-emission home delivery vans have proved successful and are to be extended, with the electricity provided by green sources. These are examples of some of the concerns and reactions, but can appear piecemeal if not part of a coordinated approach.

In May 2006 Tesco added a community dimension to its steering wheel, reflecting its emerging corporate responsibility dimension. This has encompassed a wide range of initiatives and developments, many focused on distribution, given its significance (12 per cent) to Tesco's carbon footprint. Its targets include reducing distribution emissions per case by 50 per cent by 2012 (from 2006 levels) and increasing waste recycling to 80 per cent. Many of the steps to meet such targets also bring commercial benefits. For example in transport, having better fill rates for vehicles, utilizing double-decker vehicles, reorganizing flows and looking at multi-nodal operations all increase efficiency and reduce emissions impacts. More energy-efficient distribution centres and the use of solar and other alternative energy sources fit the same pattern.

This is not to say that Tesco does not still have issues in terms of its practices. The scale of its business attracts attention and some practices, eg air freighting fresh produce or even organic produce, would seem to be at odds with sustainability. No doubt, though, if consumers begin to shun such products then Tesco will respond accordingly. Likewise the changing cost of distribution will focus its attention on efficiency and alternative methods rather than on simply passing on higher prices. Much will need to be done to meet internal targets as well as external pressures.

CONCLUSIONS AND LESSONS

This chapter aimed to understand and account for the changes in supply chains in food retailing by examining changes in the Tesco supply chain management. The basic premise was that the transformation of retailing that the consumer sees at store level has been supported by a fundamental transformation of supply chain methods and practices. In particular, there has been an increase in the status and professionalism in supply chains as the time, costs and implications of the functions have been recognized. Professionalism has been enhanced by the transformation of supply chains through the application of modern methods and approaches. For all retailers, the importance of managing supply chains is now undeniable. As retailers have responded to consumer change, so the need to improve the quality and appropriateness of supply systems has become paramount. As the impacts of supply chains on businesses and the wider environment come under more intensive scrutiny, so performance management will become more vital.

The Tesco study demonstrates many aspects of this transformation. In response to a clear business strategy its supply chain has been reorganized and realigned. From a state of decentralization and lack of control, Tesco has moved through centralization and composites, which enabled strong control to be exercised. These in turn have led to new methods and relationships in supply systems, both within Tesco and throughout the supply chain, recognizing the benefits of coordination and integration and a focus on lean and flow processes. Supply chains do not stand still, and recognition of the need to think clearly about supply pervades the case study. The developments outlined here and the transformation described via Tesco are not permanent solutions. As consumers change their needs, so retailing must and will respond. As retailing responds, companies will modify their operations, not least their supply systems, or be placed at a competitive disadvantage. As society and the economy change priorities, so too retailers have to respond and recognize their impacts on, for example, the environment. In many cases companies can benefit from a closer study of their practices and impacts in this regard, as there may be opportunities to save resources and money, as well as time.

So what are the lessons from Tesco? In many ways Tesco is all about control. The case demonstrates that to meet modern consumer needs retailers have to be in control of their operations including the supply of products. This does not mean that retailers have to undertake every activity, but it does mean they need to know all about it, manage and organize it and ensure its applicability. Inevitably this requires considerable collaboration with partners, service providers and suppliers. Through this collaboration, the flow and pace of the supply of products can be controlled and smoothed such as to reduce the effort and expense involved. In the best cases, service rises and costs fall as the supply chain orientation takes hold. This 'best case' scenario is inevitably the result of an informed supply chain and the capture of data and its use as information in the supply system is vital. Finally, Tesco recognizes that supply chains do not stand still. In a dynamic consumer market with changing demands and business strategies (eg internationalization and diversification) there is no way in which the supply chain can remain static. Supply needs to be adaptable to ongoing changes in demand, but also requires constant strategic consideration about the value being added or taken away from the business. Environmental concerns are likely to severely challenge existing practices and make supply chain change inevitable into the future.

References

Akehurst, G (1984) Checkout: the analysis of oligopolistic behaviour in the UK grocery retail market, *Service Industries Journal*, **4**, (2), pp 198–242

Bevan, J (2005) *Trolley Wars*, Profile Books, London

Burt, S L and Sparks, L (2002) Corporate branding, retailing and retail internationalization, *Corporate Reputation Review*, **5**, (2/3), pp 194–212

Burt, S L and Sparks, L (2003) Power and competition in the UK retail grocery market, *British Journal of Management*, **14**, pp 237–54

Child, P N (2002) Taking Tesco global, *McKinsey Quarterly*, **3**, pp 135–44

Clarke, P (2002) Distribution in Tesco, presentation for Tesco UK Operations Day 2002, available from http://www.investorcentre.tescoplc.com/plc/ir/pres_results/presentations/p2002/tescouk02/philip_clarke.pdf, downloaded 23 July 2008

Coe, N M and Hess, M (2005) The internationalization of retailing: implications for supply network restructuring in East Asia and Eastern Europe, *Journal of Economic Geography*, **5**, (4), pp 449–73

Coe, N M and Lee, Y S (2006) The strategic localization of transnational retailers: the case of Samsung-Tesco in South Korea, *Economic Geography*, **82**, (1), pp 61–88

Corina, M (1971) *Pile It High, Sell It Cheap*, Weidenfeld & Nicolson, London

Dawson, J A, Larke, R and Choi, S C (2006) Tesco: transferring marketing success factors internationally, in (eds) J A Dawson, R Larke and M Mukoyama, *Strategic Issues in International Retailing*, Routledge, London

Focus (2007) Tesco: every little supply chain helps, *Focus*, October, pp 34–6

Gustafsson, K, Jönson, G, Smith, D and Sparks, L (2006) *Retailing Logistics and Fresh Food Packaging*, Kogan Page, London

Humby, C, Hunt, T and Phillips, T (2003) *Scoring Points: How Tesco is winning customer loyalty*, Kogan Page, London

Humphrey, J (2007) The supermarket revolution in developing countries: tidal wave or tough competitive struggle?, *Journal of Economic Geography*, **7**, pp 433–50

Institute of Grocery Distribution (IGD) (2008) *Retail Logistics*, IGD, Watford

Jones, D T (2001) Tesco.com: delivering home shopping, *ECR Journal*, **1**, (1), pp 37–43

Jones, D T (2002) Rethinking the grocery supply chain, in (eds) J-W Grievink. L Josten and C Valk, *State of the Art in Food*, Elsevier, Rotterdam, available from www.leanuk.org/articles.htm, downloaded 30 October 2003

Jones, D T and Clarke, P (2002) Creating a customer-driven supply chain, *ECR Journal*, **2**, (2), pp 28–37

Kelly, J (2000) Every Little Helps: an interview with Terry Leahy, CEO, *Tesco Long Range Planning*, **33**, pp 430–9

Kirkwood, D A (1984a) The supermarket challenge, *Focus on PDM*, **3**, (4), pp 8–12

Kirkwood, D A (1984b) How Tesco manages the distribution function, *Retail and Distribution Management*, **12**, (5) pp 61–5

MacLaurin, I (1999) *Tiger by the Tail*, Macmillan, London

Mason, T (1998) The best shopping trip? How Tesco keeps the customer satisfied, *Journal of the Market Research Society*, **40**, (1), pp 5–12

McIlwhee, L (2006) Delivering our growth, presentation for UK Retail Trip, available from http://www.investis.com/plc/presentations/deliver_growth.pdf, downloaded 23 July 2008

Palmer, M (2004) International restructuring and divestment: the experience of Tesco, *Journal of Marketing Management*, **20**, pp 1075–105

Palmer, M (2005) Retail multinational learning: a case study of Tesco, *International Journal of Retail and Distribution Management*, **33**, (1), pp 23–49

Powell, D (1991) *Counter Revolution: The Tesco story*, Grafton Books, London

Reardon, T, Henson, S and Berdegue, J (2007) 'Proactive fast-tracking' diffusion of supermarkets in developing countries: implications for market institutions and trade, *Journal of Economic Geography*, **7**, pp 399–431

Retail Week (2007) The world according to Leahy, *Retail Week*, 23 March, pp 16–18

Retail Week (2008) Central lines, *Retail Week*, 8 February, pp 33–5

Reynolds, J (2004) An exercise in successful retailing: the case of Tesco, in (eds) J Reynolds and C Cuthbertson, *Retail Strategy: The view from the bridge*, Elsevier Butterworth-Heinemann, Oxford

Rowat, C (2003) Factory Gate Pricing: the debate continues, *Focus*, Feb, pp 46–48

Seth, A and Randall, G (1999) *The Grocers*, Kogan Page, London

Seth, A and Randall, G (2005) *Supermarket Wars*, Palgrave MacMillan, Basingstoke

Simons, D and Taylor, D (2007) Lean thinking in the UK red meat industry: a systems and contingency approach, *International Journal of Production Economics*, **106**, pp 70–81

Smith, D L G (1998) Logistics in Tesco: Past, present and future, in (eds) J Fernie and L Sparks, *Logistics and Retail Management*, Kogan Page, London

Smith D L G (2006) The role of retailers as channel captains in retail supply chain change: the example of Tesco, unpublished PhD thesis, University of Stirling

Smith, D L G and Sparks, L (1993) The transformation of physical distribution in retailing: the example of Tesco plc, *The International Review of Retail, Distribution and Consumer Research*, **3**, (1), pp 35–64

Smith, D L G and Sparks, L (2004) Logistics in Tesco: past, present and future, in (eds) J Fernie and L Sparks, *Logistics and Retail Management*, 2nd edn, Kogan Page, London

Sparks, L (1986) The changing structure of distribution in retail companies, *Transactions of the Institute of British Geographers*, **11**, (2), pp 147–54

Sparks, L (2008) Tesco: every little helps, in (ed) Kazuo Usui, *The History of Top Retailers in Europe*, Dhobunkan, Tokyo (in Japanese)

Stites, P (2007) Fresh and Easy store service centre presentation for Tesco in the US, available from http://www.investorcentre.tescoplc.com/plc/ir/pres_results/presentations/p2007/tesconov07/storeserv.pdf, downloaded 23 July 2008

Uwins, S (2007) Fresh and Easy home office presentation for Tesco in the US, available from http://www.investis.com/plc/presentations/fresheasy.pdf, downloaded 23 July 2008

Womack, J P and Jones, D T (2005) *Lean Solutions,* Simon and Schuster, London

8

Temperature controlled supply chains

David Smith and Leigh Sparks

INTRODUCTION

Consumers expect food in retail stores to be of good quality, to have a decent shelf-life and to be fit for purpose. If a retailer can present products attractively and provide good shelf-life, then there is more chance of the products being purchased and satisfying consumer needs. Managing the supply chain to maintain quality and 'fitness' of food products therefore has direct cost and service implications. Many dimensions have to be managed. One of these dimensions is the need for an appropriate temperature regime. Many food stores contain products supplied and retailed at a number of different temperatures. Failure to maintain an appropriate temperature control can adversely affect the product's appearance or shelf-life at one end of the spectrum, or could potentially make consumers ill or even kill them at the other end. Temperature controlled supply chains (TCSCs) could be said to be a matter of life or death.

WHAT IS A TEMPERATURE CONTROLLED SUPPLY CHAIN?

At its simplest, a TCSC is a food supply chain that requires that food products be maintained in a temperature controlled environment, rather than exposing them to whatever ambient temperatures prevail at the various stages of the supply chain. This basic description, however, hides a complex and potentially expensive process. The length and complexity of such supply chains are determined by the natures and sources of the products, the legal and quality assurance requirements on food safety, and the distribution facilities available from production to consumption. Recently they have been affected by the need to deliver food safety and integrity throughout the supply chain (Deloitte/Cmi, 2003). As internationalization has increased both in terms of global sourcing and local store development, so concerns about the temperature integrity for products have become a more significant concern.

There are several food temperature levels to suit different types of products: for example we could identify frozen, cold chill, medium chill and exotic chill. Definitions of the exact temperatures do vary. However, a broad grouping for the United Kingdom might indicate a regime as follows. Frozen is minus 25 degrees Celsius for ice cream; minus 18 degrees for other foods and food ingredients. Cold chill is zero degrees to plus one degree for fresh meat and poultry, most dairy and meat-based provisions, most vegetables and some fruit. Medium chill is plus five degrees for some pastry-based products, butters, fats and cheeses. Exotic chill is plus 10 to plus 15 degrees for potatoes, eggs, exotic fruit and bananas. If a food supply chain is dedicated to a narrow range of products then the temperature will be at the level for that product set. If a food supply chain is handling a broad range of products then an optimum temperature or a limited number of different temperature settings is used. Failure to maintain appropriate temperature regimes throughout a product's life can shorten the life of that product or adversely affect its quality or fitness for consumption.

It should be immediately obvious that the management process in TCSC is a complicated one. Chilling and freezing products are in themselves hard, but maintaining appropriate temperatures throughout a product's life, in both storage and transit, is complicated. How, for example, can a retailer ensure that products are always under the appropriate temperature regime when they travel from a field in New Zealand to a refrigerator in a shop in Tobermory?

This chapter explores the requirements and developments in food-based temperature controlled supply chains. It aims to raise the issues that retailers and logistics service providers have to consider. It is also important to note of course that TCSCs are not solely the concern of the food industry. There are for example similar issues in the global pharmaceutical industry, focusing on legal requirements, standards compliance, packaging developments and the potential break points in the TCSC. The broad issues covered in this chapter can have wider implications for other supply chains.

THE IMPORTANCE OF TEMPERATURE CONTROLLED SUPPLY CHAINS

The TCSC in food is a significant proportion of the retail food market and one that has been increasing steadily (McKinnon and Campbell, 1998). CH Robinson/Iowa State University (2001) suggest that over half the spend in US supermarkets is on temperature controlled products. Frozen food in the United Kingdom has been increasing in volume by 3 to 4 per cent on average per annum for the last 40 years. Developments in products such as ready meals and prepared salads have further expanded the market. Analysts see the meal solution sector continuing to increase very rapidly (Gorniak, 2002). 'Fast food' chains have captured a huge market share and are reliant on frozen product. The importance of products requiring temperature control, both to consumers and retailers, has thus been increasing, and seems set to increase further.

Even products that we often take for granted may require some form of temperature control. Prepared sandwiches for example require chilled storage of ingredients. These are then combined to make the finished product, which in turn requires temperature control storage, distribution and display (Smith *et al*, 2001). Failure to maintain adequate control (for example placing prawn sandwiches in the sun) generates obvious risks. More subtly, an inability to maintain temperature control will reduce shelf-life in the product, which is any case often very time-limited. This increases wastage and complicates the supply dynamics, adding costs. Similarly, much of the bread in supermarket in-store bakeries is brought to the store frozen, and baked/heated on the premises. Some fish products may have been previously frozen and thus are not suitable for consumer re-freezing. It is important that the temperature regime in the supply chain is secure and compliant for quality and safety reasons and that consumers are aware of this history, so as to maintain their own appropriate regimes to, and at, the home.

On the supply side, changes in the location of product sources and the removal of wholesalers from the channel have had major effects. Technological changes in production and distribution have also allowed a transformation of the supply network. As production and distribution technological capabilities have developed, so the ability for national and international, rather than local, sourcing and distribution has emerged. Products can be brought across the world to satisfy demands for products 'out-of-season' or of an exotic nature, as well as for reasons of lower purchase or cost price. Internationalization of supply of even indigenous products is common. The system developments needed to meet the demands for quality and consistency, including temperature control aspects, do impact on the channel composition (eg Dolan and Humphrey, 2000). The handling systems to manage the air freighting of for example tomatoes from the Canary Islands, baby sweet corn from Egypt or flowers from Malaysia require a considerable technological development. They also represent a fundamental organizational and relationship shift. It is possible, as environmental concerns continue to increase in importance, that the true cost of TCSC on an international basis will mitigate against such global food transfers. However, the need to maintain appropriate TCSC even on a local level will remain.

CH Robinson/Iowa State University (2001) argue that TCSCs are more important than 'ordinary' retail supply chains as they have inherently more complexity and complications:

> The (logistics) challenge is more formidable when the materials and products require temperature control. The shelf-life is often short for such products, placing even greater importance on the speed and dependability of the transportation and handling systems. Temperature controlled products also require specialized transportation equipment and storage facilities and closer monitoring of product integrity while in the logistics system.
>
> Adding to the logistics complexity is the seasonal demand for many temperature controlled products... arising from natural production conditions and consumer demand... In addition, carriers of temperature controlled products confront unique requirements and incur greater costs than carriers of dry products. (pp 1–2)

Some of the uniqueness and increased costs derive from this need to ensure temperature control. There is extra cost incurred in the requirements for handling temperature controlled products, and also in the need to monitor temperature regimes in the supply chain.

As the number and range of temperature controlled products have increased, and a number of market failures have occurred, so the issue of food safety has become more central (Henson and Caswell, 1999; Lindgreen and Hingley, 2003). Failures of food safety in the United Kingdom (not all of course associated with failures of temperature control) are common on a localized and individual level. For example there is a high level of personal food poisoning in the United Kingdom, although the extent to which this is a result of product or channel failure rather than an individual consumer's lack of knowledge or care is unclear. More publicly notable have been national events ('food scares') such as listeria in cheese, salmonella in eggs and chickens, BSE in cattle and E. coli 0157 in meat. These national events raise concern and comment about food safety. There is thus a perception over the safety of supply of food and food chains, which in turn has focused attention on risk assessment and risk management. Such concerns are not of course restricted to the United Kingdom. Deloitte/Cmi (2003) point to similar issues in the United States and note that the issue of food safety has been ranked first in a CIES survey of food retailing issues in 2002, compared to not being ranked at all in 1999. TCSCs gain importance therefore from the risks associated with failure and from the steps necessary to minimize these risks. Some of the steps are voluntary and company-specific, others are required by recent legal developments (see later).

As a consequence of risk assessments and the major problems in food safety, TCSCs have become a focal point for the development of food safety legislation across Europe. Although such legislation introduces requirements that cover a broad range of issues, one key aspect is the temperature conditions under which products are maintained. Such legislation, combined with increasing retailer liability for prosecution, has put great pressure on the standards of control throughout the food supply chain, particularly in the case of temperature control. For these reasons, TCSCs are often seen as a specialist discipline within logistics. To some extent this is understandable given the need for specialist facilities – warehouses, vehicles, refrigerators, etc – to operate chilled or frozen distribution channels. This specialist market is itself increasing in scale and scope, both as the market expands and as operational and managerial complexity increases.

However, it is not all cost and regulation, as there are operational and commercial benefits to be gained from proper TCSC management. These benefits might include an increase in shelf-life and freshness and thus better customer perception of products and the retailer. This increase in product quality and perception is the direct result of maintaining the correct temperature for that product group steadily and constantly throughout its supply chain journey. One major effect of an increase in shelf-life and freshness has been that consumers can notice the difference between product supplied through a fully temperature controlled supply chain and that supplied through a partially temperature controlled supply chain, and so make product and retailer choice decisions accordingly. Whilst it is generally the case today that the major food retailers maintain chill and cold chain integrity and thus have totally controlled TCSCs, this has not always been the case.

CHANGES IN TEMPERATURE CONTROLLED SUPPLY CHAINS

The TCSC has developed and changed since the 1980s. In the past in the United Kingdom, the supply chain often consisted of single temperature warehouses dedicated to narrow product ranges of food, eg butters, fats and cheeses at plus five degrees Celsius, dairy-based provisions, meat-based provisions, fresh meat and poultry, fruit and vegetables and frozen products. The design, equipment and disciplines were only partially implemented so that there was incomplete integrity of the temperature control. Products were exposed to periods of high ambient temperature, which affected the shelf-life and the quality of the product. Single temperature systems also meant that many more deliveries were needed. Such systems were essentially inefficient and ineffective.

Such a situation existed in the 1980s in Tesco (see Smith, 1998; Smith and Sparks, 1993; Sparks, 1986). In the mid-1980s the Tesco temperature controlled supply chain consisted of a large number of small single temperature warehouses, each specializing in the storage, handling and delivery of a narrow product range. Examples of these sets of product ranges were: fresh produce; fresh meat and poultry; butters, fats and cheeses; chilled diary provisions; chilled meat provisions; and frozen foods. Each set was managed by a different specialist logistics service provider organized on behalf of the manufacturer and supplier. The deliveries to the retail stores took place two or three times a week with the temperature controlled vehicle going from one store to another delivering the appropriate number of pallets of products. The delivery notes and product checking were conducted at the back door of the store and the cost of delivery was included in the price of the product. Fresh meat and poultry were controlled on an individual case basis and charged by weight as each case had a different weight.

There are several limitations of this model of a TCSC. It was expensive to expand to meet large increases in overall growth in volume as it requires the building of more and more single temperature warehouses. The retail delivery frequency was limited. The delivery volume drop size per store was small and vehicles used were 'undersized' because of problems over retail access. At that time there also was not full awareness of the importance of maintaining total integrity of the chill chain.

The strategy that Tesco decided upon was to build a small number of new large multi-temperature 'composite' warehouses that would store, handle and deliver the full range of product sets, all from the same location. The manufacturers and suppliers of all the product sets make daily deliveries into the composite distribution centre. The composite delivery frequency to the retail stores increased to daily. The delivery vehicles had movable bulkheads and three temperature controlled evaporators so that up to three different temperature regimes could be set on the one vehicle. The benefit was improved vehicle utilization and improved service to retail. Chill chain integrity disciplines were implemented rigorously from supplier to retail shelf.

There are other aspects to this change. Distribution and retail agreed a policy of not checking the goods at the retail back door, which improved the speed with which the goods could be transferred into the temperature controlled chambers at the store. This improved chill chain integrity. The goods were delivered in green reusable plastic trays, on 'dollies', or on roll cages, which improved handling at the store, both in terms of speed and quality. New store designs permitted the use of full length vehicles, so improving efficiency.

Another major change in supply chains between the 1980s and 2000s has been the increasing pace of the order and replenishment cycle (McKinnon and Campbell, 1998). Today, with many fresh products, there is no stock held in the retail distribution centre overnight. Stock holding in frozen products has also declined to below 10 days. Lead times have continued to be reduced. One of the key drivers of this increase in pace has been the development of information technology, which has enabled a large volume of data to collected, processed and transmitted at faster speeds. Today data are collected from the point of sale and used in calculating future customer demand, which in turn forms the basis of the orders placed on suppliers. The scale, control and skill of the retail logistics operation has improved so that even distance-sourced products can be rapidly transported to their destinations via the regional distribution centres. The move to centrally prepared meat and poultry rather than having butchers at the retail stores is one example of this (Lindgreen and Hingley, 2003). Another example is the sourcing of produce from Spain direct from the growers into the distribution centres (see Box 8.1). These changes, encouraged by information technology amongst other factors, require changes in supply chain facilities and operations to ensure chill chain integrity.

Box 8.1 Spain

Produce direct from Spain

Spain has become one of the major providers of produce to the rest of Europe. In the late 1990s, major UK supermarkets started to purchase produce direct from Spanish suppliers rather than through UK wholesalers. The total direct flow of produce from Spain solely to UK is over 1,000 vehicles per week.

For example, iceberg lettuce is grown in large volumes between October and May in Murcia and Almeria in south-east Spain under direct contract between the retailer and the growing cooperatives. The retailers' quality assurance and technical departments provide the grower with the product specification and transport temperature control requirements from Spain to UK.

There are two methods of direct delivery into the UK supermarket distribution network. The first is to fill the vehicle in Spain solely with iceberg lettuce. The delivery is split once it arrives in the UK by sending the vehicle to two distribution centres. The second method is to combine several produce products, eg iceberg lettuce and courgettes, while the vehicle is still in its originating region in Spain. This combined product volume fills the vehicle, which then delivers the whole load to a single distribution centre in the UK.

The distance from Murcia to central England is 1,500 miles. The deliveries flow through daily. The total process from harvesting to customer is four days:

- Day one: the iceberg lettuce is harvested, cooled, packaged and loaded into temperature controlled vehicles set at plus three degrees.
- Day three: the iceberg lettuce arrives direct at the UK supermarket temperature controlled distribution centre where it is checked in. Within three hours it is allocated and picked for a retail store, ready to go out on the next delivery.
- Day four: the iceberg lettuce is on display in the retail store, available for the consumer to purchase.

The code life on direct iceberg lettuce is one day above 'normal' deliveries. This extra day can be used for rolling stock in the distribution centre. The ability to roll stock means that full loads of iceberg lettuce can be delivered direct to the distribution centre. Any stock that is not allocated to a store and picked immediately (due to demand) can be rolled over to supply the next day's orders.

The range of products delivered direct has increased from the original Golden Delicious and Granny Smith to now include Braeburn and Royal Gala on top fruit, white seedless grapes, nectarines, peaches, iceberg lettuces, Galia melon and and broccoli.

The seasons of other products direct from Spain are December/January: soft citrus; January/May: tomatoes and broccoli; June/August: Galia and honeydew melons.

Source: author interviews

Following the implementation of centralized distribution, attention turned to the condition of TCSC for the inbound product sets from the supplier and manufacturer into the regional distribution centres. The examination of the logistics of the inbound supply chain revealed that there were huge opportunities to improve transport efficiency. The increasing pace of the retail supply chain had resulted in most suppliers of temperature controlled product sets sending their vehicles long distances, but only partly filled, to the various retailers' regional distribution centres. So for example, suppliers' vehicles carrying fruit and vegetables from a supplying region like Kent, were following each other to distant regional distribution centres in northern England and Wales, each with a partially full vehicle to the same destination. Clearly there was an opportunity for the consolidation of supply.

This process of consolidation saw the appointment of designated logistics service providers in the appropriate regions to manage and operate temperature controlled consolidation centres, accumulating full vehicle loads of temperature controlled products to despatch to the composite distribution centres. These consolidation centres also conducted quality assurance testing of the product. There were two benefits of placing the quality assurance function in the consolidation centres. The first was that they were close to the suppliers so that any problems could be dealt with face-to-face where required. The second benefit was that these vehicles did not then need to undergo quality assurance checking when they arrived at the distribution centre. This improved the turnaround time of the inbound vehicle, increasing its productivity and profitability, and also enabled the handling operation to commence earlier and so keep the goods in bay clear for the next set of deliveries. This was especially important in the early evening when a very high volume of produce harvested that same day is delivered.

Some of the effects of these changes to the Tesco supply chain are shown in Table 8.1. This summarizes the last 15–20 years of temperature control supply and the ways in which this has changed. Over the time period the shelf-life for these products has increased considerably. In the case of vegetables it has doubled, and for top fruit the increase is even greater. This provides better product for longer for the consumer and is more efficient for the retailer. It does, as the table indicates, require a major reorientation of the supply chain and a dedication to standards. The overall effect has been to provide fresher product more quickly and cheaply to the retail store and to lengthen the shelf-life and quality time of a product for the consumer.

The discussion above is centred on developments in Tesco. Similar operations and developments have been introduced in other major food retailers. These have been needed to handle the massive expansion of demand in the temperature controlled sector in recent years and to compete with the market leader.

Table 8.1 Tesco case study: enhancement in shelf-life

Stage	Soft fruit	Top fruit	Veg	Temperature controlled supply chain status and improvement action
Pre-1980				Single temperature produce centres (3). Ambient and plus five degrees Celsius. Code dates not a legal requirement. Shelf-life managed at retail. Retail ordered from local suppliers without any technical support.
1980 to 1986				Two further produce centres. Operating procedures remained the same. Suppliers normally loaded in yard or from ambient bays. Many vehicles have curtain sides.
1986				Notice that code dates to become a legal requirement for produce. Produce Technical Team established shelf-life and introduced QC checks at distribution centres. 78/48 hour ordering cycle to retail.
1987	2 CD + 2 CL = 4 days total	5 CD + 2 CL = 7 days total	3 CD + 2 CL = 5 days total	Code dates **CD** introduced for loose and pre-packed produce. In addition to the selling code dates there were additional days where product would be at its best. This time was called '**Customer Life**' – **CL**. QC in produce depots to enforce specification. Two further produce centres. Code of practice introduced for suppliers included distribution centre controls and vehicle standards, eg no curtain siders.
1989	2 CD + 4 CL = 6 days total	5 CD + 9 CL = 14 days total	3 CD + 5 CL = 8 days total	Six composite distribution centres opened. Separate temperature chambers of +3, +10, +15 for produce. Composite multi-temperature trailers deliver at +3 and +10 degrees Celsius loading from sealed temperature controlled loading bays. **Customer life** extended by 2 days for soft fruit, by 5 days for top fruit and 3 days for vegetables. No increase in code dates. Consumer demand for fruit and vegetables **doubled** as a consequence of the introduction of strict temperature control disciplines throughout the supply chain.
1990				Food Safety Act: to meet due diligence HACCP (Hazard Analysis Critical Control Points) analysis introduced throughout the supply chain. The result was more consistent shelf-life but no increase in days. Retail stores only allowed to buy from suppliers with technical approval.

Table 8.1 *continued*

Stage	Soft fruit	Top fruit	Veg	Temperature controlled supply chain status and improvement action
1995	2 CD + 5 CL = 7 days total	5 CD + 10 CL = 15 days total	3 CD + 6 CL = 9 days total	Produce temperature controlled consolidation hubs introduced. Six further hubs added over next three years. QA control introduced at hubs so quality checked before produce despatched to the composites. Hubs located close to supplier regions so prompt resolution of problems with supplier management.
				Shelf-life review shows increase of one day across all vegetables, soft fruit and stone fruit. Salads become inconsistent because of harvesting during the night before dew point. But there was a greater benefit of starting despatch earlier, especially from Spain. Retail order lead time 48/24 hours.
1997				Composite distribution centres change produce chamber temperatures to +1 and +12 degrees Celsius with tighter variation of +/-1 degree from +/-2 degree before. There was no change to shelf-life because the supply chain disciplines fully in place.
1998	2 CD + 5 CL = 7 days total	6 CD + 10 CL = 16 days total	4 CD + 6 CL = 10 days total	Technical departments given targets to increase produce shelf-life. One potential improvement was to introduce US-type variety control. The benefit is only possible because of the very strict total supply chain temperature control. One extra day of code life for stores.
2000				Continuous replenishment introduced. The benefit is split deliveries into retail stores with different code dates for retail without any loss of shelf-life for customer.
2002	2 CD + 5 CL = 7 days total	7 CD + 10 CL = 17 days total	5 CD + 6 CL = 11 days total	Further supply chain improvements in shelf-life to extend code dates by one day, no change to shelf-life life to improve availability on selected lines, ie core vegetables, top fruit, stone fruit but not salads or soft fruit. Three potential methods are: a) atmospheric control especially during the three-day delivery from Spain; b) humidity control; c) ethylene control.

Source: author interviews

ISSUES IN TEMPERATURE CONTROLLED SUPPLY CHAINS

The discussion above and comments in the introduction allow the identification of a number of key issues in TCSC. Here, three are identified for further discussion; the issues of costs, food safety and HACCP, and partnerships.

Costs

The basic supply configuration in the temperature controlled channel is not really much different to those in ordinary retail distribution channels. The demands placed on the components, however, are far more extreme and thus the issue of costs of facilities and operations is important.

TCSCs place strict conditions on the design, equipment and discipline of the operation, which makes the cost greater than for ambient products. Temperature controlled storage facilities need to be maintained at the appropriate temperature with accurate recording and cooling equipment, including the capacity to cope with high ambient temperatures, especially in the summer. Vehicle docking bays need air bags that inflate around the vehicle to prevent exposure to ambient temperatures. For frozen storage facilities, the loading and unloading bays should be at zero degrees. Vehicles require appropriate insulation, refrigeration and control panels to set and maintain the product at the correct temperature. An important facet of this transport refrigeration is that it is not designed to remove heat from the product (as in 'normal refrigeration') so it is essential that the heat is taken out of the product before it is loaded onto a vehicle. If not, heat will transfer to other products causing them to be exposed to a temperature outside the designated range. Some vehicles have bulkheads and several evaporators so that different sections can be set at different temperatures. The benefit of this is that vehicle utilization is improved, but operating procedures are made more complicated. This also affects costs. The cost of a multi-temperature refrigerated trailer could be three times that for an ambient trailer. The cost of warehousing could be double. This cost/structure difference means that there is a commercial imperative to reduce 'excess' activities, thus promoting concepts such as 'leanness' and flow.

Warehouse operatives and drivers must behave in accordance with the requirements for chill chain integrity to protect the product. The cost of losing a trailer load of product through overheating is not only high but also severely impacts on service level to retail and the consumer, because the pace of the supply chain does not leave time to recover with alternative product. Such cost considerations have enabled niche operators to enter and develop the market for frozen and chilled distribution. There is also a specialist association in the United Kingdom to assist this sector of the logistics industry (Cold Storage and Distribution Federation – http://www.csdf.org.uk/) and to liaise with government on regulations in this sector.

Food Safety and HACCP

As noted earlier, the integrity of temperature controlled supply chains is important for food safety (see Deloitte/Cmi, 2003). This places an obligation of care and duty of implementation on the supplier, retailer and logistics. In the United Kingdom, for example, the Food Safety Act of 1990 defined the storage, handling and transportation requirements for food products including temperature control for certain categories. One of the provisions of the Act makes it an absolute offence to sell food that is unfit for human consumption. Food that has 'gone off' due to inadequate temperature control falls into this category. The Act, however, allows for a defence of 'due diligence' against any charges. Thus a business may be able to mount a defence based on evidence that all reasonable precautions had been exercised to avoid the commission of the offence. In terms of temperature control, this implies that there needs to be a system of control, maintenance, monitoring and recording (for evidence) of the temperature regimes in the supply chain.

The Food Standards (Temperature Control) Regulations of 1995 made it an offence to allow food to be kept at temperatures that could cause a risk to health. This again implied a tightening of systems in the chain. This was effectively codified by the General Hygiene Act of 1995, which required all food businesses to adopt a risk management tool such as Hazard Analysis Critical Control Points (HACCP). Loader and Hobbs (1999) see this as a change in philosophy, representing a move away from an end product food safety inspection approach to a preventative, scientific focus with the responsibility for risk management placed on the food business proprietor. As a result, HACCP and other systems (Sterns et al, 2001) have been vital in establishing process controls through the identification of critical points in the process that need to be monitored and controlled (see Box 8.2).

These Acts in the United Kingdom were in essence national responses to approaches being recommended in Europe and codified in EU legislation. The food scares in the United Kingdom of the late 1990s also brought forward a response. The Food Standards Act 1999 created the Food Standards Agency (FSA) in April 2000. The Act was intended to induce all those involved in the food supply chain to improve their food handling practices, including temperature control.

Box 8.2   HACCP

Hazard Analysis Critical Control Points (HACCP)

It is important in the application of the disciplines of an integrated temperature controlled supply chain to understand the principles of the obligations of suppliers, retailers and logistics service providers.

All have a duty of care for the product. To meet this duty of care they must demonstrate that they have applied due diligence in the structure and execution of their operation, ie that they have taken all reasonable methods to ensure the care of the product.

One of these reasonable methods is Hazard Analysis Critical Control Points (HACCP) and is central to the discipline of chill chain integrity in logistics. The quality assurance department conducts a survey of the supply chain under its control with the objective of identifying those circumstances where the product might be exposed to unsuitable conditions, ie hazards. It ranks these hazards according to the importance of the risk, eg high, medium, low. Procedures are then put in place at an appropriate level to prevent that risk.

So to express this differently: identify the hazards, analyse their importance, identify which are critical and set up control procedures at these points. Once HACCP is put in place it becomes a strong argument that due diligence is being practised.

For temperature controlled supply chains, there are big benefits from putting the physical and operational procedures in place along the whole length of the supply chain. This investment reduces a high risk to a low risk. By stabilizing the temperature throughout the life of the product, suppliers and retailers can concentrate on other aspects that can add value to the product, eg growing varieties.

If we take the example of the movement of chill goods from distribution centre to retail stores on multi-temperature vehicles, then the risk to food safety is high and the risk of occurrence is high. The critical control points for loading at the distribution centre are:

- temperature setting stated on load sheet and run sheet;
- loader checks load sheet and sets temperatures for compartment;
- loader secures bulkhead;
- loader switches refrigeration on and ticks relevant temperature on load sheet;
- once loading complete a supervisor checks settings and switches against load sheet and signs off if correct;

- load sheet handed into goods-out office;
- driver checks digital readings (usually at the front of unit, visible in rear-view mirror) against load sheet and if correct, signs off and hands in to goods-out office;
- goods-out clerk checks if temperatures on load sheet and run sheet match, and if correct, allows vehicle to leave;
- goods-out supervisor undertakes daily checks to assure compliance.

Source: author interviews

Partnerships

This onus on due diligence and the responsibility of businesses had a major effect on systems of control and monitoring of performance. It also had an effect on the business relationships and governance in place. If a retailer, for example, wishes to be protected from claims, then it has to ensure that its suppliers are undertaking good practices, in addition to its own practice. This is not only true for retailer brand products, but for all sourced products. As such, traceability and tracking become more funda- mental and good partnerships become crucial. As costs rise in introducing new systems, increasing the depth and quality of partnerships is both a safeguard and offers possible cost benefits. As a result, partnerships expanded considerably post-1991 in the United Kingdom (Fearne and Hughes, 2000; Lindgreen and Hingley, 2003; Loader and Hobbs, 1999; Wilson, 1996). Food retailers today are keen to have such partnerships and to use them in their marketing, as seen in the numerous 'farm assured' type schemes. Such partnerships and changes in organization of the supply chain are not restricted to UK suppliers. Dolan and Humphrey (2000) show how in Africa the requirements of the leading UK retailers have transformed the horticultural sector in scale and operational terms, leaving smaller producers in a precarious position. This scale dimension is linked closely to the legal requirements and the costs of compliance and potential chain failure.

FUTURE DEVELOPMENTS AND CONSTRAINTS

TCSCs have undergone considerable changes in recent decades. This process is likely to continue, driven as it is by tightening legislation and risk awareness, the increased costs of supply and the demands on the chain from increased volume and pace of operation. A number of future issues can be explored.

First is the question of risk and integrity. There are a number of 'gaps' in the current TCSC. For example, at the retail outlet, few stores have a chilled reception area that docks with the incoming distribution vehicle. The majority have an ambient delivery bay that is exposed to the outside temperature. The delivery reception area requires an operational discipline such that chilled and frozen product is not left exposed to ambient temperature for more than 20 minutes. The retail operational staff have to move the chilled and frozen pallets, roll cages, etc promptly into the relevant temperature controlled chambers. Finally, when the product is being taken to the chilled or frozen retail shelf or cabinet within the store for replenishment, the same 20-minute rule applies. The potential for problems is clear. Another 'gap' occurs in the 'forgotten' segment of the supply chain – the length of time from selection of product by a consumer to purchase and then transport home could be considerable and affect the product adversely. As electronic commerce expands, so issues of home delivery confront much the same problem. If the homeowner has always to be present then such services are more limited and/or costly. But dropped deliveries of temperature controlled products increase the risks for the consumer.

Secondly, there is likely to be further technological development. In the future, electronic temperature tagging could become the norm, so that operators throughout the TCSC will be able to monitor current and previous conditions. Such monitoring could be real-time online for some products or could be packaging-based for others, eg colour-coded packaging changing colour if temperatures go outside allowable ranges. Advances in packaging environments leading to enhanced shelf-life time may also accompany such monitoring advances. Associated developments in technologies such as RFID will bring additional potential protection but also raise data management and control issues.

Finally, there are issues brought about by globalization and partnership trends. Whilst there have been benefits to the introduction of current procedures and practices, concern is mounting about the environmental costs of monocultures and the extreme distribution distances that are travelled. Given the costs of compliance to meet western food safety concerns, it might be more beneficial to look for more local sourcing. The internationalization of retailing acts as a counter to this, however, and may allow retailers to build deeper partnerships across the globe and to utilize their experience to enhance the quality of the local supply chain. However, consumer demands may not allow time in the supply chain for such global solutions. The future organizational shape and the role of partnerships remain therefore subject to change (Zuurbier, 1999).

References

CH Robinson Worldwide Inc / Iowa State University (2001) *Temperature Controlled Logistics Report 2001–2002*, CH Robinson Worldwide, Inc

Deloitte Consulting/Cmi Consulting (2003) *Delivering Integrity in the End-to-End Food Supply Chain*, Deloitte Consulting/Cmi Consulting, London

Dolan, C and Humphrey, J (2000) Governance and trade in fresh vegetables: the impact of UK supermarkets on the African horticultural industry, *Journal of Development Studies*, **37**, (2), 147–76

Fearne, A and Hughes, D (2000) Success factors in the fresh produce supply chains, *British Food Journal*, **102**, pp 760–72

Gorniak, C (2002) *The Meal Solutions Outlook to 2007*, Reuters Business Insight, London

Henson, S and Caswell, J (1999) Food safety regulation: an overview of contemporary issues, *Food Policy*, **24**, pp 589–603

Lindgreen, A and Hingley, M (2003) The impact of food safety and animal welfare policies on supply chain management: the case of the Tesco meat supply chain, *British Food Journal*, **105**, (6), pp 328–49

Loader, R and Hobbs, J E (1999) Strategic response to food safety legislation, *Food Policy*, **24**, pp 685–706

McKinnon, A C and Campbell, J (1998) Quick response in the frozen food supply chain, available at http://www.som.hw.ac.uk/logistics/salvesen.html, accessed 10 July 2002

Smith, D L G (1998) Logistics in Tesco, in (eds) J Fernie and L Sparks, *Logistics and Retail Management*, Kogan Page, London

Smith, D L G and Sparks, L (1993) The transformation of physical distribution in retailing: the example of Tesco plc, *International Review of Retail, Distribution and Consumer Research*, **3**, pp 35–64

Smith, J L, Davies, G J and Bent, A J (2001) Retail fast foods: overview of safe sandwich manufacture, *The Journal of The Royal Society for the Promotion of Health*, **121**, (4), pp 220–23

Sparks, L (1986) The changing structure of distribution in retail companies, *Transactions of the Institute of British Geographers*, **11**, pp 147–54

Sterns, P A, Codron, J-M and Reardon, T (2001) Quality and quality assurance in the fresh produce sector: a case study of European retailers, American Agricultural Economics Association Annual Meeting, Chicago, August, paper downloaded from http://agecon.lib.umn.edu/ on 11 July 2002

Wilson, N (1996) The supply chains of perishable products in Northern Europe, *British Food Journal*, **98**, (6), pp 9–15

Zuurbier, P J P (1999) Supply chain management in the fresh produce industry: a mile to go?, *Journal of Food Distribution Research*, **30**, (1), pp 20–30

9

On-shelf availability in UK grocery retailing: a case study

John Fernie and David B Grant

INTRODUCTION

In their major international study of retail out-of-stocks (OOS) Corsten and Gruen argued that 'availability of products is the new battleground in the fast moving consumer goods industry' (2003, p 603). The study of stock-outs is not new; in the United States in the 1960's, the *Progressive Grocer* published the first major study on how grocery customers reacted to stock-outs (1968a, b) and Schary and Christopher's 1979 study of grocery customers in London revealed that a high proportion of customers (48 per cent) chose to shop elsewhere when faced with a stock-out.

In the intervening years the grocery retail industry has been transformed, especially in the United Kingdom. At the time of the Schary and Christopher study, manufacturers' brands dominated the shelves of a fragmented retail industry. If consumers could not find their favourite brands in one store, a competitor would be able to provide it in a nearby location. Almost 30 years later the rise of retail grocery giants, such as Tesco with over 30 per cent of the UK grocery market, has led to a retail-controlled supply chain and the predominance of retailer, rather than manufacturer, brands.

Accessibility is now measured in driving times to superstores rather than short trips between butchers, bakers, fishmongers and supermarkets in the high street. Store loyalty has become as important, if not more important, than brand loyalty as evidenced by the largest grocers' ventures into non-grocery areas such as banking and other service-related sectors under their corporate brand umbrella.

In order to improve operational efficiencies UK grocery retailers streamlined their supply chains. From centralization of distribution in the 1980s companies began to integrate primary and secondary distribution to reduce lead times and take inventory out of the retail supply chain. Fernie and Sparks (2004) claimed that the United Kingdom had one of the most efficient supply chains in the world in the 1990s / early 2000s.

Despite these logistical innovations, on-shelf availability (OSA) was deemed to be a major cause of concern for British consumers (ECR UK, 2004) and media attention focused on J Sainsbury when *The Sunday Times* published a report indicating that in a 30-item shopping basket, on average Sainsbury had 10 per cent OOS with the worst performing store only having two-thirds of items available (Fletcher, 2004). It was around this time that Justin King was appointed as Chief Executive of J Sainsbury and he set out an agenda to 'Make Sainsbury's great again'. He undertook market research with Sainsbury customers and found that their greatest source of dissatisfaction was OOS. Zentes *et al* (2007) provide a detailed discussion of Sainsbury's problems as a case study.

However, this pattern was being repeated throughout the grocery sector and had become the focus of attention for Efficient Consumer Response (ECR) UK and IGD, formerly the Institute of Grocery Distribution, the main UK trade associations for addressing issues pertaining to the sector. It is the purpose of this chapter to investigate the main causes of the OSA/OOS problem and discuss measures that have been undertaken to tackle OSA. Primary research was carried out with one major grocery retailer to evaluate how OSA initiatives from its headquarters were implemented at distribution centre (DC) and store level. It is first necessary to give a background to the research that has been published to date on this topic.

LITERATURE BACKGROUND

Consumer reaction to stock-outs

Research into consumer reactions to stock-outs spans four decades and these studies identify five main reactions by consumers to a stock-out in store:

1. They buy the item at another store (store switching).
2. They delay ordering or purchasing the item (postpone purchase at the same store).

3. They do not purchase the item (a lost sale).
4. They substitute the same brand (different size or type).
5. They substitute another brand (brand switching).

Research by IGD (2003) shows that 65 per cent of UK consumers looking for a specific grocery item will adopt one of the first three reactions, thus not buying in that particular store on that occasion if a stock-out occurs. In 1979, the figure from the Schary and Christopher study was 78 per cent. Despite the retail changes that have occurred since 1979, the degree of store switching is remarkably high for a sector that prides itself on customer loyalty programmes! Compared with the more general results of Corsten and Gruen (2003) the figure for the United Kingdom is high compared with other markets, where the average is 31 per cent.

Many studies discuss in-depth the causal factors that prompt consumer reactions to stock-outs such as the product category, the nature of the brand loyalty, consumer type and the immediacy of need (Emmelhainz *et al*, 1991; Gruen *et al*, 2002; Sloots *et al*, 2005; Verbeke *et al*, 1998). The latter work not only investigated brand equity/loyalty but also the hedonic value of products. Thus, customers who possess high brand equity / high hedonic values on a product are likely to switch brands or stores to acquire the product. Further, they will do so without serious consideration of their own 'personal logistics costs' or paying to have their groceries delivered by the retailer (Teller *et al*, 2006).

Campo *et al* (2000) identified three drivers that influence consumer reactions. They are the opportunity cost of not being able to consume immediately, the substitution cost of using a less preferred product or brand, and the transaction cost of the time required to acquire the invaluable item. Corsten and Gruen (2003) showed that consumers switch more in some categories rather than others, especially with brands that do not have a personal attachment associated with them. For example, they found more substitution occurred with paper towels compared with feminine hygiene products.

Academic research on customer reactions has been reinforced by reports from trade organizations. ECR UK has held conferences, seminars and written influential reports on the topic. In addition to the three factors identified by Campo *et al* (2000), ECR UK (2004) discussed the profile of shoppers and noted that consumers tended to perceive OOS as higher in promotional rather than non-promotional items.

Similarly, IGD's main logistics conference in 2004 focused upon this theme and commissioned research, published in 2005, on consumers' responses to stock-outs in three different product categories – health and beauty, frozen food and dairy products. Similar results were found in Corsten and Gruen's survey, where OOS in health and beauty products led to consumers shopping in other stores since substitution was more likely to occur in the other categories due to the immediacy effect.

The causes of retail out-of-stocks

The Corsten and Gruen (2003) research indicates that most OOS situations occur at the store level, primarily through ordering and replenishment practices. However, they did point out that the problem of replenishment from within store was more important in their work than findings from the Coca-Cola Research Council / Anderson (1996). Replenishment within store became a key issue for UK grocery retailers in the early 2000s and is known as the 'last 50 yards' problem. Figure 9.1 shows that 35 per cent of OOS problems occur with shelf replenishment in the store and 15 per cent from the regional distribution centre (RDC) to the store.

This situation was aggravated by the growth of internet ordering for groceries and the use of store-based picking strategies for e-fulfilment to home shoppers. Pioneered by Tesco in the mid-1990s, the other major grocery chains abandoned their dedicated picking centres for store picking in order to achieve greater market penetration at lower cost (Grant *et al*, 2006). The problem with this strategy was that already congested backrooms were becoming more cluttered as RDCs delivered stock to meet demands of both store and home shoppers. Inevitably the possibility of an OOS situation increased (Fernie and McKinnon, 2003).

It is normally at the store or RDC level that most retail shrinkage occurs in the supply chain, ie consumer, employee and supplier theft, which

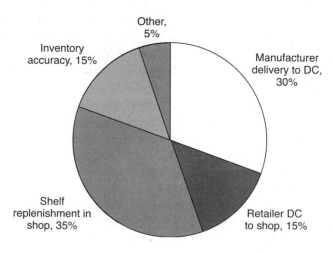

Figure 9.1   Root cause analysis of retail out-of-stocks
Source: Dybell, 2005

leads to inaccurate ordering and flawed forecasts. In the United Kingdom the average shrinkage rate is 1.4 per cent of sales and is one of the highest in Europe (Centre for Retail Research, 2005). Of particular concern to retailers, however, is that 14.4 per cent of shrinkage can be attributed to 'internal errors', such as processing errors, accounting mistakes and pricing discrepancies. For example, poorly trained staff at checkouts can scan items incorrectly thereby causing inaccurate sales data to be transmitted to suppliers.

Methods to improve on-shelf availability

Corsten and Gruen (2003) advocated an integrated approach based on process responsiveness, operation accuracy and incentive alignment to address the causes of OOS. The process improvements were related to assortment planning and space allocation, ordering systems, inventory control and store flow replenishment. Operational accuracy remedies were focused upon the accuracy of inventory levels and the ability to measure and identify on-shelf availability. Clearly technological advances such as radio frequency identification (RFID) can improve inventory measurement and accuracy in the future. The final remedy, incentive alignment, is about scheduling staff to improve shelf filling in addition to optimizing overall management objectives rather than sub-objectives by functional area.

In the United Kingdom, ECR UK has been the medium through which the OSA/OOS problem has been addressed by all members of the grocery supply chain; ECR UK is affiliated with IGD. In its initial report in 2004 it commented upon a combination of processes and approaches to tackle OSA. Similar to the Corsten and Gruen study, ECR Europe has identified seven 'levers' that can be used to improve OSA; see Figure 9.2. These are measurement 'levers' that need 'managerial attention' (levers 1 and 2); replenishment and in-store execution, namely merchandizing (3 and 4); inventory accuracy (5); promotional management and ordering systems (6 and 7). These levers have subsequently formed the basis of the ECR UK availability agenda. In line with the measurement levers, the ECR UK Availability Survey is now the established method for measuring OSA of the largest grocery stores (15,000 – 50,000 square feet) in the United Kingdom; this quarterly survey deals with 350 stores and 200 fast-selling lines across 11 departments.

In the wake of initial quarterly reports, ECR UK has also sought to investigate OSA issues that have arisen out of its reports and case studies from IGD conferences (IGD, 2005). In 2005 three subgroups were established – Availability Insights, New Product Introduction and Promotions,

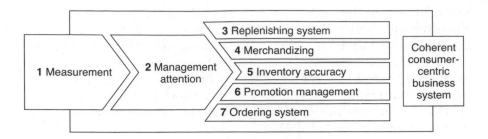

Figure 9.2 ECR Europe 'Seven improvement levers'
Source: ECR UK, 2004

and Convenience (ECR UK, 2006). The last group mirrored the larger Availability Survey by undertaking a quarterly OSA survey across seven convenience store retailers, 97 products and 11 categories.

As noted earlier, the major survey focuses on larger stores; however, the largest chains have strongly moved into the convenience store market during the last five to 10 years. The new product / promotions group was established to glean a better understanding of the impact that new product launches and promotions have on availability, whereas the insights group has tended to focus on the health and beauty category because of its consistent poor performance in the Availability Survey.

In summary, some of these recent initiatives are being trialled by various grocery retailers where they believe they have a problem and can improve the situation. Our research objective was to undertake an in-depth investigation of one firm and examine its OOS/OSA initiatives to address the three overarching problems that have been identified in the literature and trade studies: the effect on OOS/OSA from in-store picking for home delivery, promotions, and store size.

METHODOLOGY

In the ECR UK reports and IGD conferences, generic information is given on causes and possible solutions to the OSA problem. Indeed, numerous case studies are given on best practice in order to further the dissemination of results to all companies involved in supplying products to stores. In our research, we focus upon one major grocery retailer that was experiencing acute OSA/OOS problems. We argue that exploring how companies deal with supply chain management and supply chain challenges is best achieved through case studies (Ellram, 1996). A case study strategy has the ability to answer 'how' questions and to put existing theory into a new light, which again can generate new hypotheses as well as provide in-depth insight into a previously little-explored phenomenon (Ellram, 1996). Thus, this research consists of a single case study of the focal retailer to determine how it uses extant theory in its setting, or develops new insights related to gaps in theory.

Since the authors and researchers were involved in the research process, the research method was considered to be participant observation. This method is different to action research, which requires a combination of participative action and critical reflection and where the researcher both contributes to the change process and evaluates the change process during the participation (Näslund, 2002). While we participated in meetings and discussed evidence of our findings during the research process we did not substantially contribute to the company's decision-making process. Our role was to informally provide knowledge transfer between ourselves and the company based on our research interests and scope of the research project.

This research is strongly deductive in nature, drawing from the 'industry-standard' ECR UK framework identified in Figure 9.2. This enabled the researchers to test the principles advocated by ECR UK in order to compare results from this work to ongoing IGD-initiated research. Furthermore, the research from the case study allowed us to generate a conceptual framework for further research in this area, which is presented in the conclusions. The research was conducted in a series of phases. This is summarized in Table 9.1, which shows how the issue of OSA was perceived to be important at senior management level even before the new supply chain director was appointed. The later phases of the research dealt with the implementation of the Focus on Availability Strategy at both RDC and store level.

Initially the supply chain director and other senior management were approached to discuss their evolving logistics strategy and approaches to OSA. A series of face-to-face and telephone interviews were undertaken between 2003 and 2006 to chart progress on the company's strategy.

A part of the strategy was to take one store and align its processes to focus on OSA; interviews were also held with the management team implementing this project in Scotland, particularly the depot 'availability champion' responsible for coordinating the project. From June to August 2005, visits and interviews were conducted at the Scottish RDC and nine stores in the 'central belt' of Scotland, ie the 50-mile wide strip between the cities of Glasgow and Edinburgh that contains about 60 per cent of Scotland's 5 million population.

Semi-structured interviews took place with managers of the stores to determine if the project improved availability, levels of inventory, communications between store and DC. Furthermore, any problems with

Table 9.1 The research process

	Applicable ECR improvement levers	Research questions	Data collection methods
Phase 1 (2003–2006)	Levers 1 and 2	To what extent is OSA/OOS an integral part of logistics strategy? What measures have been undertaken to improve OSA? How successful were these measures?	Semi-structured interviews with supply chain director (2003) and successor (2006); telephone interviews with senior manager responsible for OSA; use of monthly independent audit of OSA across all stores.
Phase 2 (June to August 2005)	Levers 1, 3, 5 and 6	To what extent was senior management strategy implemented in the Scottish region? What practical measures were undertaken to improve the flow of product from RDC to store? How successful were these measures?	Semi-structured interviews with management team at the Scottish RDC, especially the 'availability champion'; participant observation of the process of replenishment and communication from RDC to nine stores in the region; interviews with these store managers on the success or otherwise of implementation; use of monthly reports to audit OSA performance.
Phase 3 (November 2005 to February 2006)	Levers 1, 3, 4, 5, 6 and 7	To what extent does in-store picking for internet shopping affect OSA levels? What is the impact of in-store promotions on OSA? What is the relationship between OSA and store size?	Semi-structured interviews were held with managers of stores in the Edinburgh region, 'availability champion' of one store, home shopping manager of another store and a convenience store manager; monthly audit data to measure performance in relation to size, promotions and internet shopping (March 2005 – February 2006), complemented by in-store OSA monitoring.

implementation were discussed. Lastly, the flow of products from DC to shelf was observed and a practical application of stock allocation improvements was acquired.

The company operates an audit procedure whereby an independent company produces OSA reports every month, by store and department; thus it was possible to chart the success or otherwise of these initiatives. For supermarkets, 200 products are checked of which 160 are store-specific and the remaining 40 are items on promotion. Convenience stores only have 120 store-specific products and no promotions. These reports were made available to the authors.

The final part of the project focused upon five stores in the Edinburgh area in order to discuss in-depth some of the key issues which were identified in the ECR UK general availability reports and other literature discussed earlier. The following research questions were proposed:

- To what extent does the use of store-based picking for home shopping affect levels of OSA?
- What is the impact of in-store promotions on OSA?
- What is the relationship between OSA and store size?

To answer these questions, interviews were held with the availability champion at one store, the home shopping manager at another and the store manager of a convenience store within the chain. Audit data were collected from March 2005 to February 2006 and availability results were matched for:

- the home shopping store against a store in the area of comparable size;
- two supermarket stores to measure promoted lines compared to those not on promotion;
- one supermarket store in relation to the convenience store.

FINDINGS

At the time of the initial interviews with senior management regarding the company's logistics strategy, a major restructuring of its network and systems was being undertaken. The company had been a leader in logistical innovation in the 1960s and 1970s and its efficient retail distribution had been a key contributor to its healthy profit margins. Unfortunately many of its original DCs were 25–35 years old and a new, sophisticated network of 'fulfilment factories' were planned for the 2000s. OSA had become an issue for the company and it focused much of its attention on accurately forecasting and planning promotions from suppliers to the store. Using collaborative planning software the company's buyers would agree with suppliers the level of promotion over a 13-week period, refining case quantities to match actual demand at their end of the planning cycle. The company focused upon its 1,000 best-selling lines of which around one-fifth were continuously promoted.

With the advent of home shopping aggravating the 'last 50 yards' problem the company began to experience acute OSA difficulties. Like many of its predecessors in the 1980s, network changes involving a mixture of old and new systems created short-term pressures and profitability shortfalls. The problem for the company was that the new high-tech network was 'pushing' product out to stores but overstocks were occurring in backrooms of stores and not reaching the shelves. Demand and supply were not synchronized, leading to marquees or tents being built in the back yards of stores to protect overstocks from the weather.

New management were appointed to the company, including a new supply chain director to tackle the range of problems identified above. After an initial audit of the situation he commented: 'There is nothing here I haven't seen before, it's just I've never seen it all at the same time and in the same place before.'

The first problem tackled was the stores; if product were in the store it had to be on the shelf. A Focus on Availability Strategy was formulated by taking one store and aligning all of its processes to focus on OSA. By achieving early success in reducing gaps and backroom stock, the company and its staff realized the benefits of such an approach. The marquees were dismantled and stock was reorganized within the warehouse so that everything had a place. Systems were then reviewed to action on-shelf 'gaps' and to establish causes for OOS or overstocks. Local forecasting teams were established in each RDC.

Having achieved significant improvements in-store, it was then necessary to integrate store operations with supply chain improvements to reduce lead times and reduce costs. This meant more flexible working practices in RDCs' synchronization of inbound deliveries and aligning transport schedules with store processes.

By mid-2006 a more retail-centric culture was created, OOS was reduced by 75 per cent and stock backroom levels were reduced by 53 per cent. In logistics, depot productivity had increased by 20 per cent, logistics network volumes increased by 10 per cent and the automated sites were achieving volumes two and a half times greater than in 2004.

The implementation of the Focus on Availability Strategy in Scotland

The RDC in Scotland is one of the most recent within the company's network, prior to the 'fulfilment factory' plan of 2001. Built in 1997, it is a composite distribution centre and is semi-automatic where carousel sorters channel product for picking by warehouse staff. The opening of this RDC made delivery to Scottish and Northern Ireland stores more efficient as prior to 1997 these stores received stock from Yorkshire and Lancashire in England. Nevertheless, a pilot project was introduced to Scottish stores in late 2004 and 2005 to reorganize the backroom and yard of stores and integrate both incoming deliveries from the RDC and returns of trays, pallets, trolleys and waste packaging.

The principle behind the project was to change the way inventory was handled within the store. The main change in the backroom was the removal of some racking and the use of U-shaped trolleys to allocate overstocks from replenishment of the shelves and depot delivery. This ensured that the night shift, for example, puts all stock on the shelves and overstocks in the 'U-shapes' according to need for replenishment. Prior to 8 am, the stock control team review 'gaps' and readjust forecasts prior to the inventory system being updated. The day team then replenish from the 'U-shapes' and do 'gap' counts on the busiest days, ie Thursday through Sunday.

During visits to the stores and interviews with management, it became clear that the changes being implemented in store back rooms were eliminating excessive stock. The shift to almost a 'just-in-time' basis had been challenging but had brought an element of discipline into stock allocation. Some problems still needed to be resolved, for example shelf facings, especially during promotions, often had two much or too little allocation. Also, there were restrictions on night and early morning deliveries for some stores, which led to embarrassing 'gaps' for fresh products first thing in the morning.

Interviewees felt that communications with RDC management were good but that problems with cage and pallet stacking led to unloading difficulties and damage to products. The accumulation of returns, stock, trays, etc was creating space problems in the yard, although the depot availability champion stressed that one truck per day was designated to pick up returns from stores and such an accumulation was due to some stores not managing their returns on a daily basis. The success of the project was confirmed from the audit data of September 2004 to July 2005, which showed an overall availability improvement from 90 to 94 per cent and promotions improvement from 89 to 96 per cent. In Scotland the scores were better, with one store achieving 98 per cent availability.

The Edinburgh survey

As noted above, the purpose of the research into the Edinburgh stores was to gain a deeper insight into issues such as the impact of home shopping picking, promotions and store size on OSA. Audit data were collected and analysed between March 2005 and February 2006 to answer the research questions outlined in the methodology.

From the audit data availability results were not dissimilar between the store that carried out internet delivery and a similar-size store that did not: 96.2 per cent to 96.9 per cent respectively. This seemed surprising considering that store-based picking models for home shoppers were deemed to be partially responsible for OOS. In Edinburgh, however, the main store responsible for home deliveries had its backroom extended for the purpose of processing internet orders. The use of such a dedicated site minimizes the effect of home shopping on the 'last 50 yards' problem.

Further, this store generates daily and weekly reports provided by personal shoppers who pick orders in store. These personal shoppers therefore provide an accurate real-time review of what home shoppers are experiencing with regard to product availability and this is communicated to stock control and store management. These reports are invaluable to store management and complement the monthly audit reports. A store manager stated, 'Although the audit reports are important because it is how the company assesses performance, the daily reports we receive are the most important to me since they provide me with a view of how availability is now, not how it was last month.'

All products that are substituted because of an OOS situation are communicated to the department manager to carry out a root cause analysis of why this has occurred. When a more detailed analysis of audit results was carried out, it was apparent that the internet store performed poorer than the conventional store on produce and fresh food categories, including organic items. This is a concern for store management in that: 'Our internet shoppers tend to be more affluent customers who purchase a lot of organic and fair trade products' (store manager).

Contradictory results to those initially expected were also found when comparing audit results for promoted items compared with those not being promoted. The average availability for lines excluding promotions was 95.5 per cent compared with 97.7 per cent for promoted items. It was noted earlier that the company as early as 2003 had focused on improving OSA for promotions. The new store operations project had enhanced OSA: 'Throughout the day, department managers' priority is to ensure that all shelves offering promoted items are full and dressed and an employee is allocated to this task alone every morning' (store manager).

Promotional items have been allocated extra shelf space in recent years and departmental managers can override system-generated orders if they feel that such orders will not meet demand. Coordination with the retail support team at the RDC is important to realize these orders.

The final part of the Edinburgh research was to compare audit data between a conventional superstore and a convenience store. The differences were marked, the superstore achieving 96.9 per cent compared with 89.5 per cent at the convenience store.

The company has acknowledged that availability targets are more difficult to achieve with smaller stores and have set targets accordingly: 93.5 per cent compared with 95.5 per cent for supermarkets. Nevertheless, the 89.5 per cent actually achieved is well below the target and this store failed to meet its availability target on nine occasions. This failure by categories included fresh foods (nine times), produce (eight), baking (six) and grocery (five). This was particularly unfortunate in that milk, bread and produce are the most popular lines in this convenience store.

The causes of this poor performance can be related to supply from the RDC and store replenishment issues. The company had developed a large network of convenience stores in recent years and in some regions, such as the south-east of England, it has a dedicated distribution network that supplies convenience stores. In Scotland this is not the case and all stores, regardless of size, are served by the Scottish RDC. Store managers can get frustrated by this state of affairs. 'Convenience stores are bottom of the food chain in terms of out-of-stock products. If my store and X superstore both sell out of something, and there is only one case in the RDC, the supermarket will get it' (convenience store manager).

Similarly, if an error occurs in replenishment from the RDC such as 'overs/unders' to store, the convenience store is affected more than a superstore, which has larger backrooms and receives more frequent deliveries to rectify any systems errors. Store replenishment is also a problem as shelf stackers and warehouse teams have become part of the rejuvenated solution to OSA in large stores, whereas small staff numbers in convenience stores invariably have to leave shelf filling to serve customers.

CONCLUSIONS

The research undertaken with this major UK grocery retailer demonstrates how it has addressed OSA/OOS problems to improve levels of availability. Extant research by Corsten and Gruen (2003) and ECR UK (2004, 2005, 2006, 2007) highlighted the measures that could be used to improve OSA. The 'seven levers' advocated by ECR UK (2004) have been implemented by this company. Measurement levers (1 and 2) have been acted upon through the audit procedures carried out by an independent company on a monthly basis. In addition, at the store level, daily and weekly reports keep departmental managers up to date on availability issues on a more regular basis.

Replenishment and in-store execution (levers 3 and 4) have been the focus of much managerial attention. The first task of the new supply chain director was to ensure that if the product were in the store it had to be on the shelf. The Focus on Availability Strategy was formulated by taking one store and aligning all processes to focus on OSA. Stock was reorganized in the backroom so that everything had a place. This meant introducing a new system in the backroom to ensure the proper rotation of stock on receipt of deliveries from the RDC. Inventory accuracy (lever 5) has improved with local forecasting teams at RDCs and stock control teams within stores readjusting forecasts prior to the inventory system being updated.

Regarding our research question on the impact of promotions on OSA, promotional management and ordering systems (levels 6 and 7) had been a feature of the company's logistical strategy before the appointment of a new management team. The company focused on the best-selling 1,000 lines, of which one-fifth were promoted at any one time. They then worked with suppliers to match supply with demand through a 13-week planning cycle. It is perhaps not unexpected that the Edinburgh store survey showed that promoted items had better OSA than non-promoted items, especially as a member of staff in store is allocated the task to ensure that all shelves with promoted lines are full and dressed every morning.

The two other research questions in the study that were analysed during the survey were the impact on OSA of store picking for home delivery and store size. Although the literature (Fernie and McKinnon, 2003; Fernie and Sparks, 2004) suggests that store picking has aggravated the OSA problem, this was not the case in the Edinburgh store. Here, the store backroom was extended to give a dedicated site for internet orders. Furthermore, personal shoppers provide real-time input to stock control by reporting gaps on the shelves, OOS and substitution levels.

The main problems facing the company in Scotland are poor OSA levels at convenience store level. Unlike some other regions, these stores are serviced by the same RDC that serves all stores in the region. The primary research reinforces the view that convenience stores are low in the priority list when stock problems occur at the RDC and low staffing levels in these stores mean that many of the operational procedures carried out in large stores have been less successful in smaller stores.

Our overall conclusion stemming from investigation of the three research questions is that OSA issues can be overcome by simple techniques that focus on human resources. Extending a store backroom to handle more stock is easy. However, we determined that the key difference between good and poor OSA levels at this company revolved around management and staff commitment to solving the problem; ie having dedicated staff to address promotional items and personal shoppers for in-store picking versus having insufficient staff to stock shelves and service customers in the convenience store.

This chapter has provided a view of one company's approach to solving OOS/OSA problems from 2004 through 2006. Clearly much progress has been made but work remains to be done in some areas. Nevertheless, this case study shows how an integrated approach from head office through RDCs to stores, including providing sufficient assets and human resources, created a 'can do' culture to improve not only OOS/OSA but depot productivity and overall network volume capacity.

Acknowledgements

The authors would like to thank Messrs Ricardo Junk and Michael Clement for their help in conducting the fieldwork.

References

Campo, K, Gijsbrechts, E and Nisol, P (2000) Towards understanding consumer response to stock-outs, *Journal of Retailing*, **76**, (2), pp 219–42

Campo, K, Gijsbrechts, E and Nisol, P (2003) The impact of retailer stock-outs on whether, how much, and what to buy, *International Journal of Research in Marketing*, **20**, (3), pp 273–86

Centre for Retail Research (2005) *European Theft Barometer: Monitoring the costs of shrinkage and crime for Europe's retailers*, Centre for Retail Research, Nottingham

Coca-Cola Research Council / Anderson Consultancy (1996) *Where to Look for Incremental Sales Gains: The retail problem of out-of-stock merchandise*, Coca-Cola Research Council, Atlanta, GA

Corsten, D and Gruen, D (2003) Desperately seeking shelf availability: an examination of the extent, the causes, and the efforts to address retail out-of-stocks, *International Journal of Retail and Distribution Management*, **31**, (12), pp 605–17

Dybell, J (2005) *Learning Together to Deliver Great Availability*, Presentation to the IGD Availability 2005 Conference, London, 15 June

ECR UK (2004) *Availability – A UK Perspective*, IGD, Watford

ECR UK (2005) *Availability 2005*, IGD, Watford

ECR UK (2006) *Availability 2006*, IGD, Watford

ECR UK (2007) *Availability 2007*, IGD, Watford

Ellram, L M (1996) The use of the case study method in logistics research, *Journal of Business Logistics*, **17**, pp 93–138

Emmelhainz, L W, Emmelhainz, M A and Stock, J R (1991) Logistics implications of retail stock-outs, *Journal of Business Logistics*, **12**, (2), pp 138–47

Fernie, J and McKinnon, A C (2003) Online shopping: the logistical issues, in (ed) P Freathy, *The Retail Book,* Prentice-Hall, Maidenhead

Fernie, J and Sparks, L (2004) *Logistics and Retail Management: Insights into current practice and trends from leading experts,* Kogan Page, London

Fletcher, R (2004) Basket case, *The Sunday Times,* 17 October

Grant, D B, Kotzab, H and Xing, Y (2006) success@tesco.com: *Erfolg im Online-Lebensmittelhandel oder 'Wie macht das der Tesco?'* in (eds) P Schnedlitz, R Buber, T Reutterer, A Schuh and C Teller, *Innovationen In Marketing Und Handel,* Linde, Vienna

Gruen, T W, Corsten, D and Bharadwaj, S (2002) *Retail Out-of-Stocks: A worldwide examination of extent, causes and consumer responses,* Grocery Manufacturers of America, Washington DC

IGD (2003) *Retail Logistics,* IGD, Watford

IGD (2005) *Retail Logistics,* IGD, Watford

Näslund, D (2002) Logistics needs qualitative research – especially action research, *International Journal of Physical Distribution & Logistics Management,* **32,** pp 321–38

Progressive Grocer (1968a) The Out-of-Stock Study, Part 1, October, pp 1–16

Progressive Grocer (1968b) The Out-of-Stock Study, Part 2, November, pp 17–32

Schary, P B and Christopher, M (1979) The anatomy of a stock-out, *Journal of Retailing,* **55,** (2), pp 59–70

Sloots, L M, Verhoef, P C and Franses, P H (2005) The impact equity and hedonic level of products on consumer stock-out reactions, *Journal of Retailing,* **81,** (1), pp 15–34

Teller, C, Kotzab, H and Grant, D B (2006) The consumer direct services revolution in grocery retailing: an exploratory investigation, *Managing Service Quality,* **16,** (1), pp 78–96

Verbeke, W, Farris, P and Thurik, R (1998) Consumer response to the preferred brand out-of-stocks situation, *European Journal of Marketing,* **32,** (1), pp 1008–28

Zentes, J, Morschett, D and Schramm-Klein, H (2007) Case Study: Sainsbury's, in *Strategic Retail Management: Text and international cases,* Gabler, Wiesbaden, Germany, pp 286–95

Part 4

Emerging issues: technology and environmental logistics

10

The development of e-tail logistics

John Fernie and Alan McKinnon

INTRODUCTION

Non-store shopping is not new. Traditional mail order goes back over a century. The 'big book' catalogues had experienced slow decline with the advent of more upmarket 'specialogues'. Also, the tradition of selling to friends and family has continued with party plans, most notably Ann Summers, and door-to-door selling through Avon and Betterware catalogues. These 'low tech' forms of selling accounted for around 4–5 per cent of all retail sales in the United Kingdom and the United States until the turn of this century, when the 'higher tech' options have dominated the marketplace. Initially, the 'hype' exceeded reality and after the dot com boom in the late 1990s, a considerable shakeout of the industry took place throughout the next decade as internet shopping began to experience steady growth. This chapter will discuss the growth of e-commerce, the evolving market and consumer responses to online retailing. The logistical challenges faced by the retail sector will then be discussed, especially the difficulties encountered in solving the 'last mile' problem in the grocery sector.

THE GROWTH OF E-COMMERCE

Whilst it is generally accepted that e-commerce has grown considerably in the 1990s and the early part of this century, accurate, reliable figures are difficult to ascertain because of the need to agree upon a widely accepted definition. Most research has focused upon business to consumer (B2C) transactions, although few companies in this sector have made a profit. It has been the business to business (B2B) and consumer to consumer (C2C) sectors that have produced real benefits to customers and hence increased profitability for the partners involved. In C2C markets, intermediaries such as eBay are online auctioneers brokering deals between bidders and sellers. Similarly B2B exchanges, such as WorldWide Retail Exchange, promote online auctions and collaborations between partners to reduce costs. Businesses involved in these e-commerce markets are infomediaries in that they are trading information and are facilitators in reducing trans-action costs between buyer and seller.

The problem with the B2C model compared with C2C and B2B models is the requirement to trade goods and services that are tangible and need to be stored and transported to the final consumer. Additionally, a market presence and brand identity are necessary ingredients to wean customers away from their traditional methods of buying behaviour. Yet despite these apparent drawbacks, the 'hype' associated with this new form of trading led many analysts to discuss the notion of disintermediation in B2C markets. Traditional retail channels were to be disrupted as new players entered the market with online offers. Not surprisingly, conven-tional retailers reacted passively to the new threat in view of their investment in capital assets. Pure e-tailers, with the exception of niche players, sustained losses with numerous bankruptcies and others being taken over by major retail groups.

As the market began to settle down in the mid-2000s, a multi-chan-nelled approach became the norm for all players in the market. In the United Kingdom, the catalogue-shop retailer, Argos, has achieved prof-itable growth through the additional of internet shopping. Schuh, the specialist footwear retailer, not only sells through its shops and the web but uses eBay to dispose of unwanted stock. Boden, initially launched as a mail order company, now has 56 per cent of its UK sales via the internet.

This approach is confirmed by research in the United States undertaken by the Boston Consulting Group (see Ganesh, 2004). In a survey of 63 retailers of various sizes and categories, they found that the most valued customer is the multi-channel customer. Retailers are utilizing cross-channel coordination whereby websites promote stores and catalogue offers. It is not unusual for customers to walk into stores with website printouts. More important to our discussion here is the whole issue of returns management.

Around 25 per cent of all goods purchased online are returned, hence the ability to handle returns can improve customer retention.

The market

One of the reasons for over-optimistic forecasts for e-commerce growth in the 1990s was consumer acceptance of the internet and widespread adoption of PC usage. In 2008, estimates of the number of worldwide users of the internet were around 1.41 billion with three-quarters of this figure represented by 20 countries (see Table 10.1). Compared with the estimates for 2002 in the previous edition of this book, growth in usage has been substantial, especially in India (1,200 per cent), China (700 per cent) and Brazil (not recorded but now 50 million users). The initial early adopters, such as the United States, Canada and the United Kingdom, have had relatively slow growth as market penetration levels reach or exceed 70 per cent.

Table 10.1   The largest users of the internet worldwide

	Country or region	Internet users	Penetration (% population)	% of world users
1	United States	218,302,574	71.9	15.5
2	China	210,000,000	15.8	14.9
3	Japan	94,000,000	73.8	6.7
4	India	60,000,000	5.2	4.3
5	Germany	54,932,543	66.7	3.9
6	Brazil	50,000,000	26.1	3.6
7	United Kingdom	41,042,819	67.3	2.9
8	France	36,153,327	58.1	2.6
9	Korea, South	34,820,000	70.7	2.5
10	Italy	33,712,383	58.0	2.4
11	Russia	30,000,000	21.3	2.1
12	Canada	28,000,000	84.3	2.0
13	Turkey	26,500,000	36.9	1.9
14	Spain	25,066,995	61.9	1.8
15	Mexico	23,700,000	21.6	1.7
16	Indonesia	20,000,000	8.4	1.4
17	Vietnam	19,323,062	22.4	1.4
18	Argentina	16,000,000	39.3	1.1
19	Australia	15,504,558	75.3	1.1
20	Taiwan	15,400,000	67.2	1.1
Top 20 Countries		1,052,458,261	25.0	74.8
Rest of the World		355,266,659	14.5	15.2
Total World – Users		1,407,724,920	21.1	100.0

Source: Miniwatts Marketing Group, 2008

To give an indication of the optimism exhibited by commentators in the mid-1990s with regard to the scale of online retail sales penetration, The *Financial Times* produced a conservative estimate of sales in Europe by 2000 in 1995. The author estimated that 10 to 15 per cent of food sales and 20 to 25 per cent of non-food sales would be made by home shopping (Mandeville, 1995). In reality, online grocery sales throughout Europe were around 0.24 per cent in 2000 with non-food sales only making an impact in computer software, CDs, books and videos. The position was much the same in the United States where online sales accounted for around 1 per cent of all retail sales in 2000 and 2001 (Reynolds, 2001). This slow growth in sales at that time can be attributed to consumers using the web for informational rather than transactional purposes in addition to purchasing other services rather than retail. For example, Forrester Research showed that of the US$20 to US$30 billion estimate of the online consumer market in the United States in 1999, only 60 per cent accounted for the physical distribution of goods (Laseter *et al*, 2000). The other 40 per cent accounted for digital delivered goods, such as airline and event tickets, banking services and auctions (Forrester and IMRG, in the United Kingdom, tend to give over-inflated sales figures as these goods are often cited as 'retail' sales).

More recent research indicates that retail sales online have been buoyant in the 2000s in the United States and Europe. In Europe, online sales were estimated to be around 2 per cent of all retail sales in 2005 with forecasts of this figure increasing to 5 per cent in 2010. The United Kingdom currently has the largest share of the market and, along with France and Germany, is expected to maintain around two-thirds of the European market in 2010. In the United Kingdom, the market has grown from £362 million (0.2 per cent of retail expenditure) in 1998 to £19.5 billion or 6.7 per cent of retail sales (Verdict Research, 2008). Verdict forecast that by 2012 online retailing will account for 14 per cent of retail sales or £44.5 billion. Although offline growth is faltering in the late 2000s as recession impacts upon high street sales, the online market continues to grow as shoppers take advantage of comparative price shopping on the web.

The e-commerce consumer

Internet connectivity, as revealed in Table 10.1, depicted a diverse international consumer market. This concealed the different stages of development of these markets and the geodemographic profile of internet consumers. As the market matures, the profile of the consumer begins to be more representative of the population it serves. In the early stages of development the profile of the e-commerce shopper was a young, male professional living in a middle-class neighbourhood. As the technology becomes more accepted the gender and socio-economic mix has changed. CACI, the market research group, undertakes an analysis of online behaviour and buying activity of adults (over 18 years of age) in the United Kingdom. Box 10.1 provides the detailed classification of eTypes, which shows an online lifecycle from infrequent online purchases – virtual virgins, chatters and gamers and dot com chatters to frequent online purchases – surfing suits and wired living. CACI has updated this classification into eight groups, embracing lifestage and internet usage levels, and 28 types, denoting online behaviours. This has been achieved through its own Ocean database, which has 40 million names and addresses classifying individuals by affluence, lifestyle, geographical and lifestage attributes.

Box 10.1   UK online consumers

Segmentation of online consumers in the UK

Group 1. Virtual virgins

Of those online, this group is least likely to have bought online. Less than two per thousand will have made any form of online purchase last month. Their time online is half the national average and they are likely to have started using the internet more recently than other people.

With the exception of chatting, this group does internet activities less frequently than average. Because of their relative inexperience they are more likely to worry about security and delivery problems with buying online purchases and to consider the process to be difficult.

People in this group are two times more likely to be female compared to any other group. The elderly and children are more commonly found in this type than any other.

Group 2. Chatters and gamers

This group, predominantly young males, might spend as much time online as the most avid type of internet user; however they tend not to be buyers. Only one in five will ever have made an online purchase. They may consider shopping online to be difficult and their fear of delivery and security problems is above average.

These people are avid chatters and gamers who use news groups and download as frequently as the most active and experienced surfers. Nearly half are under 25. The schoolchildren in this type are more likely to connect from school/university than any other e-type, although connection from home is still the most frequent.

Group 3. Dot com dabblers

As average internet users, these people have mixed feelings regarding the pros and cons of online shopping. Around 40 per cent will have made some form of purchase online and, with the exception of chatting, their interests spread to all forms of internet activity.

These people may see benefits of the internet in convenience and speed of delivery. Alternatively a specialist product not available elsewhere may have introduced them to buying online. In any event their enthusiasm for e-commerce is not yet complete.

Group 4. Surfing suits

Although they spend less time on the internet than average these people can be quite enthusiastic online purchasers. They are more likely than average to have bought books, software, hardware, holidays, groceries, insurance and tickets for events online.

Shopping online is seen to offer benefits such as range of product information, speed of ordering, price advantages and an element of fun. They are less likely to fear e-commerce.

They control their time on the internet and surfing: searching, e-mail and news groups tend to be preferred to chat, games or magazines.

Group 5. Wired living

These are cosmopolitan young people and the most extensive internet users, spending four and a half hours online each week. They are more experienced than most online and on average they have been using the internet for three years. Over 70 per cent will have purchased over the internet, covering between them the full gamut of products available for purchase. Over 60 per cent of these people are educated to degree level.

These people use the web as part of their lifestyle. Preferred interests tend to be newsgroups, news and magazines, with only an average interest in games or chat.

Source: CACI, 2000

Much of this discussion on the e-shopper has focused upon the PC and the internet as the medium of choice. For much of the 1990s, however, the development of TV shopping was often mooted as the likely channel to dominate the e-commerce market. Television shopping channels were already common in the United States and by the early 1990s had entered the UK market. Penetration of cable and satellite TV was low in Europe compared with North America, but the arrival of digital TV (DTV) was seen as the catalyst for the growth of interactive TV. Much of this optimism has failed to materialize. DTV services have not proved as popular as expected and operators have made losses or have gone out of business. At this time, evidence from the United States suggested that the motivations for watching TV are very different from PC usage. The latter is individualistic compared with the companionship associated with the television. Pace Microtechnology, one of the companies involved in making set-top boxes for existing analogue TV sets, undertook research into consumer attitudes to DTV services in the late 1990s (Ody, 1998). Most potential consumers are interested in DTV because of the enhancement of traditional features (better picture quality, sound, more channel choice) rather than to use it for shopping purposes.

Reynolds (2002) indicates that convergence between the two technologies will take time because the two markets are sufficiently dissimilar. This is reflected in the early adopters of cable and satellite TV who tended to be from lower income socio-economic groups – a different market segment from the early adopters of the internet. Nevertheless, the increased sophistication of mobile phone technology and portable music services has meant that TV services are in decline compared with internet services as a primary media source.

Longitudinal surveys undertaken by various authors in the late 1990s have shown how the e-tailing market matured both in terms of the customer base and the range of online offerings. In the United States the peak period of demand for internet retailing is between Thanksgiving and Christmas. Lavin (2002) draws upon consumer surveys undertaken by consultancy companies during Christmas 1998 and 1999 and her own primary research of retailers' websites during the same period. She comments that the profile of the web shopper had changed, e-tailers had worked to meet rising consumer expectations, and the 'first to market' advantage of early adopters had been eroded away. The customers of 1998 were predominantly male, technologically proficient and relatively affluent. More significantly they were not mainstream shoppers and had low expectations for their online purchase experience. She equates this with the innovator and early adopter stages of the adoption lifecycle. A year later with a rapidly growing market, the profile of the online customer had changed to a more balanced gender and age with overall lower average incomes. These are more likely to be mainstream shoppers with higher expectations from their purchase experiences. Although the market has grown considerably in the last decade, internet sales always experience a peak at Christmas and other special event days, such as Valentine's Day.

Morganosky and Cude (2002) undertook one of the few early studies on the behaviour of online grocery shoppers. Their research was based on a longitudinal study of consumers of Schnucks Markets, a St Louis-based chain of supermarkets operating in Illinois, Missouri and Indiana. The first two surveys in 1998 and 1999 asked Schnucks's online shoppers to fill in a questionnaire online on the completion of their order. The final survey re-contacted respondents from the 1999 survey to track their shopping behaviours in 2001. The results here did have some parallels with the work of Lavin (2002) in that the consumers were more sophisticated and had moved on from being 'new' users to experienced online shoppers. This is further reflected in their willingness to buy most or all of their groceries online and to improve their efficiency at completing the shopping tasks. Online grocery shoppers bought for the family. They were younger, female and better educated with higher incomes. The final survey showed that customer retention rates were good. The main reason for defections was the relocation to another part of the United States where the same online service was not available.

In the United Kingdom, Ellis-Chadwick *et al* (2002) completed a longitudinal study of internet adoption by UK multiple retailers from 1997 to 2000. Again, as in Levin's study, the primary research was largely based on reviewing retail websites over this four-year period to ascertain how internet business models were being developed. They report a six-fold increase in the number of retailers offering online shopping to their customers. Other researchers in the early 2000s followed this lead of examining websites of UK fashion retailing (Ashworth *et al*, 2006; Marciniak and Bruce, 2004; Siddiqui *et al*, 2003) and speciality stores in the United States (Feinberg *et al*, 2002) with a focus on either the supply side – retailers' use of the website for transactional or informational purposes – or the demand side – the evaluation by customers of the ease of navigation, interactivity and product information of these websites. (Readers are referred to the *International Journal of Retail & Distribution Management*, vol 33, no 2; vol 34, nos 4/5 and vol 34, no 7, which has special issues on online shopping and e-commerce in the retailing sector.)

In the above 2006 double issue, the editors Doherty and Ellis-Chadwick critically review research on internet retailing to that time by undertaking a content analysis of papers published in all journals from 1996 to 2005. They classify the research into three themes: the retailer perspective, the consumer perspective and the technological perspective. Most initial research focused on the retailer perspective, undoubtedly because of the managerial challenges involved. Hence, some of the research cited above in the late 1990s/early 2000s focused on retailers' adoption of the internet as a channel to market. As the web became an accepted technology, research then moved more to the online behaviour of consumers from consumers' characteristics to their online experiences and the incorporation of established consumer behaviour models to an online environment. Finally, the technological perspective has demanded less attention although there have been meaningful contributions on website design, software tools and e-commerce infrastructure.

These studies, and other more sector-specific consultancy / trade organization investigations, indicate that retailers are responding to this changing market environment. As the market matures, consumers tend to behave in a similar fashion to dealing with traditional retail outlets. The basics of convenience, product range, customer service and price will always feature in a consumer's 'evoked set' of attributes. Above all, retailers have become brands and customer loyalty has been established through continually high levels of service. It is not surprising therefore that traditional retailers with strong brand equity can gain even more leverage through a sound web strategy. They have the trust of the consumer to begin with and the capital to invest in the necessary infrastructure. Many dot com 'pure players' needed to build a brand and tackle the formidable challenge of delivering to customers' homes. This is why it took so long for Amazon.com to register a profit.

All of this research shows that e-tailing has been most successful to date where a multi-channel 'click and bricks' approach is adopted. In this context, we are referring to non-food products where traditional department stores and clothing specialists have considerable experience of dealing with the non-store shopper through their catalogues and 'low tech' selling techniques. These companies were well equipped to deal with home deliveries and a returns policy. Similarly the early e-tailing specialist pioneers with CDs, books, videos and computing equipment already had an infrastructure to deal with home-based orders. The grocery sector is much more complex and home delivery is more associated with food service and added-value products. Nevertheless, the sector has attracted considerable attention in the literature, and we turn to a more detailed assessment of the market and the online issues pertaining to grocery in the next section.

THE GROCERY MARKET

Despite the fact that online grocery sales account for a small proportion of retail sales in most country markets, this sector has attracted most attention from researchers and government bodies, including the DTI in the United Kingdom at the beginning of the millennium (DTI, 2001). Grocery shopping impacts upon all consumers. We all have to eat! However, our populations are getting older so shopping is more of a chore; conversely, the younger, time-poor, affluent consumers may hate to waste time buying groceries. The relatively slow uptake of online grocery shopping in the United States can be attributed to the lack of online shopping availability in that most online initiatives were promulgated by pure players because of the relative fragmentation of the US grocery market. In 2008 there remain several US states, mainly rural ones, that do not have local e-grocery services.

This fragmented market initially encouraged entrants into the supermarket store-based market. In the late 1980s this came in the form of Warehouse Clubs and Wal-Mart Supercenters; by the 1990s dot com players began to challenge the traditional supermarket operators. Unfortunately these pure players have gone into liquidation, scaled down their operations or have been taken over by conventional grocery businesses.

Why have pure players failed? Laseter *et al* (2000) identify four key challenges:

1. limited online potential;
2. high cost of delivery;
3. selection/variety trade-offs;
4. existing entrenched competition.

Ring and Tigert (2001) came to similar conclusions when comparing the internet offering with the conventional 'bricks and mortar' experience. They looked at what consumers would trade away from a store in terms of the place, product, service and value for money by shopping online. They also detailed the 'killer costs' of the pure play internet grocers, notably the picking and delivery costs. The gist of the argument presented by these critics is that the basic internet model is flawed.

Even if the potential is there, the consumer has to be lured away from existing behaviour with regard to store shopping. Convenience is invariably ranked as the key choice variable in both store patronage and internet usage surveys. For store shoppers, convenience is about location and the interaction with staff and the store experience. Internet users tend to be trading off the time it takes to stop. However, as Wilson-Jeanselme (2001) has shown, the 58 per cent net gain in convenience benefit is often eroded away by 'leakages' in the process of ordering to ultimate delivery. Furthermore, the next two key store choice variables in the United States tend to be price and assortment. With the exception of Webvan, pure players offered a limited number of stock-keeping units (SKUs) compared with conventional supermarkets. Price may have been competitive with stores but delivery charges push up prices to the customer. In the highly competitive US grocery market, customers will switch stores for only a 3–4 per cent differential in prices across leading competitors. Ring and Tigert

(2001, p 270) therefore pose the question, 'What percentage of households will pay substantially more for an inferior assortment (and perhaps quality) of groceries just for the convenience of having them delivered to their home?'

Tanskanen *et al* (2002) argue that these e-grocery companies failed because an electronic copy of a supermarket does not work. They claim that e-grocery should be a complementary channel rather than a substitute and that companies should be investing in service innovations to give value to the customer. Building upon their research in Finland, they maintain that the 'clicks and bricks' model will lead to success for e-grocery. Most of the difficulties for pure players relate to building a business with its associated infrastructure. Conventional retailers have built trust with their suppliers and customers. The customer needs a credible alternative to self-service and the Finnish researchers suggest that this has to be achieved at a local level where routine purchases can be shifted effectively to e-grocery. To facilitate product selection, web-based information technology can tailor the retail offer to the customer's needs. The virtual store can be more creative than the restrictions placed on the physical stocking of goods on shelves; however, manufacturers will need to provide 'pre-packaged' electronic product information for ordering on the web.

Online grocery retailing still accounts for a very small percentage of sales in most markets around the world; indeed, most online grocery development has occurred in the United Kingdom, the United States and parts of Asia. Planet Retail (2004) shows that Tesco dominated the market through its operations in the United Kingdom, Ireland, South Korea and its share in Safeway's Groceryworks.com operation in the United States. Peapod, owned by Ahold, and Sainsbury are also in the top five retailers, so European companies dominate this market.

Tesco has also dominated the UK grocery market with estimates of around 45–50 per cent share of the UK grocery online market (Hackney *et al* 2006; Wilson-Jeanselme and Reynolds, 2006). Tesco's success has been achieved through its innovative marketing strategy in the early–mid-1990s to challenge and eventually surpass Sainsbury as the number one grocery retailer in the United Kingdom. The launch of Clubcard and the online business allowed Tesco to glean a better understanding than the competition of its offline and online customers. Whilst others dithered on whether to follow Tesco's lead on both loyalty card and grocery home delivery, Sainsbury, Asda and Safeway (now Morrisons) fell further behind in the overall grocery market. Tesco's use of the store-based fulfilment model (see later section) allowed it greater UK market penetration before slowly adopting a picking centre approach in areas where demand intensity was high.

Tesco's internet sales in 2007/08 account for 3 per cent of the company's sales and 4 per cent of the profits. It is now difficult to disaggregate the online grocery sales from all online sales because of the launch of the non-food Tesco Direct operation in 2006. It is safe to assume, however, that grocery accounts for much of the sales in that the Tesco Direct business has been experiencing difficulties, with the suspension of clothing sales and the withdrawal of online flower sales in 2008.

One of Tesco's main challengers in the online grocery market, Ocado, questions the profitability of Tesco's operation, hinting that costs from the online business are being displaced into other parts of the company's balance sheet (*The Sunday Times*, 25 November 2007). Ocado, which has 18 per cent of the online grocery business, adopted the centralized picking model, similar to Webvan in the United States. The selling of upmarket Waitrose products online from the Hatfield distribution centre has been a slow roll-out process that still makes a post-tax loss after seven years of operation. Ocado claims that its approach is 'greener' through less use of energy than the competition and that the picking centre approach improves product availability thereby reducing waste.

THE LOGISTICAL CHALLENGES

Forecasts of the growth of online retail services are invariably demand-driven and assume that it will be possible to deliver orders to the home at a cost and service standard home shoppers will find acceptable. This is a bold assumption. Over the past decade many e-tail businesses have failed primarily because of an inability to provide cost-effective order fulfilment. Several market research studies have identified delivery problems as a major constraint on the growth of home shopping. Anderson Consulting (quoted in Metapack, 1999), for example, found that six of the 10 most frequently quoted problems with online shopping were related to fulfilment. As Verdict Research (2000) noted, 'Persuading customers to buy direct once is relatively simple. Keeping them coming back is far more difficult and is dependent on their satisfaction with all stages of the delivery experience.' Available evidence suggests that the level of consumer satisfaction with this delivery experience has been rising. By 2003, just over two-thirds of UK online shoppers reported that they were very satisfied 'across all delivery criteria' (Verdict Research, 2004). Roughly 15 per cent of consumers, however, gave 'inconvenience/having to wait in' as a reason for not having goods delivered to the home.

Arguably, the greatest logistical challenges are faced by companies providing a grocery delivery service to the home. They must typically pick an order comprising 60–80 items across three temperature regimes from a total range of 10–25,000 products within 12–24 hours for delivery to customers within one to two hour time-slots. For example, Tesco is currently picking and delivering an average of 250,000 such orders every week. New logistical techniques have had to be devised to support e-grocery retailing on this scale. Online shopping for non-food items has demanded less logistical innovation. Catalogue mail order companies have, after all, had long experience of delivering a broad range of merchandise to the home, while some major high street retailers have traditionally made home delivery a key element in their service offering. Online shopping is, nevertheless, imposing new logistical requirements. First, it is substantially increasing the volume of goods that must be handled, creating the need for new distribution centres and larger vehicle fleets. Second, many online retailers are serving customers from different socio-economic backgrounds from the traditional mail order shopper. As they live in different neighbourhoods, the geographical pattern of home delivery is changing. Third, online shoppers typically have high logistical expectations, demanding rapid and reliable delivery at convenient times (Xing and Grant, 2006).

DEFINITION OF THE HOME DELIVERY CHANNEL

The home delivery channel terminates at the home or a nearby customer collection point. It is less clear where it begins. For the purposes of this review, the start of the home delivery channel will be defined as the 'order penetration point' (Oldhager, 2003). This is the point at which the customer order, in this case transmitted from the home, activates the order fulfilment process. This physical process usually begins with the picking of goods within a stock-holding point. Only when picked are the goods designated for a particular home shopper. Distribution down-stream from this point is sometimes labelled J4U, 'just for you'.

With the move to mass customization, an increasing proportion of customer orders are penetrating the supply chain at the point of production. Consumers, for example, can configure a personal computer to their requirements online and relay the order over the web straight to the assembly plant. Where this occurs the home delivery channel effec-tively starts at the factory.

Within multi-channel retail systems, this order penetration point is the point at which home deliveries diverge from the conventional retail supply chain, which routes products to shops. For example, in the case of those supermarket chains that have diversified into home shopping, the order penetration point is either the shop or a local fulfilment (or 'pick') centre, where online orders are assembled. Both of these outlets draw supplies from a common source, the regional distribution centre. It makes sense, therefore, to regard the home delivery channel for grocery products as starting at the shop or the pick centre.

While the upper levels of the home delivery channels for grocery and non-food products are markedly different, the last link in the chain (the so-called 'last mile') presents similar logistical problems for different types of online retailer. We will examine first the 'upstream' fulfilment process and then focus on the 'last mile' problem.

Distribution of online purchases of non-food items

The distribution of these items normally exhibits the following characteristics:

1. They are generally supplied directly to the home from the point of production or a central distribution centre. Each order comprises a small number of items (often just one) and the order picking is centralized at a national or regional level. A large proportion of the orders are channelled through the 'hub-and-spoke' networks of large parcel carriers or mail order companies.
2. Within these J4U delivery networks, each order must be individually packaged at the central distribution point. This not only increases the volume of packaging in the supply chain: it also takes up more space on vehicles in both the forward and reverse channels.
3. Within home shopping systems, whether catalogue- or internet-based, there is a large flow of returned product. Typically, around 30 per cent of non-food products delivered to the home are returned to e-tailers, in contrast to 6–10 per cent for 'bricks and mortar' retailers (Nairn, 2003). This requires a major reverse logistics operation comprising the retrieval, checking, repackaging and redistribution of returned merchandise.

Wide fluctuations in online demand for particular products, particularly newly released items, can cause the flow of freight through home delivery channels to surge. This was illustrated by the distribution of new Harry Potter books through the Amazon.com networks to arrive on the doorsteps of tens of thousands of households on the day of publication.

Distribution of online grocery sales

In contrast to the average general merchandise order, which comprises 1–3 separate items, the average online grocery order contains 60–100 items, many of which are perishable and need rapid picking and delivery. This requires localized order picking either in an existing shop or a dedicated fulfilment/pick centre. Over the past few years there has been much discussion of the relative merits of store-based or fulfilment centre picking.

The main advantage of store-based fulfilment is that it minimizes the amount of speculative investment in new logistical facilities for which future demand is uncertain. Webvan, for example, was planning to build a network of 26 new automated warehouses, at a cost of approximately US$35 million each, to provide e-grocery delivery across the United States. Fewer than half of these warehouses were set up before the company went bankrupt in 2001. As a pure player in the e-grocery market, Webvan did not have an established chain of retail outlets and would have had to form an alliance with an existing retailer to adopt the store-based model. Several British supermarket chains, such as Sainsbury, Asda and Somerfield, as 'bricks and clicks' retailers, had the option of pursuing store-based or pick-centre fulfilment and opted initially for the latter. Tesco, by contrast, opted for the store-based model.

Basing home delivery operations at existing shops allows retailers to improve the utilization of their existing assets and resources. Retail property can be used more intensively and staff shared between the store and online operations. It is possible to pool retail inventory between conventional and online markets, improving the ratio of inventory to sales. This also gives online shoppers access to the full range of products available in a supermarket to which most of them will be accustomed. Another major benefit of shop-based fulfilment is that it enables the retailer to achieve a rapid rate of geographical expansion, securing market share and winning customer loyalty much more quickly than competitors committed to the fulfilment centre model.

On the negative side, however, integrating conventional and online retailing operations in existing shops can impair the standard of service for both groups of customer. The online shopper is disadvantaged by not having access to a dedicated inventory. Although a particular product may be available on the shelf when the online order is placed, it is possible that by the time the picking operation gets underway 'conventional' shoppers may have purchased all the available stock. Where these in-store customers encounter a stock-out they can decide themselves what alternative products to buy, if any. Online shoppers, on the other hand, rely on the retailer to make suitable substitutions. Substitution rates are reckoned to be significantly higher for store-based fulfilment systems than e-grocers operating separate pick centres. For example, Ocado, the only UK e-grocery to rely solely on a pick centre, claims that it can achieve substitution rates of less than 5 per cent, whereas customers using its store-based competitors sometimes experience substitution rates more than twice this level (McClellan, 2003). In comparing substitution rates, however, allowance must be made for differences in product range. Ocado's range of around 12,500 products is less than half that of the major supermarket chains engaged in online shopping.

Doubts have been expressed about the long-term sustainability of store-based fulfilment. As the volume of online sales expands, conflicts between conventional and online retailing are likely to intensify. At the 'front end' of the shop, aisles may become increasingly crowded with staff picking orders for online customers. In practice, however, much of the picking of high-selling lines is done in the back store room. It is at the 'back end' that space pressures may become most acute. Over the past 20 years the trend has been for retailers to reduce the amount of back storage space in shops as in-store inventory levels have dropped and quick response replenishment becomes the norm. This now limits the capacity of existing retail outlets to support the online order fulfilment operation. New shops can, nevertheless, be purpose-built to integrate conventional retailing and online fulfilment. The Dutch retailer Ahold has coined the term 'wareroom' to describe a dedicated pick facility co-located with a conventional supermarket (Mees, 2000).

Most of the purpose-built fulfilment centres so far constructed are on separate sites. They offer a number of logistical advantages over store-based picking. As their inventory is dedicated to the online service, home shoppers can check product availability at the time of ordering and, if necessary, alter their shopping list. The order picking function should also be faster and more efficient in fulfilment centres as they are specially designed for the multiple picking of online orders.

To be cost-effective, dedicated pick centres must handle a large throughput. The threshold level of throughput required for viability also depends on the breadth of the product range. It is very costly to offer an extensive range in the early stages of an e-tailing operation when sales volumes are low. Offering a limited range can cut the cost of the operation but make it more difficult to lure consumers from conventional retailing. Another inventory-related problem that retailers using pick centres have encountered is the difficulty of disposing of excess stocks of short shelf-life products. When over stocking occurs in a shop, consumer demand can be stimulated at short notice using price reductions or in-store merchandizing techniques. It is more difficult using electronic media to clear excess inventory of fresh produce from fulfilment centres that consumers never visit.

Several studies have argued that store-based fulfilment is more appropriate in the early stages of a retailer's entry into the e-grocery market (eg Fraunhofer Institute, 2002). It represents a low risk strategy and allows new business to be won at a relatively low marginal cost. As the volume of online sales grows, however, the cost and service benefits of picking orders in a dedicated centre steadily increase until this becomes the more competitive option. Several break-even analyses have been conducted to estimate the threshold online sales volume at which the fulfilment centre model is likely to be superior. Tesco appears to have reached this threshold volume in the south-east of England. In 2006 it opened its first dedicated fulfilment centre in south London, known as a 'Tesco.com only store', because it has a similar format to a conventional shop but is used solely for the picking of online orders. The viability threshold for such dedicated operations will vary from retailer to retailer depending on the size and layout of shops, the nature of the upstream distribution system, the product range and the customer base. It will also be highly sensitive to the allocation of retail overheads between the conventional and online shopping operations.

A further complicating factor is the geography of the retail market. The relative efficiency of the two types of fulfilment is likely to vary with the density of demand and level of local competition in different parts of the country. In a mature e-grocery market, dedicated pick centres may serve the conurbations, while store-based distribution remains the most cost-effective means of supplying the rural hinterlands. The US e-grocer Peapod has a policy of using store-based fulfilment when penetrating new local markets, working in collaboration with retail chains. Once volumes have reached an adequate level, as in Chicago and San Francisco, the company has invested in 'distribution centres'.

Experience in the United Kingdom suggests that most new entrants to the e-grocery market opted for the fulfilment model prematurely. Sainsbury, Somerfield and Asda all set up pick centres and closed them down within a few years. It is now generally acknowledged that at the present level of e-grocery sales in the United Kingdom, the store-based distribution model, pioneered by Tesco, is the most cost-effective. By supplying orders mainly from its existing shops Tesco dominates the UK internet grocery market, is developing similar businesses in Ireland and South Korea, and has established itself as the world's largest online grocery retailer.

The 'last mile' problem

In making the final delivery to the home, companies must strike an acceptable and profitable balance between customer convenience, distribution cost and security. Most customers would like deliveries to be made urgently at a precise time with 100 per cent reliability. This would minimize waiting time and the inconvenience of having to stay at home to receive the order. Few customers would be willing to pay the high cost of time-definite delivery, however.

The relationship between the width of home delivery 'windows' and transport costs has been modelled for the London area by Nockold (2001). Expanding the window from 180 minutes to 225 minutes and 360 minutes was found to cut transport costs by, respectively, 6–12 per cent and 17–24 per cent. Eliminating the time constraint completely yielded cost savings of up to a third. Similar research undertaken in Helsinki has indicated that transport cost savings of 40–60 per cent are possible where carriers can deliver at any time during the 24-hour day (Punakivi and Tanskanen, 2002). Such flexibility can usually only be achieved where a system of 'unattended delivery' is available. It is estimated that around 50–60 per cent of UK households have no one at home during the working day. An average of 12 per cent of home deliveries in the United Kingdom then fail because there is no one there to receive the goods, imposing a direct cost on carriers of approximately £682 million in 2006 and causing considerable inconvenience to online shoppers (IMRG, 2006). A good deal of creative thinking has been applied to this problem.

Figure 10.1 provides a classification of the main forms of unattended delivery that have so far been developed (McKinnon and Tallam, 2003). A fundamental distinction exists between unsecured and secured delivery. Unsecured delivery, sometimes called 'doorstepping' in the United Kingdom, involves simply leaving the consignment outside the house, preferably in a concealed location. This eliminates the need for a return

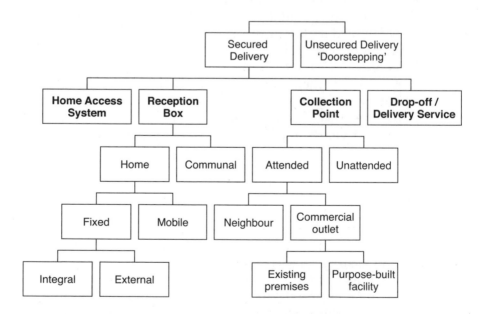

Figure 10.1   Classification of unattended delivery systems
Source: McKinnon and Tallam, 2003

journey and can be convenient for customers, but obviously exposes the order to the risk of theft or damage.

When no one is at home, the delivery can be secured in four ways:

1. Giving the delivery driver internal access to the home or an outbuilding.
2. Placing the order at a home-based reception (or 'drop') box.
3. Leaving it at a local collection point.
4. Delivering the order to a local agency which stores it and delivers it when the customer is at home.

1. Home access systems

A prototype home access system was trialled in the English Midlands. This system employed a telephone-linked electronic key pad to control the opening and shutting of the garage door. The key pads communicated with a central server, allowing the 'home access' agency to alter the pin codes after each delivery. When the driver closed the door, the key pad device issued another code number confirming that the delivery was made. At the same time a confirmation message was sent to the customer's mobile phone or e-mail address. It was found that this system could cut average drop times from 10 to four minutes and, if coupled with a five-hour time window, achieved a productivity level (measured in drops per vehicle per week) 84 per cent higher than the typical attended delivery operation (Rowlands, 2001). Despite these operational advantages, this system failed commercially. Since then two other home access systems have been launched in the United Kingdom, one involving the pin-number-activated release of a physical door key from a secure box, the other integrated into the lock. They can give delivery staff access either to the home or an outbuilding (Rowlands, 2007). So far there has been limited uptake of these systems and concern remains about the risks posed for home security.

2. Home reception boxes

Several types of reception box have so far been developed.

Fixed, integral boxes

These can either be built into the house at the time of its construction or 'retrofitted'. One system, installed in a few upmarket houses in the United Kingdom, comprises three chambers for ambient, chilled and frozen product and provides access directly into the kitchen.

Fixed, external boxes

In the short/medium term, there is likely to be more rapid uptake of external boxes, which are much cheaper to install and do not require structural modification to the property. Early models had a key pad that communicated with a service centre and could be activated by a single-use pin code issued to a delivery driver. In an effort to cut costs, most boxes now sold to consumers in the United Kingdom lack this communication interface and are not integrated into the suppliers' or carriers' IT systems (Rowlands, 2006).

Mobile reception boxes

Mobile reception boxes are filled by the supplier at its premises, delivered to the customer's home and secured temporarily to an outside wall. The main system of this type, which operated for several years in the United Kingdom, connected the box to an electronic device resembling an intercom by means of a steel cable. The supplier or carrier retrieved the box once it had been emptied and used it to recover any returned items. After a trial with a major UK supermarket chain, this system did not prove commercially viable in the UK B2C market.

Communal boxes

Communal boxes are more suited to apartment blocks and generally comprise banks of lockers.

3. Collection and delivery points (CDPs)

These are locations where customers can pick up goods that they bought online or return online purchases. Weltevreden (2008) distinguishes two types of CDP: 'locker points' where collection is unattended and 'service points' where staff are in attendance to retrieve the order. The most successful of the locker point systems in Europe employs luggage locker technology that has been extensively used in railway stations and airports around the world. These locker banks have been adapted to the role of order collection by establishing a communication link with a service centre, which issues pin codes to delivery drivers and customers. They are used primarily in a B2B capacity at present for the distribution of spare parts to service engineers, catalogues to sales representatives, etc. Efforts are now being made to attract B2C business. Several unattended CDP systems involving more sophisticated automated storage and retrieval technology have either failed or not yet progressed beyond the prototype stage. To secure business from e-tailers and carriers, networks of locker banks need to be established to offer wide geographical coverage. Substantial capital investment is therefore required to give a high proportion of online shoppers local access to this type of CDP.

Service points, on the other hand, are generally based in existing outlets, such as small convenience stores, petrol stations, railway stations or self-storage premises. In the United Kingdom, the Royal Mail offers a 'Local collect' service, which gives consumers the opportunity of diverting an order to a local post office for collection. This service only applies, however, to consignments delivered through the Royal Mail's own carrier networks. Other operators of attended CDPs, the largest of which in Europe is Kiala with roughly 4,500 outlets in several countries, have open networks that any carrier or e-tailer can use (Rowlands, 2006). Weltevreden (2008) estimates that, in 2006, there were around 2,700 serviced CDPs in the Netherlands. Nineteen per cent of online shoppers had used one, though these CDPs accounted for only around 1.4 per cent of total online retail sales.

Having to travel to a CDP significantly reduces the convenience of home shopping and may only be acceptable to a small proportion of online shoppers. One market survey has suggested that for around 55 per cent of home shoppers in the United Kingdom the most popular form of unattended delivery is leaving goods with next-door neighbours (Verdict Research, 2004). CDPs can, however, serve a useful role as an alternative delivery location when it is not possible to make a home delivery. Repeating the delivery to the home is generally more expensive, increases the consumer waiting time and may again result in a delivery failure. Moreover, when consumers exhaust their delivery opportunities, they may have to travel significant distances to the carrier's depot to collect the consignment. A case study in Winchester found that the use of CDPs in the event of a failed home delivery could reduce 'customer mileage' by over 80 per cent (McLeod *et al*, 2006). Dropping an item off at a local CDP for consumer collection can therefore yield substantial cost and service benefits.

4. Local drop-off and delivery

This represents an extension to the collection point service, where the company not only receives the order on the customer's behalf but also delivers it to his or her home at a convenient time. When the goods arrive, the customer is notified by e-mail, phone or mobile text message and asked to specify a narrow time-window within which the goods can be delivered.

To date, there has been very limited investment in home reception facilities. Many of the companies marketing innovative solutions to the last mile problem have gone out of business, while others have redirected their attention to the faster growing and more lucrative B2B market for the unattended delivery of shop orders, spare parts and catalogues. Investment in a fixed box at an individual home can only be justified at present where the customer makes regular use of an e-grocery service. The volume of non-food product being delivered to the home is still much too low to make such an investment worthwhile for the average household. It was estimated in 2003 that only around 22 packages were delivered annually to the average household in the United Kingdom (Foley *et al*, 2003).

It is likely that, for the foreseeable future, CDPs strategically located in or around retail outlets, transport terminals and petrol stations offer the best prospects of commercial viability. They appear to strike a reasonable balance between the conflicting demands of customer convenience, delivery efficiency and security. They can also integrate flows of B2C and B2B orders to achieve an adequate level of throughput.

ENVIRONMENTAL IMPACT OF ONLINE RETAIL LOGISTICS

Concerns have been expressed that online retailing is likely to generate more transport and impose a heavier burden on the environment than store-based retailing (Hesse, 2002). Some e-tailers, on the other hand, now advertise their service as being good for the environment. The British online grocer Ocado, for example, contends that each of its vans 'takes 15 cars off the road' (*London Evening Standard*, 20 June 2007).

Limited empirical data are available to test these conflicting claims, though much does suggest that, under certain circumstances, online retailing can be less damaging to the environment. Matthews *et al* (2001), compared the externalities associated with the distribution of books through a conventional retail channel and from an online bookseller and came to the conclusion that the latter was less environmentally damaging. According to their calculations, which included 'trucking, air freight, production, packaging and passenger trips', energy consumption, air pollution, greenhouse gas emissions and the quantity of hazardous waste were, respectively, 16, 36, 9 and 23 per cent lower in the case of online retailing. Following a review of nine European attempts to model the impact of online grocery retailing on traffic levels, Cairns (2005) concluded that:

> If delivery vehicles directly substitute for car trips, the kilometres saved per shopping load are likely to be substantial – with reductions in the order of 70 per cent or more. Even with very stringent operating constraints or very low levels of customer demand, reductions of 50 per cent or more are predicted.

She nevertheless acknowledges that the use of grocery home services 'by people who do not currently drive for food shopping, and increases in car use for other purposes, could counterbalance the travel reductions suggested by the models' (p 82). Claims that online retailing is intrinsically 'greener' than conventional retailing appear premature, therefore, and require much more research. Edwards *et al* (2008) examine the methodological issues that have to be resolved when comparing the environmental impact of the two modes of retailing on a consistent basis.

CONCLUSIONS

Despite the collapse of the dot com bubble, online retailing has been enjoying healthy growth in recent years and this is predicted to continue. The future rate of growth will partly depend on the quality and efficiency of the supporting system of order fulfilment. After a shaky start, many e-tailers have established effective logistical systems and built up customer confidence in the delivery operation. This has been most easily achieved in the non-food sector, where well-developed home delivery systems already existed and, in essence, only the ordering medium changed. E-grocery logistics has presented more formidable challenges. In retrospect, the initial rush to build dedicated pick centres appears reckless. Store-based fulfilment offers a surer path to market growth and profitability, though doubts remain about its longer-term sustainability if online grocery sales continue to grow at their current rate. The more successful 'bricks and clicks' retailers may eventually have to invest in new facilities to accommodate future growth. As consumers' commitment to home shopping strengthens they too are likely to start investing in home reception facilities, partly to liberate themselves from the need to 'stay in' for deliveries. Online retailers may also promote a switch to unattended delivery by passing on some of the resulting transport cost savings in lower delivery charges. This trend could be further reinforced by local authorities keen to constrain the growth in van traffic in urban areas and have more deliveries made during the night on uncongested roads. Much more research is required, however, on the relative environmental impact of the various forms of e-fulfilment reviewed in this chapter.

References

Ashworth, C, Schmidt, R, Pioch, E and Hallsworth, A (2006) Web-weaving: an approach to sustainable marketing, *International Journal of Retail & Distribution Management*, **34**, (6), pp 497–511

CACI (2000) *Who's Buying Online?*, CACI Information Solutions, London

Cairns, S (2005) Delivering supermarket shopping: more or less traffic? *Transport Reviews*, **25**, (1), pp 51–84

Department of Trade & Industry (DTI) (2001) @ Your Home, New markets for customer service and delivery, Retail Logistics Task Force, Foresight, London

Doherty, N and Ellis-Chadwick, F E (2006) New perspectives in internet retailing: a review and strategic critique of the field, *International Journal of Retail & Distribution Management*, **34**, (4/5), pp 411–28

Edwards, J B, McKinnon, A C and Cullinane, S (2008) Carbon auditing online versus conventional retail supply chains: issues associated with picking, packing and delivering a robust methodology, Proceedings of the 2008 Euroma Conference, Groningen

Ellis-Chadwick, F, Doherty, N and Hast, C (2002) Signs of change? A longitudinal study of internet adoption in the UK retail sector, *Journal of Retailing and Consumer Services*, **9**, (2), pp 71–80

Feinberg, R, Kadam, R, Hokama, L and Kim, I (2002) The state of electronic customer relationship management in retailing, *International Journal of Retail & Distribution Management*, **30**, (10), pp 470–81

Foley, P, Alfonso, X, Brown, K, Palmer, A, Lynch, D and Jackson, M (2003) *The Home Delivery Sector in the UK 1995 to 2010*, De Montfort University / Freight Transport Association, Leicester

Fraunhofer Institute (2002) *Consumer Direct Logistics*, ECR-Europe, Brussels

Ganesh, J (2004) Managing customer preferences in a multi-channel environment using web services, *International Journal of Retail & Distribution Management*, **32**, (3), pp 140–46

Hackney, R, Grant, K and Birtwistle, G (2006) The UK grocery business: towards a sustainable model for virtual markets, *International Journal of Retail & Distribution Management*, **34**, (4/5), pp 354–68

Hesse, M (2002) Shipping news: the implications of electronic commerce for logistics and freight, *Transport Resources Conservation and Recycling*, **36**, (3), pp 211–40

IMRG (2006) E-tail delivery cost benefit analysis (www.imrg.org)

Jones, D (2001) Tesco.com: delivering home shopping, *ECR Journal*, **1**, (1), pp 37–43

Laseter, T, Houston, P, Ching, A, Byrne, S, Turner, M and Devendran, A (2000) The last mile to nowhere, *Strategy & Business*, (20), September

Lavin, M (2002) Christmas on the web: 1998 v 1999, *Journal of Retailing and Consumer Services*, **9**, (2), pp 87–96

Mandeville, L (1995) *Prospects for Home Shopping in Europe*, FT Management Report, Pearson, London

Marciniak, R and Bruce, M (2004) Identification of UK fashion retailer use of websites, *International Journal of Retail & Distribution Management*, **32**, (8), pp 386–93

Matthews, H, Hendrickson, C and Soh, D L (2001) Environmental and economic effects of e-commerce: a study of book publishing and retail logistics, *Transportation Research Record*, **1763**, pp 6–12

McClellan, J (2003) Sweet smell of success, *Guardian*, 4 September

McKinnon, A C and Tallam, D (2003) Unattended delivery to the home: an assessment of the security implications, *International Journal of Retail & Distribution Management*, **31**, (1), pp 30–41

McLeod, F, Cherrett, T and Song, L (2006) Transport impacts of local collection/delivery points, *International Journal of Logistics: Research and Applications*, **9**, (3), pp 307–17

Mees, M D (2000) The place of the food industry in the global e-commerce universe: Ahold's experience, paper presented to the CIES conference on Supply Chain for E-commerce and Home Delivery in the Food Industry, Berlin

Metapack (1999) *Be-ful-filled*, Metapack, London

Morganosky, M A and Cude, B J (2002) Consumer demand for online food retailing: is it really a supply side issue?, *International Journal of Retail & Distribution Management*, **30**, (10), pp 451–8

Nairn, G (2003) Not many happy returns, *Financial Times*, 5 February

Nockold, C (2001) Identifying the real costs of home delivery, *Logistics & Transport Focus*, **3**, (10), pp 70–71

Ody, P (1998) Non-store retailing, in (ed) J Fernie, *The Future for UK Retailing*, FT Retail and Consumer, London

Oldhager, J (2003) *Strategic positioning of the order penetration point*, International Journal of Production Economics, **83** (3) pp 319–29

Planet Retail (2004) Global grocery e-commerce trends, Press Release, 1 November

Punakivi, M and Tanskanen, K (2002) Increasing the cost efficiency of e-fulfilment using shared reception boxes, *International Journal of Retail & Distribution Management*, **30**, (10), pp 498–507

Reynolds, J (2001) The new etail landscape: the view from the beach, *European Retail Digest*, **30**, pp 6–8

Reynolds, J (2002) E-tail marketing, in (ed) P J McGoldrick, *Retail Marketing*, 2nd edn, McGraw-Hill, London

Ring, L J and Tigert, D J (2001) Viewpoint: the decline and fall of internet grocery retailers, *International Journal of Retail & Distribution Management*, **29**, (6), pp 266–73

Rowlands, P (2001) Why access is the key, *Elogistics Magazine*, **15**, Nov/Dec

Rowlands, P (2006) Unattended delivery solutions – finally picking up? *Efulfilment Magazine*, Spring

Rowlands, P (2007) Delivering to people who aren't at home – how you can deal with it, *Efulfilment Magazine*, Spring

Siddiqui, N, O'Malley, A, McColl, J C and Birtwistle, G (2003) Retailer and consumer perceptions of online fashion retailers: website design issues, *Journal of Fashion Marketing and Management*, **7**, (4), pp 345–55

Tanskanen, K, Yryola, M and Holmstron, J (2002) The way to profitable internet grocery retailing – six lessons learned, *International Journal of Retail & Distribution Management*, **30**, (4), pp 169–78

Verdict Research (2000) *Electronic Shopping, UK*, Verdict Research Consulting, London

Verdict Research (2004) *Verdict on Home Delivery and Fulfilment*, Verdict Research Consulting, London

Verdict Research (2008) No sign of an e-tail slowdown, Press Release, April 16

Weltevreden, J W J (2008) B2C e-commerce logistics: the rise of collection and delivery points in the Netherlands, *International Journal of Retail & Distribution Management*, **36**, (8), pp 638–60

Wilson-Jeanselme, M (2001) Grocery retailing on the internet: the leaking bucket theory, *European Retail Digest*, **30**, (9), pp 9–12

Wilson-Jeanselme, M and Reynolds, J (2006) Understanding shoppers' expectations of online grocery retailing, *International Journal of Retail & Distribution Management*, **34**, (7), pp 529–40

Xing, Y and Grant, D (2006) Developing a framework for measuring physical distribution service quality of multi-channel and 'pure player' internet retailers, *International Journal of Retail & Distribution Management*, **34**, (4/5), pp 278–89

11

RFID: transforming technology?

Leigh Sparks

Recent decades have witnessed a transformation of the retail landscape (Dawson, 2000; 2001). The way in which retailers manage their supply chains has been altered fundamentally (Fernie and Sparks, 1998, 2004; Sparks, 1998). The nature and extent of these supply chains have also changed. Retailer activity has become more global in its scope. Logistics and other activities have to be managed over greater distances than ever before. The nature of retail competition itself has changed, with an increase in business range and concentration. From being a local activity, retailing for some companies has progressed through the national level, to an international and in certain cases a global scale.

As retailers grow and seek to enhance their activities and reduce costs, they search for the most appropriate management methods, tools and activities. For some, an almost virtual organization has evolved with outsourcing being its prime activity (eg Benetton, Tommy Hilfiger). Some elements of the business, for example supply or production, can be readily outsourced (eg Tesco's distribution centres), whereas some activities remain internal (eg Tesco's Clubcard data). In either case closer relations amongst a network of contractors becomes essential. The nature of these retailer relationships varies. Some are more collaborative or associative than transaction-focused (Dawson and Shaw, 1990). In all cases, however, the need to control costs yet provide requisite service on this scale becomes a key focus of attention. An array of new concepts has therefore been introduced into the management of retail supply chains in an attempt to improve performance. For example Quick Response (QR), Efficient Consumer Response (ECR) and Collaborative Planning, Forecasting and Replenishment (CPFR) have become common techniques. To some extent, these are tools within a wider potential restructuring of supply chains and their effectiveness depends on the quality of those using the tools.

This restructuring takes a number of forms. Some involve relationship changes, others physical infrastructure investment or disinvestment. Strategic issues need consideration, but then so do tactical practices. In essence, all aspects of supply chains are being re-examined and reconsidered. Some changes are small and specific, though with considerable implications, eg GPS tracking systems in vehicles. Others are large and complex with many ramifications, eg the move to stockless distribution. Wholesale re-evaluation of approaches and practices may be required to meet environmental and sustainability challenges. One common aspect of many of the changes being considered and implemented is technology. Technology has been used in supply chains for a considerable time, normally to provide dimensions of control and information. There is no doubt that investment in information and other technologies can deliver huge benefits if applied to the right problems in the right ways and if the organization is structured appropriately.

Since the turn of the century the most talked about technology for supply chains has been Radio Frequency Identification Devices (RFID). RFID has been over-hyped and raised many concerns, but there seems little doubt that it holds some promise for improving key aspects of logistics and supply chain performance. This chapter examines the RFID 'journey' over recent years and considers the current issues over RFID implementation in supply chains. At the heart of the chapter is the implicit concern over whether RFID is, or could be, a transforming technology.

RFID: INITIAL HYPE AND REALITY

The last few years have been filled with claims about RFID as another potentially transforming technology. RFID has become the 'hot topic' in supply chains and retailing. Whilst RFID technology is not new, its entry into business and academic consciousness has been dramatic. Until 2000 there was virtually no wide coverage of RFID in supply chains and retailing. Since then, RFID has become a major topic of discussion. As Figure 11.1 shows, the academic literature increased dramatically between 2002 and 2005 and there was similarly an explosion of general interest in

2004 (which has tailed off somewhat in recent years). Record book publication year was 2006. These general figures mask specific issues, however. It is tempting to 'read' Figure 11.1 as the development of technological hype followed by business reality. Certainly Ngai *et al* (2008) note that the papers they record concentrate on technology and in particular on the cost and performance of the technological components as well as application sectors (of which retail is the most prominent). A similar pattern is seen to some extent in the wider business press, with interest in the subject exponentially developed by Wal-Mart's announcement in 2003 of its experiments and demands on its suppliers. The subsequent reduction in citations seems to link to a move beyond technology and into a broader set of subjects and experimentation. RFID perhaps passed into core business consideration and so received a little less coverage. The same could be argued over the book publication data, with the emergence of 'how to' guides following the books on technology and in turn being supplanted by books on sectors and practices.

RFID remains a controversial subject. There is still concern over how much of what form to implement and the implications for businesses, supply chains and indeed consumers. For these reasons RFID remains an unproven technology. Clearly there are benefits to its introduction, but do the costs outweigh these and, if so, why and in what circumstances? The RFID journey is thus one that remains incomplete.

RFID began its public journey with a degree of hype, claiming to be the 'internet of things' and to cure all supply chain evils. As one of its early proponents states:

> RFID has the potential to become one of retail's truly rare transforming technologies... the business case is compelling... RFID has the ability to reduce labour costs, simplify business procedures, improve inventory control, productivity and turnover, increase sales, reduce shrinkage, and improve customer satisfaction. (LakeWest Group, 2002, pp 1–2)

RFID of course is not a new technology, and neither are the claims about its impact wholly novel, though they do tend to hyperbole (eg '20–20 visibility in the supply chain and 100 per cent availability is just around the corner', *Retail Week*, 14 November 2003, p 25). Transponders have been around for decades. The difference now is the change in their cost, size and capability.

An RFID system typically contains the following components (see http://www.rfidjournal.com for a glossary of terms): a tag or label embedded with a single chip computer and an antenna, and a reader (much like a wireless LAN radio) that communicates with the tag. This basic system structure contains a number of alternative choices for implementation. For example, tags can be passive or active. Passive tags pick up energy from the reader to operate and communicate with the reader. In

(a) Academic papers on RFID

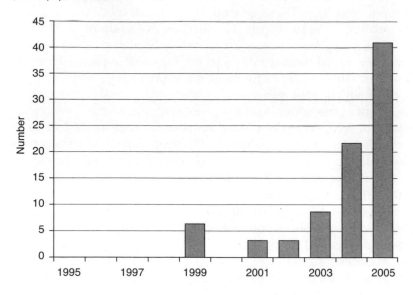

Source: Ngai et al *2008*

(b) Lexis-Nexis citations on RFID and Retail

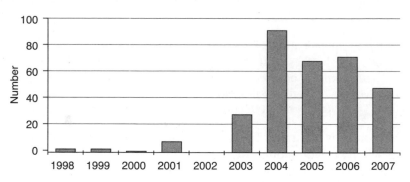

Source: Lexis-Nexis Database

(c) Books on RFID on Amazon

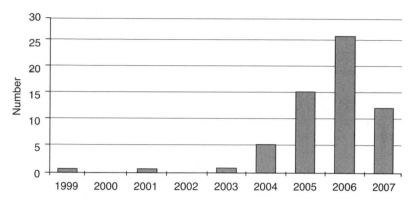

Source: Search on Amazon.co.uk, 7 August 2008
Figure 11.1   RFID literature by date of publication

essence they are simply 'read'. They have no power source and are short read-range, but are cheap and probably last longer. Active tags have an embedded power source that provides for a greater range but reduces tag life and raises costs. Active tags can store a variety of data and can be read and written to. With readers being fixed position or hand-held/movable, tags being able to transmit in a field rather than one direction, and various choices of frequency depending on the range required or the product involved, the scope for flexible systems is apparent (but so also is the potential for confusion).

Tags can be applied at a variety of levels. In the supply chain, they could be applied to every single item produced, as well as to every carton, box, crate or pallet in which the product might be handled. Non-stock items can be as easily tagged as stock items. The tag could be visibly attached to a product (possibly detachable later) or hidden invisibly or even woven into the fabric, eg a sweater or even a bank note. In comparison to bar codes, tags can be read around corners and through materials. This means that a pallet of products or a trolley of groceries could be simultaneously scanned/read as it passes by a reader or through a reader-enabled doorway.

There are also choices to be made in terms of data storage on the tag. Tags can be read-only, thus containing a unique identifier only. Alternatively tags can contain read and write capabilities allowing additional information to be held or added to each time they are read. A tag can be programmed to hold all information about a product as well as the distribution points it passed before it reached the customer. Some systems allow data to be stored on the tag in a portable dynamic database. Others allow data to be edited, added to or locked, which can be valuable in different circumstances. As might be expected given such different possibilities, one of the big issues in RFID has been the agreeing of standards for data. Other questions that need to be resolved include the choice of frequency and the ability to read chips from different countries or even companies.

Table 11.1 provides a way of thinking about RFID functions. It suggests that some of the activities within RFID are basically the replacement of current activities. For example, the RFID tag can act essentially as a 'super bar code'. Advantages derive from this area of application through the ability to do things better. However, RFID also offers the potential to be able to do new things. For example it will be possible to have remote and unattended activities to a greater extent than currently. It will also be possible to have temperature and other regimes checked by reading RFID tags. The ability to do both new things and existing things more efficiently is clearly an attraction to proponents of the technology.

Data considerations flow far beyond the tag type, etc, however. The concept of the 'internet of things' reflects the combination of transparency across the supply chain and the ability of supply chain partners to access the data. As such, databases of items, movements, locations, conditions, etc are required to be developed from RFID. The construction of such databases and their maintenance are not necessarily an easy or straightforward task. Access to the data is of course a strategic question about partnerships and sharing in the supply chain. The potential is

Table 11.1   RFID approaches

Function	Activity	Value
Super bar code	Permits faster and multiple reads of labels without opening containers; Accurate tracking via unique identifier	Faster scanning (productivity); Accurate tracking (reduce shrinkage); Real-time stock location (higher availability, increased sales); ePODs (reduced disputes)
Carry additional information (read/write only)	R/W tags may include sell-by date, etc; Added information on each tag may pose a security risk	Permits some high speed checking locally (quantity per pallet etc); Decentralized information (to be balanced against security risk)
Perform new tasks (active tags only)	Maintain records of events (eg when opened, temperature regime); Locate products by tags associated to beacon	E-seals when filling containers, provide accurate shipping manifest for customs (secure shipping lanes); Telematics related benefits

Source: adapted from http://www.ilt2003.co.uk/g/logos/MurrayBrabender_files/frame.htm, downloaded 10 November 2003

present for a transformation of approach, but realizing this potential is a different thing.

Many areas of benefit therefore have been claimed to be available through the introduction of RFID, including:

- Reduced out-of-stocks and improved shelf management – real-time product movement information can be captured using RFID and so replenishment will be more efficient, in-store product misplacement will be identified and inventory movement at warehouse and store will be more effective.
- Reduced shrinkage/fraud – RFID provides embedded tracking capabilities, which means that inappropriate product movement will be more readily identified.
- Improved productivity and streamlined processes – the abilities of RFID in terms of remote or unattended scanning, plus the speed at which this is achieved (eg a mixed pallet of goods) mean that there is the potential to reduce labour costs. Time and accuracy benefits are generated.
- Enhanced point-of-sale checkout efficiency – these time and accuracy benefits apply equally to the store checkout.

Some of the potential benefits of RFID are therefore fairly clear. RFID claims the ability to have total visibility at the item level throughout the supply chain and to achieve this visibility with more speed, greater accuracy and fewer people than was ever thought possible. This has obviously attracted considerable attention and RFID has been being proposed for many areas of the supply chain and the retail store. Retailers as a consequence began to explore the possibilities of the technology through various trials (see Jones *et al* 2004, 2005a, 2005b; LakeWest Group and MeadWestvaco Intelligent Systems, 2003; www.rfidjournal.com, various issues; Singh *et al*, 2008; Wilding and Delgado, 2004) as for example:

- Benetton announced its intention to embed RFID tags into all of the garments in one of its lines to track items arriving at the back of store.
- Prada tagged all of its merchandise in its New York Epicenter store so store staff could access a database on all stock items available without having to check the back room. RFID tags have also been embedded in their customer loyalty cards, allowing dynamic accessorizing in the changing room amongst other personal features.
- Tesco has used RFID technology and a security camera to detect motion on razor blades in store in a smart shelf scheme run with Gillette.
- Wal-Mart asked its top 100 suppliers to put RFID tags carrying Electronic Product Codes on pallets and cases by the start of 2005.
- Marks & Spencer Food trialled a closed-loop plastic tray/dolly rewritable RFID operation to improve lead time and reduce shrinkage.

- Gap used item-level tracking of denim apparel to improve supply chain and in-store visibility.
- Figleaves.com used RFID to rationalize the picking and shipping of products so avoiding the need to expand its facilities.

More detailed information on two of the early experiments and trials in the United Kingdom are presented in Boxes 11.1 and 11.2. These provide summaries of the initial experiments that Marks & Spencer and Sainsbury carried out. They raise some of the potential benefits and issues in RFID implementation and point to some of the potential problems. Both retailers now use RFID in parts of their supply chains and 'intelligent labels' (RFID-enabled labels) can be readily seen on Marks & Spencer non-food products such as suits.

Box 11.1 RFID and Marks & Spencer

Marks & Spencer pilots RFID (2003/4)

Marks & Spencer has been looking at RFID for some time. It has had an experimental scheme in food distribution that is now ready to roll out. Marks & Spencer has also recently trialled RFID tracking tags in clothes at one of its UK stores.

The small scale (one store, four week) pilot is basically a technology test aimed at stock accuracy, so as to lower safety stock and warehouse/store contact with the merchandise. Inaccuracies from incorrect delivery, damage and other merchandise movement compound to create a large problem at store level. As a result forecasts are driven by deduced not real stock. Manual stock counts are needed to remedy this, at some cost. Ideally the goal would be to keep a minimum of stock, maintained on a real-time basis. But stock is held in store and at the warehouse due to mistrust of forecast information. Suppliers also hold safety stock. Reducing the stock held and the need for handling and counting would be a considerable benefit.

The tags are contained within throwaway paper labels called 'Intelligent labels' attached to, but not embedded in, a selection of men's suits, shirts and ties. The passive tags hold the number unique to each garment. The information associated with this number is held on Marks & Spencer's secure database and relates only to that product or garment's details, for example the size, style and colour. The intelligent label is attached to the garment alongside the pricing label and is designed to be cut off and thrown away after purchase. For items such as shirts, which are pre-packed, the tag is stuck onto the transparent shirt bag.

Two scanners are used for the tags. A portal installed at the distribution centre and the loading bay of the store allows rails of hanging garments and trolleys containing packaged garments to be pushed through and read at speed. A mobile scanner in a shopping trolley that has a hand-held reader will scan several garments at the same time out on the shop floor. This is pioneering, but hardly a satisfactory long-term solution, given its size, and Marks & Spencer has expressed some frustration at the lack of readiness of technology in this area.

Given high profile media interest in consumer privacy issues, Marks & Spencer contacted one of the leading consumer advocacy groups before the trial (CASPIAN; see www.nocards.com) to discuss privacy implications. It is understood that it took some of the concerns into account. The pilot focuses on only the store operational benefits of RFID and not on any potential links to consumers.

Marks & Spencer emphasizes that many of the figures for potential savings appear to be highly speculative and that the costs and benefits have yet to be fully understood. There may also be differential aims and costs/benefits depending on product group. Marks & Spencer believes that the business case for tagging food items is based more on efficiency and speed of handling with some degree of accuracy (hence tray-level tagging), whereas the clothing business case is primarily built on accuracy (hence item-level tagging) with some efficiency benefits. In the long run the company may benefit from its ability to run RFID within a closed-loop environment, given its retailer-brand policy. Implementation issues may therefore be somewhat reduced.

Source: Adapted from material at www.amrresearch.com, http://www. spychips.com/, www.silicon.com downloaded on 1 December 2003, Ft.com 25 November 2003 and Retail Week, 14 November 2003, p 26

These experiments and testing show that there is a belief and willingness to see RFID implemented in the supply chain, but that it may not be as simple or straightforward as first envisaged. From these early experiments there are a number of ways of thinking about the problems of implementing RFID (Table 11.2). Whilst RFID has been used in some business sectors for some time, the extension to the retail supply chain presents new problems. These are due to the scale of the retail supply chain (one Woolworth's distribution centre for example has over 100,000 dollies and cages, before even item-level scale is considered) and the environmental characteristics under which the systems will have to operate. As such there are always

Box 11.2   RFID and Sainsbury

The value of RFID for the retailer: the Sainsbury's case (2002/3)

Sainsbury's RFID trial was predicated on a basis of an information-enriched supply chain. The trial focused initially on tracking chilled goods with one supplier, a single depot and a single store, before it was widened to other goods in the line going to the store. The RFID tags were applied to recyclable plastic crates. The tags were programmed with:

- the description and quality of the product in the crate;
- the use-by dates of these products;
- the crate's own ID number.

Programming was achieved at the end of the production line. Goods were then read at the depot's goods receipt area and on delivery to the store.

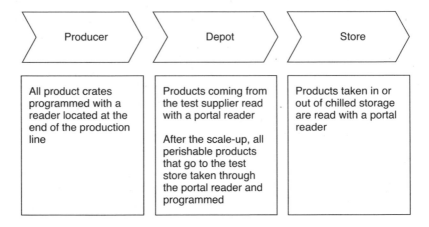

Figure 11.2   The Sainsbury process

Benefits achievable from a full-scale implementation were estimated to be £8.5 million per annum based mainly on retail store replenishment productivity, reduction of stock loss and on removal of checking stock and codes. Payback for the system was estimated to be between two to three years. These benefits were estimated without any supplier participation, which could be considerable if item stock-outs are minimized.

Source: adapted from Karkkainen, 2003, pp 532–4

Table 11.2 Problems in RFID implementation

Area	Problem	Description
Technology	Size and data storage	Functionality comes at a cost in terms of money and size. Smaller tags with increased data capacity at a lower cost are needed
	Scanning accuracy	When several items are read closely in conjunction, problems of interference arise; Tags can be faulty at production causing misreads; Readers may be insufficiently accurate
	Infrastructure costs	Readers are not yet cheap enough and will undoubtedly also develop in capabilities, causing upgrade issues
Costs	Cost vs functionality	The current cost to manufacture even the basic tags may be prohibitive; When functionality is additional then costs rise
Standardization	Product identification	All points along the distribution channel need to recognize that standardization is the key to the technology. Without standardization a global system will not work. Some steps have been made in this direction
	Manufacture and equipment standards	Standardization amongst manufacturers to avoid bespoke systems is also needed
Others	Consumer privacy	Considerable adverse reaction to the trials has been generated (see www.spychips.com), with consumer concern about personal data tracking and privacy intrusion at the forefront
	Operations and maintenance	If tags are to be reused then data management becomes an even bigger issue
	Intelligent use of data	The data collected have major impacts on people and processes. RFID is not simply a replacement technology and thus a creative vision of new processes and the skills of the people involved is needed

Source: adapted from LakeWest Group, 2002; various issues at www.rfidjournal.com

going to be technological problems as the technology is used in new situations and new generations of technology are developed. Given the scope of the possible RFID implementation in the retail supply chain, there are also always going to be issues of costs. Whilst the cost of basic tags has fallen, their potential sheer ubiquity of use in a retailer demands a huge volume. Costs therefore have to be minimal. At the same time, as this is a supply chain issue, there is also concern over the cost of implementation and compliance. To what extent can the costs and benefits of the technology be shared amongst retailers, suppliers and logistics services providers?

Quite a lot of the problems posed in Table 11.2 can be put down to the timing of technology adoption. In any innovation there are obviously leaders and laggards. In this case, as the claims for RFID are so broad, there are leaders and laggards in aspects of implementation ranging from the type of tag, the standards to be used, components of the supply chain to be tested and so on. Some of the issues may be termed 'teething troubles'; other issues may force a fundamental rethink about the whole transforming nature of the technology. Despite the bold claims of its proponents, and a widespread belief that it is a question of 'when not if', a totally transparent global supply chain at the item level still seems some way off. More likely are small-scale closed-loop developments focused on particular supply chains or problem areas.

An example of this development is provided in Box 11.3, which summarizes aspects of the introduction of Wal-Mart's RFID initiatives. From effectively a dictat in 2003, there has been a gradual recognition that a universal imposition of RFID could cause as many problems as it solves.

Box 11.3   RFID and Wal-Mart

Wal-Mart and RFID

In April 2003, Wal-Mart announced an RFID pilot test on cases and pallets in 100 stores in the Texas market, going live in January 2005. This mandate to its leading suppliers was expected to be the trigger that kick-started the RFID industry in retailing globally.

The expectation and the hype were palpable. Wal-Mart claimed the pilot would:

> Help us know where inventory is all the time. We'll see better tracking and movement of inventory, faster receiving and shipping, improved quality inspection, fewer out-of-stock items resulting in improved shopper satisfaction, greater predictability in product demand and better value for the shopper as efficiencies occur.

Whilst there is no doubt there are benefits to be had in RFID, Wal-Mart has moved much more cautiously than its announcements have initially suggested. RFID did made a difference in the test situation: out-of-stocks were reduced, test stores outperformed control stores and tagged items outperformed non-tagged items within test stores. However, problems of cost, technology capability, actual extractions of benefits and supplier acceptability, reflect both teething problems and innovation reality. Whilst roll-out has occurred to more stores and more distribution centres, initial claims of a reinvention of the supply chain have not been realized.

Wal-Mart has in some cases decided that the benefits are best realized in-store and so has focused on in-store availability and ensuring product is where it should be in-store. Accuracy and time-liness are a key focus. One benefit of this being strongly pursued is that of sustainability. If RFID improves the in-store stock position this will reduce both trips in the supply system and for customers.

One of the ironies in Wal-Mart's situation may be that its distribution centres were always fairly well-run, meaning that in operational terms RFID adds little to the distribution centre efficiency. However, benefits at store level may be more significant, hence the new focus, and these benefits may be sufficient to help convince suppliers that they gain as well as Wal-Mart. However, suppliers have to be geared up to analyse and to respond to the enhanced data. Those that have embraced the possibilities have gained considerably.

In late 2007 Wal-Mart announced three new initiatives as a change in focus to its examination of RFID. These were:

1. a focus on RFID at Sam's Club at distribution centre and store level;
2. a link to promotional activity through tagging weekly product promotions at the case and pallet level;
3. a focus on tagging all products in a specific category.

The approach being adopted is to use RFID to focus on improving specific business practices rather than the previously general business roll-out. Again this should show specific benefits more clearly, both for Wal-Mart and suppliers.

Sources: Durall, 2007; Gaudin, 2008; Hardgrave et al, 2007; O'Connor, 2007; Weier, 2007, 2008

Thus Wal-Mart has stepped back from its initial position, not all suppliers are compliant and new pilots and experiments/testing are being run, focusing on a more closed-loop system and targeting particular areas of concern. For some suppliers that have become compliant in a meaningful way and have extracted data and information, there have been benefits and they are well set up for the future. Others have become compliant in part in an almost meaningless fashion, adopting 'slap and ship' RFID labelling to meet the demands. Benefits here seem minimized for the suppliers. They, like those who have not adopted any RFID processes, may struggle if the latest Wal-Mart roll-out plans become reality, though Wal-Mart's proposal to fine non-compliance has yet to be implemented and it is unclear what the real effect might be. Wal-Mart has tried to be an RFID pioneer, but even it has realized the complications of implementing the technology generally. Despite seemingly clear benefits (eg Hardgrave *et al*, 2007) the implementation is not straightforward.

Two particular problems deserve further consideration. First, and probably unexpectedly, there has been a considerable and voluble consumer backlash against RFID technology on the grounds of privacy invasion. Tags can be placed in individual items and can continue to work after a consumer has purchased the product. Individual items could be associated with individual consumers and a very detailed picture of purchase and behaviour can be drawn up. Consumer advocates have been vocal in their criticism (see www.spychips.com) and as a result, some of the early trials (eg Prada, Benetton) have been halted. Whilst RFID may have begun as a supply chain initiative, the potential for consumer identification is clear, whether done deliberately or accidentally. Any allegation of use of hidden RFID tags to spy on consumers provokes bad publicity for retailers, whatever the real situation. Marks & Spencer for example seems to have engaged with the opponents and allayed some fears through the detachability of labels.

Second, whilst a lot of thought has been given to the technology itself, not much seems to have been devoted to the handling of the data the systems could generate and the use of these data. Rewriting the supply chain using RFID is a change management project writ large. As such there is need for much greater concern over how the data are to be stored and analysed and how their use will need to focus on aspects of process and people change. The implications are considerable.

The technology itself is advancing rapidly and needs therefore to be monitored carefully. Capital costs are not going to be low, however, despite the fall in prices in tags. People, processes and technology will be affected by any implementation, particularly if the data from the systems can be applied appropriately. Given that a total supply chain solution is some way off, it is likely that retailers are going to have to run several types of systems for some time, adding further to the cost issues (ATKearney, 2003). The question for retailers is thus where best and in what form is RFID appropriately applied for the most benefit?

RFID: MORE MEASURED CONSIDERATION?

Since the initial hype, there have been many experiments and attempts to examine RFID implementation in more detail. In recent years there has been the emergence of findings from a number of academic research projects into actual views of retail RFID implementation. It is worthwhile considering a selection of these here.

Hingley *et al* (2007) outline the main benefits and problems of RFID in retail supply chains. They focus on the potential for cheaper, more visible, higher availability supply chains providing ancillary benefits in customer service and traceability. Against that they set the costs of implementation and some technical limitations. Their qualitative research focused on suppliers in the grocery sector in the United Kingdom. They found that four main issues arose:

1. The problems of sharing or allocating the costs and benefits of implementation.
2. Related to the first issue, the equity of the benefits from the development.
3. The interviewees were concerned about the difficulties of RFID implementation on some products such as loose produce and liquids, but did accept shelf-life could be enhanced by RFID.
4. It was imperative that accuracy in the systems continued to increase.

For Hingley *et al* (2007) the key message was that RFID success was dependent on collaboration and sharing in the supply chain, or else it was simply a further way to count stock.

Moon and Ngai (2008) reported on their research with five Hong Kong fashion firms focused on retailing, though some had manufacturing as well. They found that the potential for RFID was well recognized and viewed positively. The firms saw applications in improving availability, customer relationship management, marketing and promotion, and in inventory management. Difficulties were seen in the cost of implementation, dangers of incompatibilities across technologies and the potentially problematic views of staff.

Boeck and Wamba (2008) examined 10 companies in one supply chain (soft drinks) through a participant-observation research method. Their initial perception was that RFID had the potential to increase adversarial positions in the supply chain. Their study revealed a number of issues. First, it was clear that there are differential benefits across supply chains but that these are maximized by collaboration and sound supply chain and RFID implementation design. Second, there is a tendency to push the costs and actions of tagging up the supply chain. In benefit terms this could be advantageous, but the costs and benefits needed to be debated and shared. Third, this focused attention on the efficiency and effectiveness of inter-organizational processes and the role of RFID as a supply chain management inter-organizational system. RFID could not compensate for a lack of trust or supply chain orientation or else it became simply another technology underachieving its potential. As in many situations the quality of the supply chain orientation and involvement is seen as critical.

These three academic studies provide some detail on the generally accepted views of the benefits and drawbacks of RFID, about which there are many reports (eg Bhattacharya *et al*, 2007; Hardgrave and Miller, 2006; Jones *et al*, 2004, 2005a, 2005b; Koh *et al*, 2006). They continue the process outlined by Reyes and Jaska (2007). First, using the framework of Hardgrave and Miller (2006), Reyes and Jaska attempt to dispel some of the myths around RFID. These are shown in Table 11.3. From this they go on to identify an eight-step process in RFID implementation (Table 11.4). It is obviously the case that some companies have moved down this implementation plan further than others. Many are now beyond the implementation stage and are seeing benefits from their investment and initiatives. Others, however, have not yet taken the steps needed. It would seem that RFID is not the big all-encompassing supply solution (yet) but that smaller focused projects are reaping rewards.

CONCLUSIONS

The claim that a technology will transform a business is too easily made. There have been many such false dawns in retailing and retail supply systems. The technology considered here, RFID, is the latest in a long line of such potential transformations. Yet, in the end, companies still have to move boxes from a point of production to some point of consumption. The focus has to be on doing this in the most effective and efficient way. Here, the technology does have things to offer. By focusing on the detailed applications (tagging merchandise-ready units, for example) costs can be driven out of the system, control can be improved and the detailed operations of the supply chain can be enhanced. The emphasis in the next few years may well be on smaller scale, focused applications with detailed exploration of the benefits to partners. Is this a transformation? Probably not. But is it important to retailers? Definitely. Is it necessary for a wider RFID enabled supply chain? Absolutely.

Table 11.3 Understanding the RFID myths

Myth	Reality
#1: RFID is new – or RFID technology is mature and stable	Early use of RFID has existed since World War II; however, the use of passive tags in supply chain is new
#2: RFID can be used to continuously track people/objects wherever they go – anywhere	Continuous tracking would require millions of readers and antennae located in a very close proximity to produce the necessary overlapping electromagnetic fields – is not economically justified
#3: People can drive down the street and read RFID tags inside your home, thus knowing everything about you and your stuff	The read range for passive UHF RFID is about 10–30 feet, which means that a person would have to be extremely close to read the tags
#4: RFID tags contain information about everything, including sensitive personal information	RFID tags have limited storage and cannot hold all the information as suggested
#5: RFID is generating millions of terabytes of data	Yes, RFID will produce more data. However, the challenge is not how to store it, but rather how to mine it for business value
#6: You must have 100 per cent reads at 100 per cent of the read points for RFID to be useful	In theory, yes. But not practical. There are many things that could cause a missed read
#7: Major retailers have mandated that all suppliers tag all products from all stores	Currently only a small group of suppliers is tagging a small group of products going to a small group of stores
#8: RFID is costing the average Wal-Mart vendor $23 million annually	Scope of implementation, technology prices declining, and actual deployment of RFID not as difficult as expected are factors that contributed to vendors spending much less than anticipated
#9: RFID is the panacea for creating the perfect supply chain	Yes, RFID can improve supply chain performance – either in the efficiency or effectiveness of process improvements. However, not the panacea for creating the perfect supply chain
#10: RFID is replacing the bar code	While RFID does offer several advantages over bar codes, it is more likely to be a complementary technology in the present and near future. But since RFID is a data carrier, it is possible it will replace bar code at some point

Source: Hardgrave and Miller, 2006 in Reyes and Jaska, 2007

Table 11.4 Guidelines for implementation

Step in implementation	Description
Understand what RFID can and cannot do	Getting past the myths
Analysis of present system	Analyse the processes and outcomes of the present system
Build an ROI business case	Analysis of what potential benefits could be reached with RFID
Requirements analysis	Analyse the requirements and how RFID will be implemented
Prototype testing	Test the proposed RFID system
Implementation	Implement the RFID system
Monitor	Monitor the RFID system to make sure that it meets expectations
Continuous improvement	Look for improvements to processes and technology changes

Source: Reyes and Jaska, 2007

References

ATKearney (2003) Meeting the Retail RFID Mandate, November 2003, downloaded from http://www.atkearney.com/shared_res/pdf/Retail_RFID_S.pdf on 1 December 2003

Bhattacharya, M, Chu, C-H and Mullen, T (2007) RFID implementation in retail industry: current status, issues and challenges, paper presented to the Decision Science Institute Conference, Phoenix, available for download at http://tmullen.ist.psu.edu/pubs/dsi_draft_2007.pdf, accessed 1 August 2008

Boeck, H and Wamba, S F (2008) RFID and buyer–seller relationships in the retail supply chain, *International Journal of Retail & Distribution Management*, **36**, pp 433–60

Dawson, J A (2000) Retailing at century end; competing in volatile markets, *Industrial Marketing Management*, **29**, pp 37–44

Dawson, J A (2001) Is there a new commerce in Europe? *International Review of Retail and Distribution Management*, **11**, pp 287–99

Dawson, J A and Shaw, S (1990) The changing character of retailer–supplier relationships, in (ed) J Fernie, *Retail Distribution Management*, Kogan Page, London

Durall, M (2007) Wal-Mart's faltering RFID initiative ,downloaded from http://www.baselinemag.com on 1 August 2008

Fernie, J and Sparks, L (eds) (1998) *Logistics and Retail Management*, Kogan Page, London

Fernie, J and Sparks, L (eds) (2004) *Logistics and Retail Management*, 2nd edn, Kogan Page, London

Gaudin, S (2008) Some suppliers gain from failed Wal-Mart RFID edict, downloaded from www.computerwolrd.com on 1 August 2008

Hardgrave, B C and Miller, R (2006) The myths and realities of RFID, paper available for download at http://itri.uark.edu, accessed 1 August 2008

Hardgrave, B C, Waller, M and Miller, R (2007) Does RFID reduce out-of-stocks?, paper available for download at http://itri.uark.edu, accessed 1 August 2008

Hingley, M, Taylor, S and Ellis, C (2007) Radio frequency identification tagging, *International Journal of Retail & Distribution Management*, **35**, pp 803–20

Jones, P, Clarke-Hill, C, Shears, P, Comfort, D and Hillier, D (2004) Radio frequency identification in the UK: opportunities and challenges, *International Journal of Retail & Distribution Management*, **32**, pp 164–71

Jones, P, Clarke-Hill, C, Comfort, D, Hillier, D and Shears, P (2005a) Radio frequency identification and food retailing in the UK, *British Food Journal*, **107**, pp 356–60

Jones, P, Clarke-Hill, C, Hillier, D and Comfort, D (2005b) The benefits, challenges and impacts of radio frequency identification (RFID) for retailers in the UK, *Marketing Intelligence and Planning*, **23**, pp 395–402

Karkkainen, M (2003) *Increasing efficiency in the supply chain for short life goods using RFID tagging*, International Journal of Retail and Distribution Management, **31**, 10, 529–36.

Koh, C E, Kim, H J and Kim, E Y (2006) The impact of RFID on retail industry: issues and critical success factors, *Journal of Shopping Center Research*, **13**, (1), pp 101–17

LakeWest Group (2002) RFID: retail's new transforming technology, June, downloaded from http://www.lakewest.com/PDFdocs/RFID%20Retails%20New%20Transforming%20Technology_June%202002.PDF on 1 December 2003

LakeWest Group and MeadWestvaco Intelligent Systems (2003) RFID in retail: the future is now, June, downloaded from http://www.lakewest.com/PDFdocs/RFID%20In%20Retail%20The%20Future%20Is%20Now_June%202003.pdf on 1 December 2003

Moon, K L and Ngai, E W T (2008) The adoption of RFID in fashion retailing: a business value-added framework, *Industrial Management and Data Systems*, **108**, pp 596–612

Ngai, E W T, Moon, K K L, Riggins, F J and Yi, C Y (2008) RFID research: an academic literature review (1995–2005) and future research directions, *International Journal of Production Economics*, **112**, pp 510–20

O'Connor, M C (2007) Wal-Mart, Sam's Club push RFID further along, *RFID Journal*, 5 October, downloaded from http://www.rfidJournal. com/article/articleprint/3666/-1/1

Reyes, P M and Jaska, P (2007) Is RFID right for your organization or application? *Management Research News*, **30**, pp 570–80

Singh, S P, McCartney, M, Singh, J and Clarke, R (2008) RFID research and testing for packages of apparel, consumer goods and fresh produce in the retail distribution environment, *Packaging Technology and Science*, **21**, pp 91–102

Sparks, L (1998) The retail logistics transformation, in (eds) J Fernie and L Sparks, *Logistics and Retail Management*, Kogan Page, London

Weier, M H (2007) Wal-Mart rethinks RFID, *Information Week*, 26 March, downloaded from http://www.informationweek.com/story/showArticle. jhtml?articleID=198700170

Weier, M H (2008) Wal-Mart sets deadline for Sam's Club suppliers to use RFID, *Information Week*, 17 January, downloaded from http://www. informationweek.com/story/showArticle.jhtml?articleID=205900237

Wilding, R and Delgado, T (2004) RFID demystified: (a) The story so far, *Logistics and Transport Focus*, April, pp 26–31, (b) Supply-chain applications, *Logistics and Transport Focus*, May, pp 42–48, (c) Company case studies, *Logistics and Transport Focus*, June, pp 32–42

12

The greening of retail logistics

Alan McKinnon and Julia Edwards

INTRODUCTION

Logistical activities are responsible for much of the environmental cost associated with modern retailing. It is hardly surprising therefore that logistics features prominently in the environmental statements of large retailers. Most of these retailers have developed, or are in the process of formulating, environmental strategies. Some have been portraying themselves as 'green' for many years, often on the basis of a few minor cosmetic changes to their business practices. There is now much greater commitment to making retailing genuinely sustainable both in environmental and social terms. This stems partly from a requirement to demonstrate corporate social responsibility (CSR) to investors and other stakeholder groups. It also reflects increased corporate awareness of the gravity of the environmental problems confronting the planet, particularly from global warming. As consumers are becoming more environmentally-conscious, retailers' green credentials are becoming a more important competitive differentiator. Environmental initiatives can generate higher revenues and secure greater customer loyalty. They can also yield cost savings by, for example, cutting energy consumption and packaging waste. By happy coincidence, greening retail operations can represent best business practice both economically and environmentally.

In this chapter we examine the adverse effects of retail logistics operations on the environment and review a series of measures that companies can take to minimize them. The main focus will be on the lower links in the supply chain controlled by larger retailers with a logistics capability.

ENVIRONMENTAL EFFECTS OF RETAIL LOGISTICS

These effects can be divided into six broad categories.

1. Greenhouse gas (GHG) emissions

Numerous gases exert a global warming effect with varying degrees of intensity. Carbon dioxide, produced by the burning of fossil fuels in power generation and vehicles, is the most important GHG emitted by retailers, though heavy users of temperature control equipment also release refrigerant gases which can have a global warming potential thousands of times greater than CO_2.[1] Some large retailers have measured their 'carbon footprints' and disaggregated their CO_2 emissions by activity. Marks & Spencer, for example, has estimated that its logistics operations account for roughly 11 per cent of its total CO_2 emissions (Hill, 2007).

2. Noxious gases

These pollutants, such as nitrogen oxide, sulphur dioxide and particulate matter (PM10), impair local air quality and are responsible for a range of negative effects on human health, vegetation and buildings. Tightening controls on exhaust emissions over the past 20 years, mainly in developed countries, have drastically reduced the release of these pollutants.

3. Noise

This emanates mainly from vehicles and distribution centres. As a result of improvements in vehicle technology and the imposition of tougher regulations on vehicle noise, new trucks today are much quieter than those of 10–15 years ago. In retail logistics, noise abatement not only involves investing in newer vehicles with quieter engines. The sound of refrigeration equipment, the rattling of roll cages inside vehicles and even in-cab radios can cause annoyance. The range of activities performed in and around a retail distribution centre can also disturb local residents, particularly as these premises typically operate on a 24-hour/seven-day cycle.

4. Accidents

The involvement of freight vehicles in traffic accidents is generally considered to be an externality. The costs of personal injury / death, any damage to property and related use of emergency services are borne by the community at large and thus deemed to be environmental costs. Accidents occurring within distribution premises, on the other hand, are treated as an internal cost of the business.

5. Waste

Retail logistics operations generate large quantities of waste, mainly in the form of packaging material, though products that are damaged or life-expired while in the supply chain and have to be rejected can also be considered a type of logistics-related waste. In the past much of this waste went into landfill sites, occupying rural land and creating serious environmental problems (such as the release of methane, a very potent greenhouse gas), or incineration plants that release air pollutants. Today retailers must adhere to strict controls on the recycling and reuse of packaging and other waste.

6. Visual intrusion

Many people dislike the appearance of trucks and warehouses and believe that they reduce the quality of the local environment. Large trucks are often considered out of place and even intimidating in sensitive urban and rural environments, while large warehouse 'sheds' are often criticized for dominating the landscape. It is very difficult, however, to quantify and cost these subjective judgements and so, for this reason, they tend to be excluded from formal environmental assessments.

In this chapter we will focus on ways of reducing the environmental effects of transporting goods through the retail supply chain, though in a later section we also comment on the return of waste packaging and several other environmental issues of relevance to retail logistics.

FRAMEWORK FOR ANALYSING THE ENVIRONMENTAL IMPACT OF RETAIL DELIVERIES

The options for reducing the environmental impact of retail deliveries can be reviewed systematically within the framework shown in Figure 12.1. This framework, which was originally developed for the Green Logistics research project,[2] has been adapted for retail logistics operations. It essentially maps

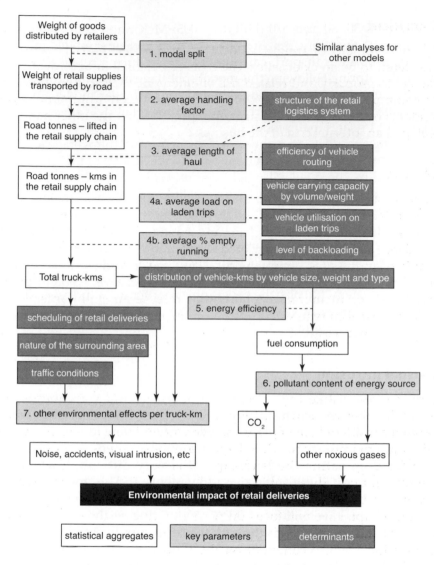

Figure 12.1 Analytical framework
Source: Adapted from McKinnon, 2008

the relationship between the quantity of goods purchased by retailers and the environmental costs of moving them through the supply chain to the final point of sale. This relationship is defined by seven key parameters.

1. *Modal split* is the division of freight traffic between transport modes. The environmental impact of these modes varies enormously. For example, the average grammes of CO_2 emitted per tonne-km for a deep sea container ship, freight train, heavy truck and long haul airfreight are, respectively,

around 14, 30, 80 and 570 (DEFRA, 2005; McKinnon 2007; www.jfhille-brand.com). Switching freight from air or road to cleaner modes, mainly rail or water-borne transport, can significantly reduce a retailer's environmental footprint. Following this modal split stage in the framework, subsequent parameters need to be calibrated for particular modes. As road is invariably the main transport mode used for retail deliveries, the rest of Figure 12.1 relates to this mode.

2. *Average handling factor:* this is a crude measure of the average number of links in a supply chain. It can be applied to the section of the supply chain controlled by the retailer. It might comprise a single link from the distribution centre (DC) to the shop or several links in the case of retailers whose control extends back to the supplier's premises, which channel products through primary consolidation centres (PCCs) upstream of the DC and/or operate an additional tier of regional/local depots downstream of the DC.

3. *Average length of haul:* this is the mean distance that goods are transported on each link in the retail supply chain. It partly reflects the retailer's sourcing strategy, but also the geographical structure of its logistics system and the efficiency of vehicle routing. The conventional view is that by sourcing more products locally, retailers can cut their transport requirements and benefit the environment. As discussed later, however, lifecycle analysis reveals that minimizing the distance that goods are transported does not necessarily minimize environmental costs.

4a. *Average payload on laden trips* and 4b, the *average percentage run empty* are two critical parameters relating to the utilization of vehicle capacity. By achieving higher levels of 'vehicle fill' retailers can reduce the amount of truck traffic required to move a given quantity of goods.

5. *Energy efficiency:* defined as the ratio of distance travelled to energy consumed, this parameter is affected by a range of factors including vehicle characteristics, driving behaviour and traffic conditions. By rescheduling deliveries to off-peak periods retailers can reduce their exposure to traffic congestion and allow the vehicles to run at more fuel-efficient speeds.

6. *Pollutant content of the energy source:* transport fuels differ in the amounts of particular pollutants that they emit. In the case of electrically-powered freight operations, there are also wide variations in the environmental impacts of different types of electricity generation. Converting from conventional diesel fuel to alternative fuels or to battery-powered vehicles recharged with electricity generated by renewable means (such as wind or water power) can significantly cut emissions of CO_2 and noxious pollutants.

7. *Other environmental effects per truck-km:* the other adverse effects that are not directly associated with energy consumption, such as noise irritation and accidents, vary with traffic conditions, the environmental sensitivity of the surrounding area and the nature of the vehicle. Upgrading vehicles to the latest environmental and safety standards and

altering the scheduling and routing of deliveries can help to reduce the level of externalities per kilometre travelled.

We will now discuss most of these key parameters in more detail and outline measures that retailers can take to modify them in a way that benefits the environment. The environmental effects of rescheduling deliveries are discussed later as a 'topical issue'.

Choice of transport mode

Retailers can switch traffic flows to cleaner transport modes both on inbound (primary) movements into their DCs and outbound (secondary) deliveries to shops. In the case of supplies sourced from other parts of the world, the main choice is between air freight and deep-sea container services. According to NTM, the Swedish Network for Transport and Environment, long-haul air freight services emit on average around 30 times more CO_2 per tonne-km than ocean shipping. As a result of a process called 'radiative forcing', the global warming impact of high-altitude emissions is two to four times greater than greenhouse emissions at ground level. Although air transport is significantly more expensive than movement by sea, the difference in rates does not adequately reflect the huge difference in environmental costs. This is because no tax is currently imposed on the fuel consumed by air freight and deep-sea shipping services. Being a much more energy-intensive mode, air freight derives much greater economic benefit from this tax-free status. In a world subject to accelerating climate change, it is likely to be only a matter of time before this environmental anomaly is corrected. As a first step in this direction, the European Commission is proposing to include aviation in the Emissions Trading Scheme from 2012. In the longer term, full internalization of the environmental costs of air freight, most of which are associated with climate change, could substantially increase air freight rates per tonne-km. When combined with steeply rising oil prices, the imposition of higher environmental charges will strongly discourage retailers from using air freight for all but the highest value, most time-sensitive products.

For the delivery of retail supplies over shorter distances, the modal options are generally road, rail and inland waterway services. Retailers have traditionally relied much more heavily on road freight services for three reasons:

1. Their DCs and shops have lacked direct rail (and waterway) connections.
2. The distances between DCs and shops are usually too short for rail and water-borne services, which are essentially long-haul modes, to be competitive.

3. Operators of rail freight and water-borne services have found it difficult to meet retailers' requirements for rapid and reliable delivery.

In recent years, however, major retailers have begun to make much more use of these alternative modes. In the United Kingdom, for example, Tesco, Asda and IKEA have switched significant volumes of longer-haul traffic from road to rail. Tesco's daily train between the English Midlands and Scotland removes approximately 4.5 million truck-kms annually from the road network and reduces CO_2 emissions by 6,000 tonnes per annum. Tesco also transports wines and spirits by inland waterway in the north-west of England.

These modal shifts by UK retailers have been supported by government grants designed to make logistics operations more environmentally sustainable. These grants are only awarded where the economic case for the modal transfer is insufficient. There have so far been few, if any, examples of retailers opting for greener transport modes at the expense of higher delivery costs.

Structure of the retail logistics system

The number and length of links in a retail supply are so intimately related that it makes sense to discuss them together under the general heading of logistical structure. In recent years the structure of modern retail logistics systems has been criticized by some environmental organizations and other commentators for being fundamentally unsustainable (eg Sustainable Development Commission, 2008). They object in particular to the wide sourcing of products, the channelling of products through centralized DCs and the replenishment of products on a just-in-time / quick response basis. Some critics argue that long-term sustainability, particularly in a low-carbon world, will only be achieved by a return to local subsistence economies, with consumption largely constrained to what can be produced locally. This would require a reversal of long-term retail trends and a return to the distribution systems of the early 20th century. Such a draconian transformation may ultimately be necessary if the gloomiest climate change scenarios were to materialize. We will confine our discussion here, however, to more modest changes to the structure of retail logistics systems, some of which are already underway and can still yield significant environmental benefits.

The consolidation of inbound supplies at retailer-controlled DCs improves the efficiency of shop deliveries and reduces their environmental impact. The alternative distribution model, which pre-dated the development of retailers' logistics systems and involved a multitude of suppliers delivering small quantities directly to each shop in the chain, was more damaging to the environment. For example, an analysis by McKinnon and Woodburn (1994) indicated that channelling grocery supplies through retailers' DCs in the United Kingdom cut CO_2 emissions by around 20 per cent relative to direct supplier deliveries to the shops.

In some retail supply chains, most notably clothing and temperature controlled food, an additional tier of primary consolidation has been inserted upstream of the DC. This has been necessitated by the move to quick response replenishment and diversification of the product range and supply base. While the addition of an extra warehousing operation and more circuitous routing of products via PCCs carry environmental penalties, these are likely to be offset by improved vehicle loading on the primary movements into DCs.

While primary consolidation has added a link to the retail supply chain, rationalization of the inward movement of imported goods can remove a link. In response to the huge increase in retail imports, mainly in deep-sea containers from the Far East, many retailers have been reconfiguring their inbound supply chains. Some have been adopting 'DC bypass' strategies, often in collaboration with shipping lines, which involve storing and handling imports at the port of entry and despatching them from there directly to the shop. This too can yield environmental benefits, as well as cutting costs and improving service quality (Bradley, 2007).

The greater the efficiency and capacity of the logistics system, the easier it is for retailers to source products from distant suppliers. The resulting lengthening of supply lines is often criticized for being environmentally damaging. In the United Kingdom, for instance, supermarket chains have been accused of extending 'food miles' by sourcing more produce from overseas, even when similar products are available locally. The food miles issue has been the subject of several major studies (eg Garnett, 2003; Smith *et al*, 2005). One conclusion to emerge from this work is that the distance a product travels can be a poor measure of its overall environmental impact. When a full product lifecycle analysis is conducted it is often found that products sourced from afar have lower environmental costs. This can occur where 'distant suppliers... operate more energy-efficient, less carbon-intensive production facilities than local suppliers and the resulting saving in production-related CO_2 exceeds the additional emissions from longer freight hauls' (McKinnon, 2008). Retailers can also cut these long-haul transport emissions by minimizing their use of air freight and maximizing the loading of sea containers. The UK retailer Boots, for example, managed to reduce CO_2 emissions per cubic metre from the transport of imported goods from the Far East by 29 per cent between 2004 and 2007 mainly by switching from air to sea, consolidating freight in 40-foot rather than 20-foot containers and reducing the amount of handling at terminals (Barnes, 2007).

Utilization of transport capacity

Transport Key Performance Indicator (KPI) surveys conducted in the United Kingdom have assessed the loading of trucks carrying retail supplies (McKinnon, 2004). This has shown that loads transported by road at the retail end of the supply chain tend to have a relatively low density because of the nature of the goods, the high level of packaging, broad assortment of products and nature of the handling equipment. For this reason, they are constrained much more by the deck area and cubic capacity of the vehicle than by the maximum weight it can carry. This is reflected by the fact that, in both food and non-food delivery operations, approximately three-quarters of the available vehicle floor area was occupied, whereas on average under 60 per cent of the weight-carrying capacity was used. Around half the available space on the vehicles was actually used. The KPI surveys also found significant amounts of empty running by trucks in the retail supply chain. Approximately 11 per cent of the journeys made in the non-food retail sector were empty. The corresponding figure for the grocery retailers was twice as high. Although 23 per cent of their lorry-kms were run empty, this was below the national average of 26.5 per cent for all road freight operations in the United Kingdom. The remainder of this section will examine three methods of improving vehicle load factors and thus cutting truck-kms within the retail distribution system.

1. Backloading of shop delivery vehicles

Rather than return to the DC empty, a shop delivery vehicle can be routed via a supplier's premises to collect orders. The resulting triangular trip can eliminate two empty journeys, substantially reducing truck-kms, energy consumption and emissions. Some retailers also use their suppliers' vehicles to make outbound deliveries to their shops on their way back to the factory. Both practices require retailers to coordinate their primary and secondary distribution to ensure balanced loading of their vehicles. Some retailers have tried to achieve this by adopting factory gate pricing and thus gaining control of the primary transport operation (Potter *et al*, 2007). Maximizing transport efficiency across 'network systems' comprising primary and secondary distribution presents formidable analytical challenges, however, and requires the application of complex software tools.

Companies have often been reluctant in the past to seek backloading arrangements. They have given precedence to outbound distribution and been afraid that delays in the backloading operation may prevent vehicles returning in time to deliver the next outbound load (McKinnon and Ge, 2006). There has, nevertheless, been a significant growth of backloading in retail supply chains in recent years. Across a sample of 10 UK food retailers, backhauls accounted for 5 per cent of total store delivery kilometres in 2006 (IGD, 2007). There is considerable potential to increase this figure. Asda, for example, estimates that it could save a further 9 million vehicle-kms per annum through backloading (Pearson, 2007).

2. Use of larger vehicles

Retail supplies in sectors such as grocery, clothing and footwear have a low density and thus 'cube-out' on vehicles before they 'weigh-out'. Increases in vehicle size can allow many retailers to consolidate loads on fewer trips, cutting vehicle-kms and emissions. The extra carrying capacity can either be gained by lengthening the vehicles or by increasing their height. In some countries, most notably Sweden and Finland, the extra carrying capacity has been gained horizontally in longer trucks, while in the United Kingdom, where height clearances are relatively high (up to 5 metres), it has been gained vertically in double-deck trailers. The benefits of using double-deck trailers (see Table 12.1) is well illustrated by the case of the United Kingdom do-it-yourself retailer Focus. By replacing standard trailers with double-deck trailers on journeys from its DC in central England to shops in northern England, it cut vehicle-kms, fuel and CO_2 emissions by almost 50 per cent (Department for Transport, 2007).

The use of larger vehicles can be subject to several physical constraints. The location of city centre stores may be unsuitable for access by double-deck vehicles and, as a result, they are often restricted to use within primary trunking operations between factories and DCs or DCs and local depots. The nature of the reception bays at shops and DCs and the amount of on-site manoeuvring space can also limit vehicle size.

3. Urban consolidation centres

These centres can be used to consolidate supplies destined for shops in inner urban areas, integrated shopping centres and airports. They reduce

Table 12.1 Travel distance, fuel and CO_2 savings from the use of double-deck vehicles

	Double-deck vehicle	Single-deck vehicles	Savings
Total distance travelled (miles)	275	532	257
Total fuel used (litres)	163.7	318.2	154.5
Total CO_2 produced (kg)	440	854	414

Source: Department for Transport, 2007

the number of vehicles accessing the retail centres and, in so doing, help to alleviate congestion and environmental impacts in the surrounding area (Browne *et al*, 2005). The final delivery leg, usually run within an agreed delivery schedule, is often performed by environmentally-friendly vehicles achieving much higher load factors than the direct shop deliveries that they replace. The main beneficiaries of these urban consolidation schemes tend to be medium-sized retailers selling lower-value, non-perishable goods.

The Bristol Consolidation Centre in south-west England serves approximately 50 retailers based in the city centre. It is located on the western fringes of the city near to the intersection of two motorways, and some 11 km away from Broadmead, the target retail area. Vehicle movements to the city centre have been reduced by 75 per cent for participating retailers. They can also take advantage of additional value-added services, such as packaging and waste collection, and can access overspill storage facilities at peak times.

The Retail Consolidation Centre serving retailers at Heathrow Airport has enabled vehicle deliveries to be reduced by approximately 70 per cent and yielded a 3,100 kg saving in CO_2 emissions per week. Goods are now delivered to the multi-temperature warehouse located on the perimeter of the airport, with an onward shuttle-based delivery service operating to a fixed timetable. Over half the retail and catering units participate in the scheme, while new retailers must join as a condition of their contract with the airport authority (Department for Transport, 2003).

Energy efficiency of retail deliveries

Retailers and logistics service providers working on their behalf can improve the energy efficiency of transport and warehousing operations in many ways. Road freight operators can apply numerous fuel economy measures, which typically yield a 1–5 per cent fuel saving (Department for Transport, 2006a). These measures include:

- providing drivers with training in fuel-efficient driving;
- offering incentives for fuel-efficient driving;
- purchasing more fuel-efficient vehicles;
- reducing the vehicle power rating to match load weight and topography;
- reducing vehicle tare (empty) weight;
- improving the vehicle's aerodynamic profiling;
- raising standards of vehicle maintenance;
- imposing tighter speed limits;
- ensuring correct tyre pressures.

Research in the United States, for example, found average fuel savings ranging from under 1 per cent for automatic tyre inflation systems to almost 8 per cent for a reduction in maximum speed from 65 mph to 60 mph (Ang-Olsen and Schroeer, 2002). Some of these measures, however, are counteracting. For example, cutting maximum speed will reduce the effectiveness of improved vehicle aerodynamics. A fuel management programme should not, therefore, simply comprise a loose collection of measures. These measures should be integrated into a coherent package tailored to the needs of particular types of retail distribution. While many truck fuel economy measures are generic and can be applied in any sector, some have been pioneered by retailers. For example, in the United Kingdom, retailers such as Marks & Spencer, TK Maxx and PC World have trialled the use of 'teardrop' trailers that slope both at the front and rear of the vehicle. When combined with additional carrying capacity, they can cut full consumption per cubic metre of load by around 20 per cent relative to a standard trailer.

Use of alternative fuels

Biofuels

Biofuels have attracted increased attention in recent years as a result of concern about climate change and energy security. Their appeal is obvious. They are produced from renewable plant materials (feedstocks) or organic waste oils and fats, and when blended with standard diesel or petrol can, depending on the source, deliver reductions in greenhouse gases emissions in the order of 20–50 per cent (Concawe *et al*, 2006).

In the case of retail logistics operations, biodiesel is considered to be the alternative fuel with the greatest potential. In Europe, it is typically mixed with diesel in low-percentage blends (B5 and B10), and when used in such low ratios, standard diesel engines require no modification (International Energy Agency, 2004). Truck manufacturers have been reluctant to approve higher percentage biodiesel blends for fear of adverse effects on engine life and performance. Undeterred, Tesco aimed to introduce a 50 per cent biodiesel blend (B50) in three-quarters of its distribution fleet in the United Kingdom during 2008.

Government policies promoting the use of biofuels and corporate commitments to switch to these fuels now appear to have been premature. Recent lifecycle (or well-to-wheel) comparisons of the environmental impacts of biofuels and conventional fuels suggest that the former are not a panacea as first thought. New evidence suggests that most forms of biodiesel, with the exception of that produced from waste vegetable oil, yield little net CO_2 benefit and, on a lifecycle basis, can

potentially generate more CO_2 than conventional diesel. Other environmental and social effects of biofuel use are also being questioned
(Environmental Audit Committee, 2008; Royal Society, 2008). The
diversion of agricultural production from food to energy crops has
substantially inflated food prices around the world and exacerbated food
shortages. The increasing demand for biofuels is also accelerating the
clearance of native tropical forests and threatening biodiversity.

Second-generation biofuels, produced mainly from agricultural
waste and forest products, may alleviate these environmental and
social concerns and prove a more sustainable means of cutting CO_2
emissions. Commercial production of these fuels is still many years
away, however, and even their effectiveness in achieving lifecycle
carbon reductions is now being questioned (Environmental Audit
Committee, 2008).

Electric and hybrid vehicles

Electric vehicles are virtually pollution-free at the point of use and
extremely quiet. They are therefore particularly well suited to home
delivery operations in which a large proportion of vehicle-kms are run in
sensitive residential neighbourhoods. One major UK retailer is planning
to make its online shopping division entirely reliant on electric vans by
2010. In assessing the overall impact of electric vehicles, however, one
must take account of the primary energy source of the electricity used to
recharge the batteries. In an effort to make its electric van operation
carbon-neutral, Tesco is installing wind turbines at some of its premises
and 'feeding' sufficient energy into the electricity grid to offset that used
in recharging vehicle batteries.

The adoption of electric vehicles has traditionally been constrained
by the limited distance range between battery recharges, and restrictions on vehicle carrying capacity resulting from the on-board energy-
storage requirements. Electric vehicles still offer less payload than
conventional delivery vans, but now have a distance range of around
250 miles (which exceeds the normal daily range of most retail-related
van deliveries).

A new generation of hybrid vans and rigid trucks, which can switch
between battery and diesel-/petrol-fuelled engines, is now being
produced commercially. Their manufacturers claim that they can achieve
fuel savings of 20–30 per cent when compared with conventional
diesel/petrol vehicles. In the medium to long term they are likely to have
extensive application in retail supply chains, particularly in multiple-drop
deliveries to shops and homes.

MANAGING WASTE WITHIN THE RETAIL SUPPLY CHAIN

The efficient management of waste in the retail supply chain involves minimizing the use of packaging in the forward distribution channel and recovering waste packaging in the reverse channel.

Packaging prevents waste by delivering products to the customer in a saleable, undamaged condition and can increase the efficiency of the distribution operation. It also, however, accounts for almost 20 per cent of UK household waste and, with enhanced environmental awareness amongst consumers and tightening government regulations, retailers are coming under increasing pressure to minimize its use.

The answer is not to eliminate packaging altogether but to minimize its unnecessary use. Research has indicated that inadequate packaging can cause more product waste than over-packaging, as a result of damage occurring in the distribution channel (Institute for European Environmental Policy, 2004). A recent pilot study has also revealed wide variations between food retailers in their use of packaging materials and in their ability to recycle it (Bassett and Charlton, 2007). Table 12.2 compares packaging reduction initiatives and targets of major UK food retailers.

In the reverse channel the main aim is either to recapture value through recycling or reuse, or to dispose of the waste in the most environmentally sustainable manner. It is now common practice for retailers to site resource recovery units (RRUs) at their DCs. Vehicles returning to the DCs first call at the RRU where packaging is removed and baled, and any trays cleaned and stored for reuse.

This systematic treatment of packaging and handling equipment, accompanied by the use of the reverse logistics channel for the return of retail products, not only maximizes the amounts recovered, but also exploits the backload capacity in returning shop delivery vehicles.

Table 12.2 UK retailer packaging reduction initiatives (as of January 2008)

Asda	25% reduction in own-brand packaging by 2008
Morrisons	15% less own-brand packaging
Sainsbury	5% reduction in packaging by 2008
Tesco	25% reduction in own-brand packaging by 2010
M&S	25% reduction in packaging by 2012

Source: Bassett, 2007 and the corporate websites of the various retailers

TOPICAL ISSUES

Night-time delivery to retail outlets

Daytime traffic congestion affects the reliability of retail deliveries, particularly as it is concentrated in and around urban areas where most shops are located. It not only impairs the efficiency of the distribution operation, but also carries a significant environmental penalty as vehicles consume much more fuel per tonne-km on congested roads. A large proportion of deliveries to retail premises are made during the working day, often during the morning peak (McKinnon and Ge, 2004). This is partly necessary to stock the shops prior to the start of trading. It can also be due to night delivery curfews and access restrictions imposed by local authorities. The Freight Transport Association (2006) has estimated that some 40 per cent of supermarkets in the United Kingdom are restricted by some form of night-time delivery curfew. If half of these curfews were relaxed, it would be possible to save around 63 million truck-kms annually and roughly 36 million litres of fuel.

Recently the UK government has been examining the possibility of relaxing night-time delivery restrictions in an effort to rationalize retail deliveries (Department for Transport, 2006b). Although complete elimination of night-time curfews would be both impractical and inappropriate, some relaxation in 'out-of-hours' restrictions would help to ease daytime congestion and cut emissions. Concern has been expressed about noise disturbance to private dwellings in the vicinity of shops and DCs during the night. Delivery vehicles are, however, much quieter today than when delivery restrictions were first imposed. Ultra-quiet vehicles, with virtually silent fridge units, tail lifts and roll cages/containers and wheels, have been developed that are well suited to evening and night-time delivery.

Carbon auditing and labelling of products

Some major retailers, such as Tesco and Migros, are committed to putting 'carbon labels' on the products they sell. These labels indicate the amount of CO_2 (in grams) emitted by a product during its production and distribution. It is argued that consumers concerned about climate change would then be able to make informed choices at the time of purchase, based on the emissions data supplied (*The Economist*, 2007). The carbon-intensity of the supply chains for individual products could become a selection criterion influencing the purchasing behaviour both of retail buyers and final consumers. In the United Kingdom, the Carbon Trust and British Standards Institution have developed a standard procedure for auditing carbon emissions across the supply chains of individual products (Carbon Trust, 2006). Several products, such as Walkers Crisps and around 30 of Tesco's own label products, already carry carbon labels.

Initial hopes that carbon labelling would eventually become universal for all goods and services now seem unlikely to be fulfilled. To date only a handful of companies have attempted to calculate carbon footprints for a few of their products. Their experience suggests that this process involves huge amounts of time, effort and cost. Some companies have reported costs of around £30,000 per product. Others have quoted average analysis costs per product of £3–4,000. Even if this lower average proves more realistic, when multiplied by the 25–30,000 products stocked by the typical superstore, the cost of carbon auditing this range could total over a hundred million pounds. To date, only basic products comprising a few basic ingredients have been carbon audited. Carbon auditing the supply chains of more complex consumer products such as TVs, computers and cars presents a much more difficult and costly challenge. There would also be a need to update the carbon estimates regularly and to establish a system of independent validation. Many managers are now asking if product-level carbon auditing and labelling are ever likely to be practical and cost-effective, especially given current uncertainty about their impact on consumer behaviour.

Relative environmental footprint of online retailing

In many countries online retail sales are growing faster than sales through conventional retail outlets. Recently, growth rates for e-tailing have been in the order of 35–50 per cent per annum in the United Kingdom, and expectations are for 30+ per cent growth rates over the next few years (Synovate, 2006). For distribution companies, the arrival of internet shopping has meant a shift in fulfilment strategies away from high-volume distribution to shops to direct delivery of individual customer orders to homes.

As discussed in Chapter 10, some online retailers have been actively proclaiming the environmental benefits of online shopping (Smithers, 2007). Very little empirical work has been undertaken to date to substantiate these claims. Research by Cairns et al (2005) and Siikavirta et al (2005) in the grocery sector and Matthews et al (2001) in book retailing have indicated that, under certain conditions, online retailing can have a lower environmental footprint than conventional retailing. Other research has cast doubt on the relative environmental benefits of online retailing (European Information Technology Observatory, 2002; Sarkis et al, 2004). Hop Associates (2002), having conducted a review of the environmental effects of e-commerce, stated that it was 'not the wiser as to whether e-commerce will increase traffic or decrease it'. A comparison of the environmental impact of the two forms of distribution is complicated by the broad range of factors that must be considered including the structure of the respective supply chains, the nature, loading and routing of the vehicles, the proportion of repeat deliveries to the home, the level of returns, the energy efficiency of shops and DCs, and consumer travel behaviour. One of the key elements in the environmental appraisal is the extent to which personal travel, mainly by car, is replaced by van traffic. The degree of substitution may be quite modest. After all, consumers frequently combine shopping trips with other activities such as the journey to and from work or the 'school run'. Also, customers ordering online may then use their car for some other purpose during the time normally allocated for shopping.

Growth in the digital transmission of products

The internet provides a new 'digital' distribution channel for some product categories (such as music, books, films and computer games), which removes the need for physical transport, storage and handling. So far the music sector has been the main beneficiary of this digital technology, owing to the diversity of the available delivery platforms. Music is also highly portable once downloaded and easily accessible via the web (OECD, 2005). As a result, digital sales have experienced rapid growth, with the United States, Japan and the United Kingdom leading the way in music downloading. Correspondingly, sales of CDs have seen year-on-year falls, with some predicting the demise of music distribution in physical formats in the not-too-distant future (Brown, 2008). Similarly, although still in their infancy, sales of digital videos are expected to grow exponentially over the next few years.

Although digital transmission eliminates packaging, transport, storage and physical displays, the environmental benefits of this type of distribution are partly offset by the growth in demand for hardware required to play these digital formats, such as personal computers, MP3 players and games consoles. Furthermore, not all digital technology has been embraced equally. Digital books and online newspapers have yet to capture the imagination of readers in the way that MP3 players and digital downloads have attracted audiences for music and films. Several companies have tried to tempt readers online by producing e-book reading devices, though the conversion of customers from hard-copy formats has remained low (Langdon-Down, 2007). Newspaper and magazine sales are, nevertheless, in long-term decline as citizens get more of their information from online and broadcast media.

While the replacement of physical distribution by digital transmission will dramatically reduce the environmental impact of logistics in a few sectors of the retail market, its contribution to the overall greening of retail supply chains is likely to be small.

CONCLUSIONS

Large retailers have been a fertile source of logistical innovation. They have pioneered many logistical management practices and technologies that have subsequently been adopted in other sectors. The more progressive retailers also appear to be taking the lead in developing and implementing green logistics strategies. This chapter has outlined the numerous environmental improvement measures that they can incorporate in these strategies. If properly coordinated, this set of measures can substantially reduce the environmental costs of retail distribution. At present many of these costs are borne by the community at large and do not appear on the retailer's balance sheet. It is likely, however, that they will increasingly be internalized in higher taxes and/or through the inclusion of logistical activities in emissions trading schemes. Those retailers that by then have minimized the environmental footprint of their logistics operations will derive a significant financial benefit. They will also have benefited financially in the meantime as many of the green measures discussed in the chapter cut costs as well as emissions. Perhaps the most important driver of improved environmental practice in retail logistics, however, will be the growing expectation of customers that the products they buy are delivered in a sustainable manner.

References

Ang-Olsen, J and Schroeer, W (2002) Energy efficiency strategies for freight trucking: Potential impact on fuel use and greenhouse gas emissions, *Transportation Research Record*, Transportation Research Board, **1815**, pp 11–18

Barnes, I (2007) Carbon auditing supply chains: making the journey presentation to the Multimodal 2008 conference, Birmingham (www.greenlogistics.org)

Bassett, C, and Charlton, A (2007) *War on Waste: Food packaging study, Wave 1*, Local Government Association

Bradley, P (2007) For speed and reliability, take the bypass, *DC Velocity*, May

Brown, J (2008) Slump in album sales could see end of CD, *Independent*, 9 January

Browne, M, Sweet, M, Woodburn, A and Allen, J (2005) *Urban Freight Consolidation Centres*, Final Report for the Department for Transport, Freight Best Practice Programme, London

Cairns, S, Sloman, L, Newson, C, Anable, J, Kirkbride, A and Goodwin, P (2005) *Smarter Choices – Changing the way we travel*, Department for Transport, London

Carbon Trust (2006) *Carbon Footprints in the Supply Chain: The next step for business*, Carbon Trust, London

Concawe, Eucar and JRC (2006) *Well-to-wheel Analysis of Future Automotive Fuels and Powertrains in the European Context*, European Commission, Brussels

DEFRA (2005) Guidelines for Company Reporting on Greenhouse Gas Emissions, London

Department for Transport (2003) *Heathrow Airport Retail Consolidation Centre, Freight Best Practice Programme*, HMSO, London

Department for Transport (2004) *The Efficiency of Reverse Logistics*, HMSO, London

Department for Transport (2006a) *Fuel Management Guide, Freight Best Practice Programme*, HMSO, London

Department for Transport (2006b) *Delivering the Goods: Guidance on delivery restrictions*, HMSO, London

Department for Transport (2007) *Focus on Double Decks, Freight Best Practice Programme*, HMSO, London

The Economist (2007) Not on the label, 17 May

Environmental Audit Committee (2008) *Are Biofuels Sustainable? House of Commons, EAC, first report of session 2007–2008, volume 1*, Stationery Office, London

European Information Technology Observatory (2002) *The Impact of ICT on Sustainable Development, Part 2 in Annual Report*, EITO, Brussels

Freight Transport Association (2006) *Delivering the Goods: A toolkit for improving night-time deliveries*, FTA, Tunbridge Wells

Garnett, T (2003) *Wise Moves: Exploring the relationship between food, transport and CO_2*, Transport 2000, London

Hill, R (2007) Your M&S, presentation to Reducing Carbon Footprint in the FMCG Supply Chain, Hilton Olympia, London, November

Hop Associates (2002) *The Impact of Information and Communications Technologies on Travel and Freight Distribution Patterns: Review and assessment of literature*, Department for Transport, London

IGD (2007) *Retail Logistics 2007*, IGD, Letchmore Heath

Institute for European Environmental Policy (2004) *Packaging for Sustainability: Packaging in the context of the product, supply chain and consumer needs*, INCPEN, London

International Energy Agency (2004) *Biofuels for Transport: An international perspective*, OECD, Paris

Langdon-Down, G (2007) Dawn of the digital book, *Guardian*, 10 December

Matthews, H, Hendrickson, C and Soh, D L (2001) Environmental and economic effects of e-commerce: a study of book publishing and retail logistics, *Transportation Research Record*, **1763**, pp 6–12

McKinnon, A C (2004) Benchmarking the efficiency of retail deliveries in the UK, *BRC Solutions* (British Retail Consortium journal), **5**

McKinnon, A C (2008) The potential of economic incentives to reduce CO_2 emissions from goods transport, paper prepared for the 1st International Transport Forum on Transport and Energy: the Challenge of Climate Change Leipzig, 28–30 May http://www.internationaltransportforum. org/Topics/Workshops/WS3McKinnon.pdf

McKinnon, A C (2007) *CO_2 Emissions from Freight Transport in the UK*, Commission for Integrated Transport, London, http://www.cfit.gov. uk/docs/2007/climatechange/pdf/2007climatechange-freight.pdf

McKinnon, A C and Ge, Y (2004) Use of a synchronized vehicle audit to determine opportunities for improving transport efficiency in a supply chain, *International Journal of Logistics: Research and Applications*, **7**, (3), pp 219–38

McKinnon, A C and Ge, Y (2006) The potential for reducing empty running by trucks: a retrospective analysis, *International Journal of Physical Distribution and Logistics Management*, **36**, (5) pp 391–410

McKinnon, A C and Woodburn, A (1994) The consolidation of retail deliveries: its effect on CO_2 emissions, *Transport Policy*, **1**, 2

OECD (2005) *Digital broadband content: Music*, Report DSTI/ICCP/IE(2004)12/ Final, OECD, Paris

Pearson, S (2007) ASDA logistics: sustainable supply chains, presentation to the Green Supply Chains conference, October, London

Potter, A, Mason, R and Lalwani, C (2007) Analysis of factory gate pricing in the UK grocery supply chain, *International Journal of Retail & Distribution Management*, **35**, pp 821–34

Rigby, E, Harvey, F and Birchall, J (2007) Tesco to put 'carbon rating' on labels, *Financial Times*, 18 January

Royal Society (2008) *Sustainable Biofuels: Prospects and challenges*, Royal Society, London

Sarkis, J, Meade, L M and Talluri, S (2004) E-logistics and the natural environment, *Supply Chain Management*, **9**, (4), pp 303–12

Siikavirta, H, Punakivi, M, Karkkainen, M and Linnanen, L (2005) Effects of e-commerce on greenhouse gas emissions: a case study of grocery home delivery in Finland, *Journal of Industrial Ecology*, **6**, (2), pp 83–97

Smith, A *et al* (2005) *The Validity of Food Miles as an Indicator of Sustainable Development*, AEA Technology/DEFRA, London

Smithers, R (2007) Supermarket home delivery service promotes its green credentials, *Guardian*, 12 September

Sustainable Development Commission (2008) *Green, Healthy and Fair – A review of the government role in supporting sustainable supermarket food*, Sustainable Development Commission, London

Synovate (2006) *Lockerbanks: Appeal and likely usage of Lockerbanks*, Report for Transport for London 06024, London

Notes

1. HFC 23, for example, has a global warming potential 11,500 times greater than carbon dioxide.
2. This is a four-year research project being undertaken by six UK universities. For more details see www.greenlogistics.org.

Afterword

John Fernie and Leigh Sparks

As we indicated in the preface, this book is the fourth in a series of insights into current practice and trends in retail logistics. The first volume, edited by John Fernie and entitled *Retail Distribution Management* gave an indication of the key issues of the late 1980s. The title of the book gave a clue to the challenges facing logistics management at that time. Attention focused upon *distribution* management and how to improve efficiency in getting goods to retail outlets. This was the era of centralization and the strategic decision whether to contract out or retain in-house the financing and management of logistical infrastructure.

The second book, *Logistics and Retail Management*, by the current editors, updated the earlier version, although notable changes in managing the supply chain were evident and the volume was essentially brand new. The earlier text had charted the beginnings of retail control of the FMCG supply chain. This was reinforced by initiatives such as quick response and efficient consumer response, which promulgated greater collaboration between supply chain partners so that costs and benefits of reducing lead times could be clearly identified, taking cost out of the system for mutual benefit. Relationship change was at the forefront of such collaboration. Incremental improvements in the logistics network were also evident. In the grocery sector, consolidation centres were built to improve vehicle utilization as retailers demanded more frequent deliveries of smaller quantities of product. Composite distribution became a feature of logistical support to retailers with large superstores/hypermarkets in that mixed loads of ambient chilled, fresh and frozen products could be stored and distributed to store more efficiently. In the clothing sector, much attention centred on the issue of domestic versus offshore sourcing and how retailers could implement QR initiatives to reduce lead times.

The third volume, published in 2004, built on the core framework of the 1998 edition but developed the subject in three main ways. To an extent the third volume represented a deepening of pre-existing issues, overlaid perhaps by the dot com hype and then decline. Thus the third edition provided more focus on fashion logistics and in particular the changing sourcing models and concepts such as fast fashion as operated by Zara and H&M, amongst others. It also focused more on the challenges of grocery and food logistics and in particular the problems and opportunities in temperature controlled supply chains. Finally and in recognition of the importance that data, information and communications had come to play in modern retailing, a section on technological developments including e-tailing, internet exchanges and initial RFID considerations, and on ERP systems, was added. Together these changes provided a more rounded view of retail logistics as practised in 2004.

This was not to suggest that retail logistics had been 'solved' – far from it. One of the characteristics of retail logistics is that it is ever-changing and that different businesses are at different stages of their development and understanding of their needs and practices. As such we concluded the 2004 edition with a series of challenges that were likely to be confronting retailers in the remainder of the decade. We identified four:

1. The need to focus on ensuring appropriate availability levels in the store.
2. The recognition that complexity in supply chains had been rising and eating into management resources and time. A drive for simplicity might therefore be required.
3. That the focus on efficiency in supply chains would need to continue to ensure appropriateness of activity for the business.
4. Multi-channel retailing was likely to become more prevalent and that as a consequence issues of return flows and cross-format and cross-channel flows might become more important.

As we have noted in the preface to this volume, we have not been disappointed! In putting together this fourth volume we have again tried to include many of the issues that have emerged in the last few years. Notably we have added in areas of fashion and food logistics, including availability and extended work on e-tailing and RFID. Perhaps most fundamentally, and making a difference to previous volumes, we have added a dedicated chapter on green logistics.

In the previous editions we have elected not to provide a summary or concluding chapter that recaps the volume or brings together core themes in some way. Instead we have attempted to examine how and in what directions retail logistics and supply chains might develop and change. The success or otherwise of this is open to debate and whilst we could argue that we selected appropriate topics in the forward-look in the last edition, it is clear we underestimated the environmental pressures that have developed.

So, what are the challenges we would emphasize as we prepare this volume in August 2008? Three big issues are forefront in our discussions: efficiency, transparency and sustainability.

1. Efficiency

In the last few months the dramatic rise in the price of oil, combined with the extension of problems arising from the 'credit crunch' has seen many economies tilt towards recession. The negativity surrounding economies generally makes it difficult not to focus on efficiency in its broadest sense. The dramatic rise in the price of fuel and the consequent rises in prices of many products have come at a time when disposable income is being severely constrained. As a consequence, demand is slackening and altering. If demand is less volatile and weakening then it could be argued that efficiency could be less of a concern. However, the vast increase in the cost of transporting products makes efficiency absolutely vital. If money can be saved by better load-fill or cleaner driving, or by not having so many voids or errors, then the overall effect will be beneficial.

For retailers therefore there are now even more good reasons to be concerned with efficiency. It would seem unlikely that cost pressures are going to diminish in the near future, and whilst consumer confidence and spending may return, being as efficient as possible does not seem like a bad strategy. So it is likely that there will be enhanced pressure to smooth flows as much as possible, to ensure as full a vehicle fill as can be achieved and to make sure that products are in their 'correct' places. Modernization of equipment and systems and training of staff will be important to ensure efficiency can be gained/delivered. Many of the likely developments will be focused on specific issues generating incremental improvements with rapid payback.

2. Transparency

A corollary of efficiency to some degree is the ability to generate transparency in the supply chain, for both internal and external stakeholders.

If a supply chain is transparent then it is likely that it can be made more efficient. The more visible the activities and the products/equipment are in the supply chain, the more likely it is that mistakes or errors will be avoided and/or problems be dealt with as they occur. In essence enhanced transparency has the potential to provide a more efficient and effective supply system and to improve availability.

Transparency has a number of dimensions, but increasingly technology is providing the means to improve clarity. However, there also has to be the willingness to allow transparency to occur across the supply chain. RFID is a pertinent example here. It has the potential to make supply chains more transparent (though at some cost), but the real benefits seem to derive at two levels: within a business and within the supply chain. If the data from RFID are not shared then true improvements from the knowledge and transparency will be much scarcer.

For retailers there is also a consideration of the scope and scale of transparency. Is it appropriate to treat all suppliers the same? Can this really be achieved and managed? Or is the real benefit to be gained from focusing attention on selected partners and ensuring they can deliver what is needed? In the short term, cost pressures could drive transactional priorities, but partnership-based transparency is likely to provide more benefits in the long term.

3. Sustainability

Probably the most fundamental change in recent years has been the recognition that supply chains and logistics are critically important in terms of green logistics and sustainability. The global issue of climate change has become so important generally that it has forced governments and businesses to consider anew practices and operations that had become entrenched. Climate change has direct effects on logistics and supply practices in many ways, but primarily it has meant that the ideas of green logistics and sustainable distribution have emerged as practical business concerns rather than fringe operational worries. They have become fundamental to the business rather than 'nice to think about'. Businesses that fail to recognize this will have problems in the future.

As climate change has focused concern it has been overlaid by other concerns such as food security. There are clear links here to sustainability and the issues raised may cause some rethinking about what can and can't be achieved in this regard. It is still too early to be certain about the evidence in many areas of these topics. The debates about the wisdom or otherwise of biofuels and the difficulties of totally accurate lifecycle analysis are practical illustrations of the problems. At a macro level the debates about the style and impact of some local production as opposed to the benefits of production for developing countries also hint at the difficulties in this area. What seems to be certain is that all practices are being challenged by the new realities. It is less clear what the best practices are to meet the new demands and/or how we transition between these states of activities. In some cases it might be possible to see small-scale changes having major impacts (eg packaging reduction) but it might also be the case that radical rethinking and transformation of activities might be required (eg the abandonment of air freight).

The impacts of many logistics and supply chain practices are going to come under harsh scrutiny at many levels. The cost and environmental impact of road transport or air freight are examples where serious questions will be asked about their sustainability. If costing regimes force businesses to internalize environmental impact costs, then the viability of such behaviour will be questioned. What will be important, however, and likely to become even more important, are questions of efficiency. It will make no sense to anyone to send lorries on long-distance journeys half full. It will possibly even become morally impossible. As such the aspects of efficiency and transparency will be used to meet the problems thrown up by sustainability.

There will of course be many dimensions to sustainability. A critical aspect in the use of resources will be the need for retailers to reduce packaging and other handling inputs and to enable reuse and recycling of packaging, product and other components. Retailers will increasingly have to demonstrate not only that they have done all they can to minimize such impacts but also that they have done all they can to maximize consumer opportunities in recycling. It needs to be accepted that some aspects will require investment by retailers, but that in many instances they benefit as well, both directly in cost terms and indirectly through customer recognition of their activities.

There are other challenges that will undoubtedly face the retail logistics industry in the coming years. However, we believe that, looking forward, the key challenges are to make the supply chain visible to aid efficiency and to rethink existing and new activities to provide as green a solution as possible, based on sound practices and efficient operations. Making supply chains and logistics work in such a turbulent and different environment is a real challenge, compounded by the new realities of what is acceptable and possible. As we have said before, logistics cannot stand still.

Index